Why Religion?

A Journey from the memory

Faten Sabri

Edited by: Lara Sabri

2021

I pray to God that He accepts this book from me and adds it to my and the following people's balance of good deeds:

My compassionate father, may God have mercy on him, who taught me how to live with dignity and honor.

My affectionate mother, may God have mercy on her, who was the symbol of dedication and devotion.

My husband ...who is the highest symbol of sincerity, loyalty, and partner of the journey.

My siblings ... who support me and share life's joys and sorrows.

My children and grandchildren... who are pieces of me.

All thanks and appreciation go

to:

The unknown soldier who taught me how to stand firmly on the ground, the example of devotion and sincerity.
The one who never refused to help me, provided me with advice and guidance, and asked God to give me the good.
To my husband, the ideal man; may God prolong his life to remain my aid.
To whose guidance lay behind every word and sentence in this book.
My dear husband, Loai Sabri.

All thanks and appreciation go

to:

Prof. Dr. Muhammad ibn Abdullah as-Saheem: Professor of theology at King Saud University.

Islam House's team of reviewers and editors.

Contents:

My Success is Through God

I have always asked God for help in my life and asked Him to facilitate useful knowledge that I can benefit from. I used to pray to Him and say: O Lord, plan for me, because I do not manage well. I saw in a dream **then, that** Prophet Muhammad, may blessings and peace be upon him, gave me a set of books, and I did not understand the interpretation of the dream. My husband began his journey as a diplomat assigned to the United Nations.

I decided to join him with the children. I felt that I had a lot of free time because I was separated from my work, family, and friends. **Then, God opened the way for me to study languages that filled this free time.**

Many friends believed that my diligence in studying languages would not add anything to my education. They also thought that it was a waste of time because I would forget what I learned as soon as we returned to our country after my husband's retirement. Back then, I never stopped repeating the supplication: O Lord, plan for me, **for** I do not manage well. Until God opened a way for me to speak with non-Muslims about Islam, and because of my proficiency in languages, it amazed everyone.

I came across many obstacles that almost stopped me from continuing. Until a moment of despair, I heard someone telling me to "go on" during a dream, which encouraged me a lot. Then God sent me an unexpected helping hand and encouragement. Based on this encouragement and distinguished professors' advice, I decided to write this summary of my experience during the home quarantine period imposed on everyone due to the Corona pandemic.

I thank God the Almighty for helping me write this book. I pray to God that this book will be the lantern that lights the way for people with bright minds and open hearts, wanting to seek the truth. I pray to Him to make it a message of goodness and peace for all by getting to know the right and innate religion. The religion of all the previous prophets of God which is represented by the tolerance of Islam and was delivered by the final Prophet Muhammed, may peace be upon him, which is: "The belief in the Creator of the universe and worshiping Him alone without an intermediary". The religion that came to correct misconceptions and to restore faith to its correct position.

The need for religion is greater than the need for food and drink. A person is by nature a religious person. If he does not find the true religion, he will then invent a religion for himself, similar to what happened with the pagan religions created by humankind. Human beings need security in this life, just as they need protection after death; the true religion gives its followers complete safety in this life and the Hereafter.

The measures of the true religion:

Belief in God:

It is essential for a person to have faith in a deity, whether the belief in the true God or in any false deity. He may call this deity god or name it anything else. His god may be a tree, a star in the sky, a woman, his boss at work, a scientific theory, or even identity in himself, but it is necessary to believe in something that follows it and sanctifies it, along with returning to it in his way of life and may die for it. This is what we call worship. Worshiping the true God frees a person **from slavery to others**.

The true God is the Creator:

Worshiping someone other than the true God includes claiming that they are gods, but God must be a creator. The evidence that He is the Creator is either by witnessing what He created in the universe or by inspiration from God who has been proven to be the Creator. If this claim has no evidence, neither from who created the universe nor from the **words** of the Creator Himself, it is necessarily invalid.

Belief in the Creator is based on the fact that things do not appear without a cause, nor chance can be a creator to the universe because chance is not a primary cause, but rather a secondary result that depends on the availability of other factors (the existence of time, space, matter and energy) in order for these factors to form something accidentally. The word "coincidence" cannot be used to explain anything because it is nothing at all.

The Creator:

- He must have preceded time, space, energy, and existence. Therefore, nature cannot possibly be a creator to the universe because nature itself is time, space, and energy. Thus, the Creator (the primary cause) must have existed before nature.
- He must also be omnipotent (having power over everything).
- He must be a decision maker, producer, originator, and initiator, to start creation.
- He must have the foresight, and must be omniscient (have perfect knowledge of all things).
- He must be one, because if this cause is perfect, it should not need any other reason. The Creator should not need to be incarnated in the image of one of His creatures, nor should He have a wife or son in any case, because He possesses all the attributes of perfection.
- He must be wise and does nothing except with superior wisdom.
- He must be fair to reward and punish.
- He must be in contact with people. He would not be God if He created them and left them.

  That's why He sent messengers to help clarify the path and inform people of His method. People who took this path deserves the reward, and punishment to those who goes astray.

Religion:

Religion is a way of life, which organizes a person's relationship with his Creator and those around him, and it is the path to the afterlife.

- It should be closer to the first human instinct, which needs a direct relationship with its Creator, without the intervention of intermediaries, and it represent the virtues and good qualities in **human beings.**
- It should be one religion; easy and simple, understandable, and uncomplicated.
- It must be a fixed religion for all generations, countries, and kinds of people, which does not accept an increase or decrease according to whims, as is the case in the customs and traditions that originate by humans.
- It must contain clear and proven beliefs; it does not need a mediator. Religion should not be taken by sentiments, but by correct and proven evidence.
- It should cover all life issues and every time and place. It should fit this life and the Life after death, build the body and not forget the soul.
- It should protect people's lives and preserve their honor and money.

Thus, those who did not follow this approach, which came in accordance with their nature, lived in a state of turmoil and instability with a feeling of restlessness in the soul. Also, he'd experience the torment of the Hereafter.

Why Islam?

- The religion of Islam is compatible with human nature.
- The religion of Islam has a proven belief that is clear and straightforward. It is far from blind faith. Islam is not satisfied with

addressing the heart and conscience by relying on them as a basis for belief only, it instead follows its principles with a convincing and compelling argument, along with clear proof and correct reasoning that holds the reins of minds and takes the path to hearts.

- The religion of Islam is a comprehensive teaching of all life aspects. It is flexible, because it is related to the human nature that God created man, and this religion came following the laws of this instinct, which is:

The faith in one God "the Creator", Who has no child or any partner, Who does not incarnate in any of His creature's image or body nor in any idol. And to have direct connection with this God by worshiping Him directly without any intermediary (priests, saints, prophets or idols, etc.).

- The religion of Islam brought answers to human beings' innate questions about the purpose of existence, the source of existence, and destiny. It establishes evidence in the issue of divinity from the universe, soul, and history on the existence, oneness, and perfection of God. In the issue of resurrection, it indicates the possibility of creating humans, the heavens, and the earth, and it indicates God's wisdom of justice in rewarding the benefactor and punishing the offender.

Humanity meets in one origin and proceeds towards one goal. Diversity and difference are a universal necessity that obligates the human being of the importance of continuing of the dialogue.

God said:

And if your Lord had willed, He could have made mankind one community; but they will not cease to differ.[1]

The purpose of this difference is acquaintance and integration between all races; the path of dialogue is the path that God's messengers took from Adam to Muhammad, peace be upon them all.

God said:

O mankind, indeed We have created you from male and female and made you peoples and tribes that you may know one another. Indeed, the most noble of you in the sight of God is the most righteous of you. Indeed, God is Knowing and Acquainted.[2]

Everyone is of one origin. Everyone came to earth with one goal: knowing God and worshipping Him alone as the Messenger of God worshipped Him, not by worshipping the Messenger himself or worshipping anything else.

To spread the message of monotheism, God sent all messengers to all nations, guiding their people to the universe realities, so they start from it and achieve the purpose which they were created for. Every nation had a messenger, and all heavenly messages across time and space have come to serve this purpose.

God said:

And We indeed sent into every nation a messenger, [saying], Worship Allah and avoided Taghut (idolatry).[3]

Each heavenly message confirms what was brought by the previous one, as the messengers, peace and blessings be upon them, graduated in delivering

---

[1] (Qur'an 11:118).

[2] (Qur'an 49:13).

[3] (Qur'an 16:.36).

the message of God. They were united in receiving the message of monotheism from God, but they had different laws according to the human need.

The Holy Qur'an, which is the book of God and His words, has not changed despite hundreds of years and the different nations and civilizations. It is still as it was revealed, and it continues to lead Muslims in their worldly life and on their way to the Hereafter.

It confirms the origins of the religions that preceded it, which were brought by the messengers for their time.

By taking the path of dialogue, the believer has realized the truth of the oneness of the source of God's message to proceed from his own faith towards the beginning of the journey on the earth.

This diversity is not considered an obstacle to the human communication. The dialogue has foundational principles, premises, and faith which enforce humans to respect them and start from them to communicate with the other.

The dialogue aims to eliminate fanaticism and fantasy, along with the projections of blind neurotic affiliations that prevent the human from understanding the reality of pure monotheism and leads to collision and destruction as is the situation now.

The dialogue of the messengers of God begins on a fundamental basis, which is the belief in all the heavenly messages.

With the Noble Qur'an's recognition of cosmic facts, and by presenting a summary of the divine messages that meet in the origin of monotheism, and by calling on its followers to recognize this origin, this final book was the culmination of this human communication.

The believer recognizes that God is the source of everything, and this is the greatest motivation for his journey in life according to God's method and law.

Therefore, the worldly life is the beginning of an eternal journey that a person resumes after death.

Islam considers that our existence in this world is for a supreme goal and purpose: God Almighty's knowledge and to worship Him by having a direct connection with Him.

Any misfortunes that happen, God knows it, and have allowed it. God has absolute wisdom, and absolute wisdom is related to absolute good. There is no absolute evil in existence.

Despite the shortness of this worldly life, it is like a place of affliction and a test for human beings, so that they are distinguished in degrees and ranks when they approach the next life.

Islam provided harmony between reason and religion, reason and the information transformed through narrated chains (Qur'an and sayings of Prophet Muhammed), along with harmony between the mind and heart.

Therefore, there is no enlightenment, renaissance, progress, beauty, or true science except by embracing the religion of Islam.

Islam has succeeded as a method, while capitalism and communism have failed. No orientalist has studied Islam and its civilization – whatever his stand from Islam is –did not admit that Islam is a Religion and a State.

However, Muslims being away from their true religion and their inability to properly spread Islam's principles has contributed in recent decades to an increase in the number of atheists, sceptics, and perplexities in the world.

People in the West advanced in science and knowledge when they abandoned the wrong beliefs based on the distorted religion they had, and adopted science and logic. Still, with their approach to science properly, they lost the values, morals, and purpose of their existence, by neglecting to embrace the correct religion.

We will examine these points in detail by narrating real-life conversations with personalities from different nationalities and cultures on this Journey.

Starting

the

Journey

Can There be Doubt about God?

There is no refuge from God except to Him!

The Qur'anic verse "There is no refuge from God except to Him" have always been on my mind growing up, but I did not fully understand it until a funny situation occurred with my son around 20 years ago. He was playing in the kitchen and wanted to touch the hot stove. He was very stubborn, and I had to hit his hand to prevent him from touching it again. He cried and started to wander around from one place to another, not knowing where to go. His father tried to calm him down and cheer him up, but the surprise was that he ran directly back to me and cried on my lap. His father laughed and said: Glory be to God.

I remembered the words of God Almighty **There is no refuge from God except to Him**[4], and I understood the verse. I said to myself that God Almighty reminds us when we are subjected to some difficulties, to always return to Him whenever we find ourselves far away from Him. I felt great joy after this incident.

[4] (Qur'an 9:118).

Coronavirus and the wisdom of God:

The catastrophes that occur on earth which affect humans, such as diseases, volcanoes, earthquakes, and floods, manifest the names and attributes of the Divine Majesty.

These catastrophes are at the same time a trial and test for a person; if the person assists and helps in these situations, that person will be rewarded. Suppose the person gets directly affected by these situations and shows patience, in that case, the person will know his Lord's Majesty through this affliction, just as he recognizes Gods attributes of beauty through the good that God provides to him. Seeing Gods attributes in the good and the bad situations gives us a clearer understanding of Gods attributes. In fact, if a person only knew the characteristics of Divine Beauty, it is as if he did not know God Almighty.

One atheist asked me one day about those who had been plagued by disasters, diseases, and similar disasters, so I simply said to him:

The worldly life is only a moment if you compare it with eternal life, a dip in heaven can make them forget any pain or distress, as Prophet Muhammed said.

The presence of calamities, evil, and pain was the reason behind the atheism of many contemporary materialistic philosophers. In 2007, Sir Anthony Flew, arguably the most influential atheistic philosopher of the twentieth century, published a book stating: "There is a God." Flew said: "The most impressive arguments for God's existence are those that are supported by recent scientific discoveries".

Then he said:

"The presence of evil and pain in human life does not negate God's existence, but it prompts us to reconsider the divine attributes of Him."

Anthony Flew considers that these disasters have their silver lining.

He also said: "The existence of evil and pain has been credited with building human civilizations throughout history". Also, he said: "No matter how many claims there are regarding the interpretation of this dilemma, the religious understanding remains the most acceptable and most consistent with the nature of life."

Any person who looks at life events in an external sense will not see the other side of a bad situation. Corona Virus (COVID-19) has taken lives, affected over a million individuals, and impacted everyone's life across the globe.

However, this should be seen as a wake-up call to humanity for several aspects of life that have been neglected by us for so many years; we will be able to adjust our standard of living from this point onwards. It includes government preparations for an epidemic, general hygiene, care for the environment, and even some of our living style.

Pollution in this period fell to its lowest levels worldwide due to the suspension of air and vehicle traffic, which in turn led to reducing emissions from these engines polluting the environment. It's like the globe and environment entered a recovery phase during the spread of Corona disease. A person must reflect and reconsider his life affairs.

This situation caused families to reunite inside their homes, as it reminded them of God's blessings, and their shortcomings in praise and thanks to the Lord of the Worlds. A person does not feel the grace except when he loses it.

People also began to realize the importance of hygiene more than ever, and were aware of the need to adopt severe prevention methods, the use of disinfectants excessively, and washing hands with soap and water at all time. Who would have expected all this?

There is no doubt that this great event re-arranged life priorities, as it showed the extent of human weakness and fragility, and the lack of preparation for such an event.

In a matter of a week, the whole world was standstill against this virus. We have heard and been dealing with fears of wars, or destruction between countries, but we have never expected that the next outbreak would be microbial.

This event broke the pride of many who thought that humans had reached the highest levels of materialism, and they became more like deities and felt that they do not need their Creator.

Corona disease kills the small and large, weak, and strong, poor and rich, simple man and king. It does not differentiate anyone. We heard about many wealthy people who fled to isolated shelters or palaces to escape the oppression of this disease. These same people were indifferent to most epidemics and conditions because they thought they could eliminate them by spending on treatment. The problem now for the wealthy is that money exists while the treatment does not exist. It's like the virus came to establish equality between humans; it does not differentiate between strong and weak. Also, it does not distinguish between rich and poor.

It is strange to see that the whole of humanity united for the first time in history to confront this microbe.

If there is no God, then from where do we get all this good?

Atheists who question why evil exists also reveal numerous fault lines in their worldview.

Questioning the existence of good is the far worthier question, for only after identifying the dominant principle can the exceptions to that principle be understood. People would forever see the extraordinary laws of physics, chemistry, and biology as incoherent if they were to begin studying these sciences with the rare exceptions that deviate from these laws. Likewise, atheists can never overcome the "hurdle of evil" until they find the humility to concede that evil is the exception in a world of innumerable phenomena that are good, orderly, and beautiful.

Consider periods of sickness versus health over the average lifetime, or impaired versus functional across human race. Consider the moments when arteries flow versus clogging throughout life or the decades of prosperity versus ruin for an average civilization. Consider the centuries of dormancy versus eruption of volcanoes, or the millennia of non-collision between planets. Where does all this prevalent good come from?

Energy and matter swimming in a world of chaos and coincidence could never produce a world where the default is suitable. Ironically, scientific empiricism attests to the second law of thermodynamics stating that the total entropy (degree of disorder or randomness) in an isolated system with no external influence will always increase and that this process is irreversible.

In other words, organized things will always break down and dissipate unless something from the outside pulls them together. As such, blind thermodynamic forces could never have produced anything useful on their own, nor made good as widespread as it is, without the Creator organizing these seemingly random, chaotic phenomena that appear into the marvelous things like beauty, wisdom, joy, and love. All this is only after proving that the rule is good and bad is the exception.

Ibn al-Qayyim says:

"Evil and pain is either benevolence and mercy, justice and wisdom, or reform and preparation for the good that happens after it, or to prevent more difficult evil than it."

In my dialogue with a Russian atheist, he asked many questions, including the troubles and pains that cause people to suffer.

I told him: Our view of evil and pain depends on our view of the reality of this worldly life, and the purpose of human existence in it, which differs between religious people and materialists.

I told him what I have read before [5]: The materialistic perspective considers that this life has no meaning behind it. If a person dies, that's it; it becomes nil. With this perspective, people will feel the urge to obtain the maximum level of pleasure. Therefore, when that person experiences any pain, he cannot comprehend it, because they cannot look at a bigger picture of a bad situation. With a limited perspective, this person will be living in life with a shallow look, and will not understand the "random" conditions that life puts him in. Therefore, the saying that there is a god who is the source of mercy and love regulating this life becomes nonsense and absurd for them, and this means that whatever prevents them from this pleasure is considered pain for them.

---

[5] *The Myth of Atheism*. Dr. Amr Sharif. Edition 2014 AD.

Knowing God:

And I did not create the jinn and mankind except to worship Me.[6]

Islamic Revelation provides us with many reasons for why God has allowed evil and suffering to exist. The problem of evil is not presented in Islam as a problem, but rather as an instrument in the actualization of God's plan, which is intertwined with human experiences in this world as an experience that it is necessary for man's spiritual development. As we mentioned, God has attributes, and the key to happiness in this life and in the Hereafter, is to know His characteristics and attributes very well. We must teach our children the names of God and His attributes.

The attributes of Majesty:

The Possessor, The All-Mighty, The Compeller, The Restorer, The Ever-Dominating, The Magnificent, The Supreme, The All-Strong, The Capable, The Powerful, etc.

The attributes of Beauty:

The Most Gracious, The Most Generous, The Source of Goodness, The Compassionate, The Most Kind, The Pardoner, etc.

Our mission in this life is to know our Creator, so when we know only His attributes of Beauty, then we don't know Him very well.

Having hardship and suffering enables us to realize and know God's attributes, such as The Protector and The Healer. For example, without the pain of illness, we would not appreciate God's attribute of being the Healer or the One who gives us health.

---

[6] (Qur'an 51:56).

Knowing God in the Islamic teachings is a greater good, and worth the experience of suffering or pain. It will ensure the fulfilment of our primary purpose, which ultimately leads to Paradise.

Indeed, We have made that which is on the earth adornment for it that We may test them [as to] which of them is best in deed. [7]

The original concept of God:

In my dialogue with an atheist woman who was previously a believer, she said that when her daughter died, she became an atheist, and she didn't want to believe in God anymore.

The woman claims that He took her daughter from her. She said that I prayed to Him and told Him: "if you keep my daughter alive and protect her from cancer and cure her, I will believe in you, but if you take my daughter, I will stop believing in you."

This lady doesn't know who her Creator is nor His mercy. She doesn't know that in any case, it must be noted that God did not make this world permanent. This world is temporary, and everything in this life is limited by time. When it's time finishes, it dies or ends.

Neither are the good things of this world everlasting nor are the bad things eternal. We are here for a short time, and we are being tested. Those who pass this test will find an endless world that is perfect and permanent, and those who fail this test shall see the consequences of their sins and corruption.

I told her: According to mathematics, any number compared to infinity is zero. So, this life is zero, we live in the zero, because if I lived 100 or 90 or

---

[7] (Qur'an 18:7).

200 years, eventually, I will leave this life. So, compared to the eternal life with the Creator, we are here in the zero.

I told her: You must understand the wisdom behind natural disasters and suffering. Natural disasters and suffering bring out the best in some people to display elevated human values and charity. The suffering of the righteous comes with promises of a great reward and blessings from God.

Let us say you knew God and believed in His existence; you realized that he is more merciful than your parents, and you acknowledged the fact that God Almighty has a paradise that displays the heavens and the earth. Do you prefer losing faith in Him, His mercy, and His everlasting paradise over this worldly life? Would you choose zero over infinity?

I told her: It is not logical to judge a play without continuing it to the end or to reject a book because you did not like the first page.

I received many questions about the protection from atheism. How can we protect our children from atheism?

As you notice, I always insist on saying that The Original Concept of God is the key to protecting our children from atheism. Our children must understand and realize their Creator's attributes, that the Creator is more merciful than their mothers.

I say and repeat that the solution is to know God's true concept because whoever knows God, knows everything. Because, of course, we did not realize our fathers' and mothers' wisdom when we were young in many behaviors, and we always wondered why the parents behave this way. Does my father love me? Why did he agree to go on this trip?

Do you love me, mom? If you love me, why do you pressure me to study and get high marks? Why do you force me to do my daily homework? Why does my mom send me to sleep every day early?

When we grew up and had children, we understood the wisdom of our fathers' behaviors, and we understood as well that no one on earth loves the best for us more than them.

In-depth knowledge of God helps us find explanations for many matters. When our awareness and expertise widen, we can guide ourselves to solve many problems.

No disaster strikes except by permission of God. And whoever believes in God – He will guide his heart. And God is Knowing of all things. [8]

I often hear about the increase in atheism due to human-caused wars and natural disasters; there is no doubt that God's acceptance of these matters to take place is only a test of their faith. These tests bring out the truth in people, whether they have full faith in God or are hesitant in their belief. Should I worship God or only mention Him in prosperity?

And of the people is he who worships God on an edge. If he is touched by good, he is reassured by it; but if he is struck by trial, he turns on his face [to the other direction]. He has lost [this] world and the Hereafter. That is what is the manifest loss. [9]

The mercy of the Creator:

In a dialogue with an atheist, I told him that it's enough to understand or believe that the Creator is waiting for us to judge us, and that He is very merciful with us. To make this idea very clear or very close to our minds, we just need to imagine that our mothers will be the one to judge us. How happy will we be? We will be so happy, relaxed, and relieved. It's enough

---

[8] (Qur'an 64:11).
[9] (Qur'an 22:11).

for us to get reassurance in this life that our mothers are waiting to judge us on the day of judgement. So, there's no need to be scared.

I gave him a simple example of the importance of knowing God. I told him: If they told you that Faten Sabri is a lion tamer with an unforgiving and robust personality. When you come to meet her, of course, you will be careful to talk to her because you don't know anything about her except that she has a formidable personality. But the people who know her will laugh at this claim and will be surprised because everyone knows very well that Faten is afraid of cats. He laughed a lot.

During the priest's visit from the Vatican and his colleague to our center, I took them to show them the mosque. While we were discussing the concept of monotheism, I was telling them that God the Almighty, is the Creator, according to our faith. Allah is the One and the Only, who does not come to earth in any animal form or human form. He is very merciful, has no son, no partner. He created us to have mercy on us, and He sent one message through many prophets to all nations. He sent this message with Prophet Abraham, Jacob, Moses, Jesus Christ, and more. We consider Jesus Christ a human messenger who was created without a father or a male same as Prophet Adam, who was created without a father or a mother. We pray to God, worship Him as Prophet Jesus did, and like what Mary, the mother of Jesus did, but we don't pray to Mary, Jesus, or Muhammed. We pray like them.

So, he said: We don't pray to Mary, but we use Mary as an intermediary to let our supplication reach the Creator. As you know, in most families, when the children want something from their father, they prefer to speak to the mother. The mother is very merciful and has a very soft heart, and she loves her children very much. So, she can take their requests and speak with their father. So that's why we talk to Mary first, to let our supplication reach the Creator.

I told him: Yes, you are right, but this is in case the children don't know the real nature of their father. They don't know that he's very merciful, more than their mothers, and he loves them more. Maybe he doesn't show this love.

He said: No, no, let me explain more about this point. Mary, for us, is like a tray. When you serve your guests, you put the juice or the water on a tray to give the visitor. So, Mary is like a tray. We put our supplication on this tray to give it to the Creator.

I told him: Okay, so who was Mary's tray? Mary prayed directly to God; she didn't use anyone for her supplication to reach her Creator. She prayed directly to Him. So, who was Mary's tray?

This story was the starting point for spreading the true concept of God and was the reason for writing my book "The Original Concept of God", in which I wanted to explain to the world that the true concept of God is the missing point now.

Not knowing the Lord of the Worlds leads to misconceptions about Him, such as being embodied in three hypostases or represented in a human being's flesh.

Distorting God's true concept in the Old Testament not only confused people's minds and put them at loss, but also caused them to resort to atheism and distract them from religion.

The Torah, which God Almighty revealed to Moses, peace be upon him, stated that God is the One and the Only. The One who is Eternal, Merciful. Exalted is the Creator of every defect or deficiency. But we find in the Old Testament (the distorted Torah) claims about specific attributes that do not fit God's Majesty (forgetting, lack of knowledge, fear, tiredness), Glory be to Him.

In my childhood, I always wondered why God Almighty mentioned in the Holy Qur'an that he created the heavens without getting tired. I was shocked by the need to say this point, as it is known that God Almighty does not get tired. Eventually, when I started my conversations with non-Muslims, I knew that Christians believe that when God created the heavens and the earth, He rested. They would always ask me why Muslims do not consider Sunday to be a holy day, and I say because God does not get tired to rest. Surprisingly, they laugh and say: yes, you are right.

Monotheism is the way of salvation:

It is very wrong to introduce Islam by saying: Islam means to believe in One God, and just stop there. We must explain and give more depth. Islam means to believe in One God, who is the Creator, and directly connect with Him. Nothing is like Him. He does not come to earth in any animal form or human form; He has no image known to humans. Our minds can only imagine objects, people and situations based on past experiences and memories. God is beyond our perception and cannot be comprehended.

Whenever we sin, we repent to Him directly. When we have a problem, we ask Him to solve the problem instantly. When we feel blessed, we must thank Him directly. We must give these details because the faith in One God already exists in many religions.

Speaking of the faith of the disbelievers of Quraish (the tribe of Prophet Muhammad) for example, the disbelievers of Quraish believed in One God because when they were asked about worshipping the idols, they said they worship idols to make them closer to Allah. So, the problem in their case was not with Tawheed Al Rububeyya, which is to believe in One God.

The problem was with Tawheed Al Ebada, which is to have a direct connection with the Creator.

Is not to God that sincere faith is due? As for those who take guardians besides Him, "We only worship them that they may bring us nearer to God." God will judge between them regarding their differences. God does not guide the lying blasphemer.[10]

Conclusion:

We conclude that what permitted calamities is God's Will. God's Will is related to absolute wisdom, and absolute wisdom is related to absolute good, as there is no absolute evil in existence. Atheism appeared because of the differences between religions which are represented in the means used to communicate with the Creator, directly or through the taking of mediators (saints, priests, idols, or prophets).

If all religions left calling to mediators and went directly to the Creator, humanity would be united and their hearts upright, and be guided to the truth. Just as everyone agrees in praying towards the Creator directly without a partner or mediator when calamities or adversities occur, so it was necessary to invite everyone in good and bad times to worship the Lord of the Worlds. As the Holy Qur'an stated:

Say, 'O People of the Scripture, come to a word that is equitable between us and you – that we will not worship except Allah and not associate anything with Him and not take one another as lords instead of Allah.' But if they turn away, then say, 'Bear witness that we are Muslims [submitting to Him].'[11]

---

[10] (Qur'an 39:3).

[11] (Qur'an 3: 64).

Earning the Pleasure of God

There is no life worth living except the life of the Hereafter:
I have always been struggling to fully understand this saying of Prophet Muhammed peace be upon him. I wanted to get out of this inner contradiction. I tried to balance between gaining happiness for myself and my loved ones in this life, yet on the other hand, I know how great the delight is in the Hereafter. The struggle continued until my father got sick. I was living in Africa with my kids and husband who was a delegate of a United Nations' project. I was sad because I lived far away from my father, who was too sick. I kept praying for his cure and happiness in this life. Eventually, he died. I was in a great pain and sadness until I saw a dream one night, which made me cry happily. I saw him laying on a bed, and he told me: come closer. So, I did, then he said: we are alive here, we are not dead. Then he pointed around him saying: Look around at those who are reading Qur'an. I exclaimed: Are you happy?
He replied with a very long tone: I am happy. I can still hear its echo in my ears till now.
I woke up happily repeating: There is no life worth living except the life of Hereafter.[12]

---

[12] Agreed on it.

The delusion of the contemporary man:

There is a beautiful story of an American physicist who once came to visit our center. He spent two hours in an argument with my colleagues at the library. It was all about proving the existence of God on a scientific basis in which he denied.

I was silently listening without interfering until my colleagues felt tired. He was overly argumentative. They all left the library without reaching any result. After that, the visitor asked me if I could persuade him in a scientific way that God does exist, and asked If I have knowledge of physical science.

I smiled and said: Oh! I have a better knowledge; I know God!

He grumbled: No, no, please I insist that there is no God, but there is science.

I replied: You cannot just refute the author's existence because you got to know the book. They are not alternatives. Science discovers the laws of the universe, but it did not create them, God did!

I continued: Anyway, forget about science for now and tell me. You want to convince me that there is no God. So, are you happy with this? Are you satisfied with yourself?

He surprised me admitting: Never, I have never felt happy in my life. I am miserable. I don't know what to do, then he cried.

I replied: Do whatever makes you happy. Do you know the Law of attraction, the law that means you get what you expect?

He answered surprisingly: Do you believe in this law?

I said: I know it, but I don't believe in it. I believe in a greater one which is "good thinking in God". We believe that God the Creator created us to have mercy on us, and not torture us. We believe that He prepared for us a Paradise whose width is the heavens and the earth, so we will get what we expect if we obey His orders. However, you believe that you are nothing, came from nothing, and will end up with nothing. Thus, you will get maybe worse than what you expect. Do you accept (Nothing) as an answer from your son when you ask him what do you want to be when you grow up? You will not tolerate this, and you will try every possible and impossible way to urge him to study, work and do his best to be a better, important, and valuable person in the future.

He uttered: I feel lost.

I answered: You will stay lost until you eventually return to God, just like how a lost child will never find peace and happiness until he finds his mother.

Touched by my words, he said: Can anyone become a Muslim?

I said: Of course. Islam is the religion of nature.

He asked: Do I only have to believe in God?'

I replied: You also must believe in His messengers and prophets from Prophet Adam to Prophet Muhammad, and to believe in the Hereafter.

He agreed: Yes, yes.

I continued: You also must accept Jesus, peace be upon him, as a messenger, not as a god or a son of God.

He said eagerly: No, Jesus is not God; he is a Prophet.

The point here is that Man should look at himself first before he becomes conceited away from the truth. Despite how technology developed around us, we still cannot develop ourselves to be mortal creatures or even be independent creatures who don't need food, drink, air or going to the restroom.

Man tries hard searching the whole universe for happiness and continuance in life, although he knows for sure that he cannot travel to the moon without special suits and in selected spacecrafts because of fearing death.

Say, "Be you stones or iron or [any] creation of that which is great within your breasts." And they will say, "Who will restore us?" Say, "He who brought you forth the first time." Then they will nod their heads toward you and say, "When is that?" Say, "Perhaps it will be soon". [13]

According to Secularism, Charles Taylor describes how western society considers Man as the center of the universe. The laciest considers himself as the master of the universe and all that he cannot see, does not exist.

Despite having all means of comfort, it is not surprising that western societies face difficulties in dealing with evil. So, a luxuriant mostly commits suicide when encountering any problem.

Victor Frankl said: "Today people have all means of living but with no meaning of life itself, which makes life as a prison that contains people rushing between the walls of life and death. They are afraid of every bite in a meaningless life where every pain or hardship is inexplicable, inevitable, and unclassifiable. It is the only sort of chaos and tragedy."

The primary purpose of life isn't to enjoy a temporary sense of happiness, but to achieve inner and deep peace through knowing and worshipping God. Achieving this aim will lead eventually to eternal bliss and true happiness. So, if this is our goal, we will go through every trouble to achieve it.

---

[13] (Qur'an 17:50-51).

Can you imagine a person never having hard time or pain? According to his luxury life, he will forget all about God. Thus, he will fail to achieve what he was created for in the first place. Compare this to another person whose painful experiences led him to God and achieve his goal. From an Islamic point of view, the person who goes through suffering knows God better, and he is closer to Him than another person who forgets God because he does not suffer. Each human being has a goal which is usually based on his beliefs; what we find in religion but not in science, is the cause and the purpose which Man seeks. Thus, religion explains the reason why we were created, but science is just a means.

When someone goes towards religion, the most frightening thing for him is the deprivation of life's enjoyment. For most people, being religious means, they need to avoid everything else; everything is forbidden. Their thought is a false judgment that pushes people away from religion. Islam corrects this misconception; it tells us that everything is permissible, and the forbidden things are few. Islam invites us to merge in society, and balance between the spiritual, physical needs, and others' rights. One of the great challenges that faces the irreligious societies is dealing with evil and bad deeds. You will find nothing but enforcing stiff punishments.

The value of the present life:

People held tests to differentiate between the students through marks and degrees before moving into a new part of life. Despite how short the exam is, it evaluates the student's fate; the same applies to this worldly life. It is a quick test for people to rank them in degrees when they face the Hereafter. The human comes out of life with his deeds only, not with anything else from his properties. Thus, people must realize that they should act in this life for rewards and high degrees in the Hereafter. People have forgotten the true meaning of life as they continuously complained from Coronavirus. God created us in a test. Pain and trouble are parts of the test. Passing the test will ease the way to eternal bliss in Paradise.

He Who created Death and Life, that He may try which of you is best in deed: and He is the Exalted in Might, Oft-Forgiving. [14]

Atheists misunderstand our goal of life as a test for our behavior and deeds. For example, how could we possibly develop patience if we do not face experiences that need patience? How could we build courage if don't we face risks? How could we have mercy on each other if there wasn't anyone in need of it?

I remember I have always been repeating: (O God, grant me wisdom, which if I have been given, I will have received much good). After moving to Africa, I met a lot of difficulties. I insisted on raising my children in a religious environment on the straight path, without causing them to become introverts. This made me acquire a lot of wisdom. Later, I realized that God had answered my prayers.

So, why the test?

Some people say: If God is merciful, why does He not just let us all enter Paradise?

God wants us all to be religious.

If you are ungrateful, then remember! God is independent of you, and He does not favor ingratitude on the part of His creatures. If you are grateful, He will be pleased with you. For no one who carries a burden bears another's load; and your returning is to your

---

[14] (Qur'an 67:2).

Lord, when He will tell you what you used to do. Surely, He knows what is in the hearts. [15]

However, if He sends us all to Paradise, it will not be fair. He will treat Moses the same as Pharaoh; all evil and innocent people will enter Paradise as if nothing happened in the worldly life. We need a criterion that decides who would deserve Paradise. One of the beautiful things in the Islamic religion is that our Creator (who knows us better than ourselves) told us that we got all we need to overcome these tests.

God does not charge a soul except [with that within] its capacity...[16] However, if we cannot overcome these hardships after doing our best, God's mercy and justice will ensure that we receive compensation somehow, either in this life or in the eternal life that lies ahead.

Knowing God in good and bad times:

Once, I was in a meeting with an Administrative from an Argentinian International foundation. My colleagues advised me not to talk to him about religion because it is a thorny issue, but I refused and said: I don't know what to do apart from talking about religion. I was their only choice because I was the only one who speaks Spanish. I started the conversation by mentioning the Creator's greatness and Oneness and making a simple comparison between the various religions. I highlighted that monotheism is the missing ring that could unify nations. He surprised me with his flushing red face and tears saying: you Muslims are way better than us.

I replied: why?

---

[15] (Qur'an 39:7).
[16] (Qur'an 2:286).

He answered: you return to God in good moments and bad moments, but we don't do this except in troubles only. We are attached to the present life while you are connected to the Hereafter.

I said: Hardships are bliss for you then.

He was moved.

We humans quickly forget for various reasons. One of these reasons is comfort and bliss. That is why God sometimes interrupts the sweetness of life with some tribulations when we cling to its luxury, and we forget the main goal that brought us to this world.

I continued: This life is a test. The human comes out of it with a passing or a failing certificate. If someone says he likes his life, it's as if he is saying that he likes the exam and doesn't want to get the certificate.

Thus, loving this life is the origin of all evil; this is how humans are locked in a maze. They can't understand the existence of these two contradictions. The test in this life could be through goodness or evilness. Usually, when the human is tested by blessings, he gets more attached to this worldly life and loses connection with his Creator. Unlike when he is tested by difficulties, he gets more attached to God. A person is not aware that the test of evil may benefit him more than harm him in this world.

The most obvious example is what happened to Man when he developed science and technology. He forgot all about religion, God, and even other people around him.

Evil is not necessarily humanmade, but it still affects humans somehow. Spreading of disease, earthquakes, and volcanoes are evil according to human beings, but they happen to preserve the ecological balance. Besides, God gives people the means to face these incidents. Recently, the human has been exposed to the coronavirus, which disrupted life's movement in many aspects. So, Man became more eager to help others, and people became unified. Even enemies stepped aside from their problem to find a solution for this danger, threatening them all. As if this danger benefits human beings mostly when civil wars stopped. We heard the prayer call "Allah (God) is greater" at some places we never imagined hearing it in as if this virus uncovered their hearts' veil.

Know that the life of this world is but amusement and diversion and adornment and boasting to one another and competition in increase of wealth and children – like the example of a rain whose [resulting] plant growth pleases the tillers; then it dries and you see it turned yellow; then it becomes [scattered] debris. And in the Hereafter is severe punishment and forgiveness from Allah and approval. And what is the worldly life except the enjoyment of delusion. [17]

The worldly life is a place of testing and affliction. This life is full of contradictions: sickness and cure, evil and goodness, heat and cold, day and night, life, and death, etc.

Man has his free will to choose. God didn't plant evil in the human soul, but God planted the freewill to choose between evil and goodness. Man will freely choose, and God will eventually judge.

And [by] the soul and He who proportioned it (7) And inspired it [with discernment of] its wickedness and its righteousness, (8) He has succeeded who purifies it, (9) And he has failed who instills it [with corruption]. [18]

---

[17] (Qur'an 57:20).
[18] (Qur'an 91:7-9).

And say, "The truth is from your Lord, so whoever wills – let him believe; and whoever wills – let him disbelieve…"[19]

An era of anaphylaxis:

Evil and goodness are inseparable through ages. It has been noticed that people become more sensitive towards evil nowadays due to their comfortable life. The common saying "to better and longer life" became our motto after we reached the moon. So, it became expected that people get more sensitive when they see the children's tears, feel the elder's weakness, and hear patients' screams.

Human's excellency:

God knows that the human tends to be lazy and neglect things, so sometimes he intends to wake us up. People have many good traits which appear clearly through hardships. Trouble reveals courage, generosity, brotherhood, and selflessness, even with animals. Afflictions such as orphanage, homelessness, or hunger bring out many good people to the world, as well as magnificent heroes around us whose pain and suffering arouse their virtues, and enable them to make history. Even in our personal life, after each failure, we start a new beginning. God shutting our way is just a sign to change our direction. So, in dealing with a problem, we must realize that our problem was not these dark, gloomy clouds chasing us, but it is truly our heavy eyelids that prevent us from seeing the sunlight. God periodically refreshes our lives through difficulties.

Therefore, as soon as people wake up from their negligence, they realize the true meaning of their existence, and they feel the urge to live for more

---

[19] (Qur'an 18:29).

remarkable and vital goals. Hence, we can say that this 'evil' plants human excellency.

Through difficulties, people don't only discover aims, but they also live with God, for God, and by God in this life and the life after[20].

The happiness of this life and the Hereafter:

Once an atheist asked me about the human's need to believe in God, and that it is enough for people to have morals and values to control them and maintain mutually respectful relations. I told him that it is meaningless to respect and love your work colleagues while neglecting your connection with your boss. To get goodness in our life, we must strengthen it with our Creator.

Besides, what could be our motivation to have morals and values? To respect laws or respect others? If you say the enforcement of laws, we will then argue that law is not available in every place and at any time. It is not enough to solve all our local and national problems. Many people who commit crimes and evil deeds are away from others and law. All these religions around us prove how much people need it in their lives. We need it to arrange and discipline our behaviors on a religious basis which cannot be covered and hidden.

The necessity of religion is proved by the presence of many religions, which most nations on earth resort to for regulating their lives and controlling their people's behavior based on religion or law. As we know, the only criterion for a person is his religious belief in the absence of regulation, since law cannot always exist with a person and everywhere.

---

[20] https://yaqeeninstitute.org/mohammad-elshinawy/why-do-people-suffer-gods-existence-the-problem-o.

The only deterrent that can affect a person is his inner belief that he is being watched and held accountable, and this belief is buried and firm in his conscience. When the person is involved in a wrong act, he tries to conceal it because he has an instinct to differentiate between the right and wrong; hence, he was able to tell that this act is outrageous, and that it is denied by common sense. All this proves the existence of religion and belief in the depths of the human psyche.

Religion fills the gap that laws don't. Human-made rules cannot supply or bind minds and hearts to it at different times and places.

It was from what I read and liked, that a person's motivation or drive to do good differs from one person to another. Each person has his motives and interests to do or adhere to specific ethics or values.

- Punishment: Can prevent people from harming each other.
- Reward: Can encourage people to behave well.
- Self-esteem: Can control the human's desires as what one loves today may hate tomorrow.
- The religious restrain: Knowing and fearing God is the strong and effective motivation[21].

Religion greatly influences moving people's feelings and emotions, whether positively or negatively.

This influence indicates that the origin of people's instinct is based on knowing God. It may be used in many cases intentionally or unintentionally as a motive to move it, leading us to the risk of misunderstanding the purposes and teachings of the true religion, which has bad impacts on the individual and the community.

---

[21] *Atheism A Giant Leap of Faith*. Dr. Raida Jarrar.

Conclusion:

Scholar Ibn al-Qayyim summarized the conclusion in these beautiful words:

"In the heart, there is a dishevel; it can't be accumulated unless we direct ourselves to God, and a desolation, can't be not be removed unless the human is left alone with Him in his solitude. Sadness exists within the heart; it will not go away unless we acknowledge the pleasure of knowing Him and our sincere treatment with Him. Anxiety exists within the heart; it won't go away unless we meet with Him and escape from Him to Him. There is a fire of heartbreak, it will not be extinguished unless we get satisfied with the destiny, His commands, and whatever He forbade us from, and for us to embrace patience on that until the time of His meeting after death. There is a strong request; the request does not stand without God being the only required. Neediness exists within the heart; only His love, His constant remembrance, and devotion to Him can fill this need, and even if one gets the world and everything in it, that need will never be met !!"[22]

---

[22] An Islamic Scholar.

The Originator of Heavens and Earth

So, flee to God!

In a visit to South Africa, we came upon a beauty that was beyond imagination. When we reached Cape Town, I got the feeling that we had gone to another world. There were beaches filled with penguins and gardens filled with birds and butterflies with breathtaking colors. While wandering and exploring this enchanting place, we met a simple older man from Malaysia, who was born and grew up in this place. He was a driver that took us on a tour in the city for ten days. I asked him if he had visited any other county, and much to my surprise, he answered: I don't know any other place except Mecca, and I don't want to know any other place except Mecca. Whenever I get an amount of money, I go to Mecca. He said that they go to Mecca in groups crossing the black continent in trips that cost them much money and effort. Yet he said that he insists on visiting Mecca whenever he has the expenses. I was very touched saying to myself: how strange is it that such a man would leave such beauty and go to a wasteland with absolutely no greenery like Mecca. At that point, I remembered the verse: **So, flee to God**[23]. Then I said to myself: God the Almighty has indeed spoken the truth; He gloriously planted seeds of being attached to Him and yearning to meet Him in our hearts. I was pleased.

---

[23] (Qur'an 51:50).

They have not appraised God with true appraisal:

They have not appraised Allah (God) with true appraisal, while the earth entirely will be [within] His grip on the Day of Resurrection, and the heavens will be folded in His right hand. Exalted is He and high above what they associate with Him. [24]

One of the amusing incidents that I recall was a conversation I had with a Chinese diplomat who spoke English fluently. He made me laugh when he said that the Creator created the universe, then got busy, and is no longer interfering in anything in it.

At first, I thought he was joking; then I realized that this is a fundamental belief in one of the religions that are widespread worldwide.

I told him that God knows everything in this universe from the tiniest to the most extraordinary thing. Not a leaf falls without His knowledge, and not a fruit comes out of its covering. He keeps count of all things.

He answered: Isn't it strange that the Creator would interfere in everything? I simply replied that the fly that seems useless to people could cause diseases and change the natural balance in the environment. Wasn't it a mosquito that caused the death of the Alexander the great?

Is it not enough for us to realize our Creator's greatness when we see that the people nowadays fear tiny microbes, which are spreading and can't even be seen? Indeed, it is only Him who knows the true value of everything!

I always recall this conversation and say to myself: **... For indeed, it is not eyes that are blinded, but blinded are the hearts which are within the breasts.** [25]

---

[24] (Qur'an 39: 67).
[25] (Qur'an 22: 46).

The greatest nations are challenging each other by showing off their military equipment, and God, The Most Glorious, shows us a challenge that can't even be seen with our eyes.

The spreading of the coronavirus made the world realize our Creator's greatness and how all our balances have been disturbed. This unseen creature has caused the nuclear and hydrogenic weapons to collapse, and the human pride collapsed as well.

The scholar Ibn-Qayyim says: "Look at the speech of the Qur'an, and you will see the King who has the absolute possession of all, Who deserves the absolute praise. The King who has full control of everything. Everything starts from Him and ends with Him. He is the All-Knowing, Who knows all that's apparent and all that's hidden. It is Him who hears and sees, gives and takes, rewards and punishes, honors and humiliates. It is Him who creates and provides, causes death and life. It is Him who judges and manages."

The glory of God is manifested in His connection with His creations:

My conversation with the Chinese person pulled me towards reading more about his faith, in which people believed that the Creator created the universe, then abandoned it and left it without guidance.

I kept searching for a way to respond to this belief's followers, which they call "Divine Neutrality".

During my **research**, I found that the Qur'an acknowledges **the** fact that God interacts with His creations through the messengers. This connection is manifested in more than one verse in the Qur'an.

[We sent] messengers as bringers of good tidings and warners so that mankind will have no argument against God after the messengers. And ever is God Exalted in Might and Wise. [26]

First, God **stressed** that there is **wisdom** behind the creation of the human being.

Then did you think that We created you uselessly and that to Us you would not be returned?" [27]

Then, He stressed that playing and amusement were never the aims of creation.

And We did not create the heaven and earth and that between them in play. [28]

Had We intended to take a diversion, We could have taken it from [what is] with Us – if [indeed] We were to do so. [29]

God **stressed** the absolute surrender and submission of the heavens and the earth.

So, is it other than the religion of Allah (God) they desire, while to Him have submitted [all] those within the heavens and earth, willingly or by compulsion, and to Him they will be returned? [30]

He created man and Jinn only to worship Him.

And I did not create the jinn and mankind except to worship Me. [31]

God shows that man was honored over other creations by the direct and genuine relation with Him through worship.

---

[26] (Qur'an 4: 165).
[27] (Qur'an 23:115).
[28] (Qur'an 21-16).
[29] (Qur'an 21:17).
[30] (Qur'an 3:83).
[31] (Qur'an 51:56).

And who is better in religion than one who submits himself to Allah (God) while being a doer of good and follows the religion of Abraham, inclining toward truth?...[32]

Worship here is meant in its general meaning, which is knowing the Lord of the Worlds and forming a connection with Him— knowing His attributes, glorifying, exalting Him, and worshipping Him alone.

Besides what's mentioned in the Qur'an, there are several logical pieces of evidence of communication between the Creator and humans. Some of them are:

Wisdom:

If a person built a building, then abandoned it without making it appropriate for accommodation, we would undoubtedly judge this person as unwise and unstable. So, as God is ideal. There must be wisdom behind creating the heavens and the earth and exploiting them for the human's service.

The instinct and common sense:

Each human being has a strong instinct to know his/her origin and the reason for their existence. Instincts always drive the human being towards knowing their founder. When someone is born, and he/she doesn't find their parents, they get this intense need of seeing them as they were the reason for his/her existence.

The stable instinct that hasn't been affected by outside effects could be led to its Creator and founder. But that's not enough. Still, it needs guidance from its Creator through messengers to guide it to the correct path and know its Creator in a way He deserves.

---

[32] (Qur'an 4:125).

We find that many people in the world have found their way towards the heavenly messages while others are still astray from the truth and are attached to materialism.

This instinct in human beings towards communicating with their Creator, knowing the wisdom behind their existence, and knowing their fate after death has forever been in people's minds. They have invented myths and philosophies about them trying to find explanations and answers to these existentialism questions.

The existence of these questions in the human's minds, and seeking towards looking for answers for them, gives us evidence that there is an unseen power that will be leading to push Man towards knowing his/her Creator. It also gives us proof that it's unacceptable that the creations would be left with such an instinct without guidance from the founder of this instinct.

Ethics:

The feeling of thirst is a clue to water's existence, even before knowing of its existence. Also, our longing for justice is a clue to the presence of the Equitable.

So, witnessing the defects in this life and injustice between people, makes it unbelievable that this life will end with the unjust people getting away with their actions and the oppressed not being paid back. There is a comfort in the idea of the existence of resurrection and the Hereafter and retribution. No doubt that the person who knows that there will be a judgment on actions won't be left without guidance, encouragement, and intimidation. This is the role of religion.

Also, the existence of the current divine religions, whose followers believe in their source's divinity, is considered direct evidence of the Creator's communication with human beings. Even if atheists deny that the Lord sent messengers or books, the books and religions' existences are strong evidence of one truth, which is Man's unbridled desire to communicate with God and satisfy his natural void.

We find that the Qur'an stresses on giving evidence on the truthfulness of the prophets and messengers in a way that was suitable to every time and place. It is not logical to believe in the Creator's existence without believing in the presence of a practice or curriculum of communication with the Creator.

One of the Creator's attributes is wisdom, and one of the characteristics of the human being is the conflict of good and evil, and freedom of choice. It is self-evident that the imperative of the Creator's wisdom becomes clear to us, and it is enough that death exists on the imperative of judgment. Death is not destruction, but rather the transition stage to a reckoning; this is the divine religion's role in showing this fact.

The glory of the Creator is manifested in His response to the distressed who call on to Him:

I once had a conversation about the Creator's greatness with a German woman married to an Argentine man, and her Argentine mother-in-law. The husband wasn't present. During the conversation, I realized that the German woman didn't believe in God's existence, but then something happened, which caused us to cry.

The mother-in-law talked to me persistently about the hardships facing us in life, and questioned how we could handle them. The conversation was very touching to the extent that she cried. Then while I was explaining the wisdom, mercy, glory, and greatness of God in sending such hardships, she asked: Then what's the solution? What should we do to face such difficulties?

I replied: Say: Ya Rab (Oh God)!

They said: How?

I showed them the way to do supplications by raising their hands and taught them the words. We all said: Ya Rab (Oh God)!

While we were saying the words, the German woman got a phone call with news that made her cry and jump in joy, hugging her mother-in-law and me. The mother-in-law kept on asking her: Did he come out? Did he come out?

The German woman replied: Yes! Yes! They both hugged me saying: We thank you, God!

I learnt that the husband had been put in jail from three weeks due to corruption in his data. He was a man of high status in the community, so this was a shock to them.

The German woman told me words that I will never forget. She told me thank you for bringing out of my heart what I didn't realize existed. I never thought that I believed in God. At that moment, I realized how great God is to answer supplications and to guide such hearts that longed to know Him.

I was delighted with what this woman admitted to me because it proved what I always repeat in my lectures to students and in my conversations with non-Muslims, there is nothing called atheism. All people know that God is there whether they admitted it or not. Our role is to get from those who claim to be atheists the faith they are hiding or trying to hide.

Now, we all urgently need to say these supplications to God at the time of this corona pandemic.

The supplications of the distressed. As if we are all in the stomach of the whale. We need to say: **There is no deity except You; exalted, are You. Indeed, I have been of the wrongdoers.**[33]

Why religion?

One Portuguese doctor asked me about the importance of converting to Islam, and why should she convert to any religion at all. She wondered why it wasn't enough to just believe in God and worship Him in her way.

She said that she believed in a Creator's existence, but she didn't think that He communicates with humans through messengers. She said that she does good deeds and helps both humans and animals, but isn't waiting for a reward from the Creator, she takes her prize and happiness from humanity instead.

I told her: Do you think the human is immortal? Is human happiness endless? When humanity ends, only God, Who does not die, will remain. I told her that by her way, she is like a student whom after twelve years of studying says: I don't want the certificate.

Imagine, if you were a member of a Social Solidarity Foundation to get a retirement salary, then the foundation declared that it wouldn't be able to pay these salaries. It will close soon; would you continue dealing with it?

A believer works and strives to help humanity for the sake of God, and gets happiness both in life and Hereafter.

I told her: Regarding the importance of the religion's existence, imagine that you are walking in a way and do not know its end. You'd have two options, either follow the instructions of the signs found on the road or try to guess, which may cause you to lose and perish.

---

[33] (Qur'an 21:87).

Also, imagine that you buy a TV, and try to use it without going back to the operating instructions. You will spoil it. The TV set coming from the same factory, for example, arrives here with the same instruction booklet that arrives to Portugal, so we must use it in the same way.

I also told her: If you want to communicate with me, for example, I must tell you the possible way, as if I tell you to talk to me by phone and not by e-mail, for example, and you must use the phone number that I provide you personally, as you cannot use any other number.

We find some people communicating with God by dancing and singing in places of worship, and others who applaud to wake God according to their belief.

It is God's greatness to make a system to be followed by all of us, organize our relationship with Him, and our relationship with those around us, which is the religion's definition.

Humans cannot worship God by following their whims because they will harm themselves first before harming others.

Some of them worship God by taking a mediator, and they believe that God comes in the form of human beings or stones. God wants to protect us from ourselves when we worship what does not benefit or harm us, but rather causes us to perish in the Hereafter. Worship other than God with Him is considered the greatest sin, and its punishment is immortality in Hell.

She asked: why does making partners with God makes the person deserve eternal hellfire?

I told her: In the manmade laws, it's well known that not adhering by the king's rights is like no other crime. What if we are talking about the KING of the kings? It's God's right to be worshipped alone, and it's human's right to have a direct connection with Him without intermediaries so they can get peace in this life and the Hereafter.

The correct religion:

Then she asked me about the correct religion that she must embrace after believing in God.

I told her: It is from God's greatness that He made the right religion easy, logical, and according to our instincts. It's to worship Him alone while doing good deeds and leaving the evil. It's the religion that all the prophets called for.

The correct religion could be distinguished through three main points[34]:

> The attributes of God in the religion.

> The attributes of the prophet or the messenger.

> The details of that religion.

The correct religion must include attributes showing the Beauty and Glory of God:

It must include a description of God and evidence of His existence.

Say: He is Allah, [who is] One, (1) Allah, the Eternal Refuge. (2) He neither begets nor is born, (3) Nor is there to Him any equivalent. [35]

As for the description of the messenger and his attributes, the religion:

Must describe how the connection between God and the messenger is established.

---

[34] *The Myth of Atheism.* Dr. Amr Sharif. Edition 2014 AD.

[35] (Qur'an 112).

**And I have chosen you, so listen to what is revealed [to you]. ** [36]
Must show that these messengers are responsible for delivering the messages from God.

**Messenger, announce that which has been revealed to you from your Lord, and if you do not, then you have not conveyed His message... ** [37]
These messengers haven't been sent to call people to worship themselves, but to worship God alone.

**It is not for a human [prophet] that Allah (God) should give him the Scripture and authority and prophethood and then he would say to the people, "Be servants to me rather than God," but [instead, he would say], "Be pious scholars of the Lord because of what you have taught of the Scripture and because of what you have studied." ** [38]
Must emphasis that the messengers are supreme in the limited human attributes.

**And indeed, you are of a great moral character. ** [39]
The messengers are human role models.

**There has certainly been for you in the Messenger of God an excellent pattern for anyone whose hope is in God and the Last Day and [who] remembers God often. ** [40]
It's illogical to accept a religion that describes the messengers as drunk or adulterers or traitors.

---

[36] (Qur'an 20:13).
[37] (Qur'an 5-67).
[38] (Qur'an 3:79).
[39] (Qur'an 68:4).
[40] (Qur'an 33:21).

As for the religion itself, it must include:

A description of the Creator:

The correct religion wouldn't describe the Creator with what doesn't fit His glory and greatness. It wouldn't show Him like an animal or stone or that He was begotten or has children. It also wouldn't show Him as to have equals from His creations.

[He is] Creator of the heavens and the earth. He has made for you from yourselves, mates, and among the cattle, mates; He multiplies you thereby. There is nothing like unto Him, and He is the Hearing, the Seeing. [41]

Allah – there is no deity except Him, the Ever–Living, the Sustainer of [all] existence. Neither drowsiness overtakes Him nor sleep. To Him belongs whatever is in the heavens and whatever is on the earth. Who is it that can intercede with Him except by His permission? He knows what is [presently] before them and what will be after them, and they encompass not a thing of His knowledge except for what He wills. His throne extends over the heavens and the earth, and their preservation tires Him not. And He is the Most High, the Most Great. [42]

Must show the purpose of existence:

And I did not create the jinn and mankind except to worship Me. [43]

Say, "I am only a man like you, to whom has been revealed that your god is one God. So, whoever would hope for the meeting with his

---

[41] (Qur'an 42:11).

[42] (Qur'an 2: 255).

[43] (Qur'an 51:56).

Lord – let him do righteous work and not associate in the worship of his Lord anyone." [44]

The obligations of the religion must be within human capabilities:

...God intends for you ease and does not intend for you hardship... [45]

God does not charge a soul except [with that within] its capacity... [46]

And God wants to lighten for you [your difficulties]; and mankind was created weak. [47]

Must give the rational proofs of the validity of concepts and facts it presents.

The message must give us clear and sufficient rational proofs to judge the validity of its content:

So, we find that Qur'an did not only give such mental proofs, but has defied atheists and polytheists to provide evidence of their beliefs.

And they say, "None will enter Paradise except one who is a Jew or a Christian." That is [merely] their wishful thinking, Say, "Produce your proof, if you should be truthful." [48]

And whoever invokes besides God another deity for which he has no proof – then his account is only with his Lord. Indeed, the disbelievers will not succeed. [49]

---

[44] (Qur'an 18:110).
[45] (Qur'an 2: 185).
[46] (Qur'an 2: 286).
[47] (Qur'an 4:28).
[48] (Qur'an 2:111).
[49] (Qur'an 23:117).

Say, "Observe what is in the heavens and earth." But of no avail will be signs or warners to a people who do not believe.[50]

Must have no contradiction between the religious contents presented in the message:

Then do they not reflect upon the Qur'an? If it had been from [any] other than Allah (God), they would have found within it much contradiction. [51]

It is He who has sent down to you, [O Muhammad], the Book; in it are verses [that are] precise – they are the foundation of the Book – and others unspecific. As for those in whose hearts is deviation [from truth], they will follow that of it which is unspecific, seeking discord and seeking an interpretation [suitable to them]. And no one knows its [true] interpretation except Allah. But those firm in knowledge say, "We believe in it. All [of it] is from our Lord." And no one will be reminded except those of understanding. [52]

The religious texts must not conflict with natural human ethical laws:

So, direct your face toward the religion, inclining to truth. [Adhere to] the true nature on which God has created [all] people. No change should there be in the creation of God. That is the correct religion, but most of the people do not know. [53]

God wants to make clear to you [the lawful from the unlawful] and guide you to the [good] practices of those before you and to accept your repentance. And God is Knowing and Wise. God wants to

---

[50] (Qur'an 10:101).

[51] (Qur'an 4:82).

[52] (Qur'an 3:7).

[53] (Qur'an 30: 30).

accept your repentance, but those who follow [their] passions want you to digress [into] a great deviation. [54]

The religious texts must not conflict with science:

Have those who disbelieved not considered that the heavens and the earth were a joined entity, and We separated them and made from water every living thing? Then will they not believe? [55]

The religious texts shouldn't be isolated from daily human life and modern civilization:

Say, "Who has forbidden the adornment of God which He has produced for His servants and the good [lawful] things of provision?" Say, "They are for those who believe during the worldly life [but] exclusively for them on the Day of Resurrection." Thus, do We detail the verses for a people who know. [56]

The religious texts should be convenient to any place and time:

...This day I have perfected for you your religion and completed My favor upon you and have approved for you Islam as religion... [57]

The Message universality:

Say, [O Muhammad], "O mankind, indeed I am the Messenger of God to you all, [from Him] to whom belongs the dominion of the heavens and the earth. There is no deity except Him; He gives life and causes death." So, believe in God and His Messenger, the

---

[54] (Qur'an 4 :26- 27).

[55] (Qur'an 21:30).

[56] (Qur'an 7:32).

[57] (Qur'an 5:3).

unlettered prophet, who believes in God and His words, and follow him that you may be guided. [58]

Conclusion:

Based on our Creator's greatness, we conclude that He has communicated with His creations, sent messengers with His true heavenly religion to all human beings as a mercy to them, and to alleviate their suffering, while many people do not realize this fact.

We find groups of people who deny God's sending of messengers. Another group of people made partners and intermediaries with the Creator and followed different ways to communicate with the Creator. Others suffered from the beliefs of their peoples and ended up leaving religion entirely.

The truth that we want to prove here is that:

- There must be a religion first.
- There must be one religion because the Creator is one (but with different laws and approaches that suit nations).
- Finally, the true religion must be Islam (believing in One God, and unifying Him in worship).

How could God accept any other religion that wouldn't call for monotheism. (Submission by believing in Him and worshipping Him alone). If we look throughout history, we won't find any other religion as clear and tolerant and pleasant as Islam.

---

[58] (Qur'an 7:158).

The Fall of the False Gods

Indeed, God will perfect His light, but the disbelievers will still dislike it:

One day in Africa at the language center, I was frustrated about the situation our world had reached, which is avoiding God's religion and turning to other religions by asking and obeying an object that wouldn't benefit them nor harm them. I was engrossed in my thoughts. Suddenly, a Muslim French language teacher interrupted me by asking about the reason behind my deep thinking.

I answered him: What bothers me and causes me to overthink is that people are ignorant about God's religion, and I feel that I have a responsibility towards that. I want the phrase "There is no god but One God (Allah)" to reach far and globally.

He then told me: Do not worry, my sister, for God has promised to preserve his religion, and God will not break his promise.

After that, I noticed how strong his faith was, and observed his certainty in God too; I then remembered the noble verse: **Indeed, God will perfect His light, although the disbelievers dislike it.** [59] I was ultimately relieved.

---

[59] (Qur'an 61:8).

The Day when there will not benefit [anyone] wealth or children:

Today during the Coronavirus crisis, we see dead people whom no one knows about, along with elderly homes filled with lifeless, anonymous bodies. Nobody knows anything about people who die on the street. Others have money and are waiting for treatments; they began to sacrifice the elderly for the sake of the young one. Patients race for hospital beds. This situation presents a scene that is similar to specific scenes from the Day of Resurrection.

The corona crisis caused some people to drop symbols from their hearts; they used to pin their illusions on these symbols. These symbols resulted in fake deities that they used to worship instead of worshipping God The Almighty. Indeed, whoever used to worship money ended up not benefitting from it. Whoever used to think that his physical science could save him was wrong because it did not save him. Whoever used to plead through stones and idols eventually kept a distance from them because he was scared, they might inflect him. We often hear about priests who urge their followers to take refuge in God directly and avoid coming to them. The light of "There is no God except Allah the One true God" is seen all over the world.

Undoubtedly, such situations push human beings to take refuge in God and turn to Him.

Below are the words of the Prophet Muhammad in its best meaning:

If you ask, then ask God [alone]; and if you seek help, then seek help from God [alone].[60]

---

[60] (Sahih Al-Tirmizi).

I remember what a Spanish elderly told me one time; he said: "In the West, we worship neither God nor Jesus. We worship women and money." Although he said it jokingly, what he said was true.

Indeed, I can remember what he said now, while the Westerns say: O God, Myself.

Have you seen he who has taken as his god his own desire:

I read once [61] that atheists traced their source of randomness and chance by using the terms design, fine-tuning, coded language, intelligence, intent, complex systems, and interconnected laws, etc. Although they never admit it, scholars refer to the Creator by other names such as Mother Nature, Laws of the Universe, Natural Selection, Darwin's Theory, etc. They do that in a miserable attempt to escape religion's logic and believing in the Creator's existence.

They are not but [mere] names you have named them – you and your forefathers – for which God has sent down no authority. They follow not except assumption and what [their] souls desire, and there has already come to them from their Lord guidance. [62]

Using any name other than "God" robs some of His absolute qualities and raises more questions. For example, avoiding to mention God is attributed to random nature and the creation of universal laws and complex interconnected systems. Man's eyesight and intelligence are traced back to a blind and foolish origin.

I read that some of Darwin's followers consider natural selection (an irrational physical process) a unique, creative force that solves all complicated evolutionary problems without any real experimental basis.

---

[61] *Atheism A Giant Leap of Faith. Dr. Raida Jarrar.*

[62] (Qur'an 53: 23).

Later they discovered the complexity of the design, structure, and function of bacterial cells. So, they started using expressions such as "smart bacteria", "microbial intelligence", "decision-making" and "problem-solving bacteria"; thus, the bacteria turned into their new god.

Man, in Islam is God's representative, and in the West is an advanced animal:

I had a conversation with a French visitor, and he discussed the issue of the origin of Man's existence on earth.

He said: The West adopts Charles Darwin's theory; we are human beings developed from Apes.

I asked: Why didn't the rest of the Apes evolve to become the rest of humanity?

I added: The theory is a set of hypotheses. These hypotheses come by observing a phenomenon, and they require successful experiments to prove them, or an observation that verifies the validity of the idea. If either experience or statement cannot prove one of the ideas that belong to the theory, the whole approach is reconsidered. Please give me an example of a living thing that evolved from another living thing.

He said: I will give you an example that happened more than 60,000 years ago.

I told him: If you haven't seen or noticed it personally, then there is no way to accept your argument.

He said: No, it was recently observed that birds' beaks might change shape in some species.

I told him: But they remained birds and based on your theory, birds must evolve into another species. Thus, the theory has no meaning.

He said: No, no, I believe in science. I read many books in this field, and I believe them.

I asked: What is the difference between you, a believer in God, and a believer of the Book of God then? You consider the person who believes in the Creator's existence as a backward person because he believed in something he did not see. Plus, the believer believes in something that raises and exalts his status, while you believe in what disgusts and condemns you! The idea that human was evolved from apes was not part of Darwin's views at all. He said that humans and monkeys go back to one standard and unknown origin called (the missing link). It had unique development, and it turned into a human being. Although we as Muslims reject entirely Darwin's words, he never said what others think he said, which is that the monkey is the ancestor of humans.

It has been proven that Darwin believed in the existence of a deity, but this idea (evolving the human being from an ape ancestor) eventually came from Darwin's followers after they added it to his theory; they were initially atheists. Of course, we as Muslims realize that God honored Adam and took him as a successor. To be evolved from an animal or something similar doesn't fit the successor.

The era of madness:

I had an interesting conversation with an American who went far in convincing me of Darwin's theory.

I asked him: Is the biological evolution a scientific or theoretical fact? Does the concept of evolution necessarily deny God's existence, or is it possible to combine the two perspectives?

He answered me: If you do not believe in modern Darwinism, you are a backward, ignorant or insane person.

He continued: Of course, modern Darwinism has no place for acceptance of the universe creator.

I told him: I don't know who is the crazy one! Darwin, the founder of this theory, said himself: "Let's assume that the eye, with its comprehensive structures, adjusts the focal length of different distances and allows various quantities of light to pass through it. Saying that the eye is formed by natural selection seems to be something that highly contradicts common sense, and I admit that." [63]

I added: Darwin believed that a great Creator is behind the first living cell, then nature handled its development, reaching to what we see from biological diversity today. Look at what you and his followers did, considering him a symbol of atheism.

I added: Darwin's theory that says we came to this world as a result of random mutations is just a theory that has not been approved. Darwin himself, the founder of this theory, admitted that he had several suspicions where he wrote several letters to his colleagues expressing his doubts and sorrow.

Darwin said: "It's extremely difficult or even impossible to imagine that a massive universe like our planet where a human with enormous humane capabilities came into existence by a sudden coincidence, or because necessity is the mother of invention. Whenever I look around me to find out the prime reason for this existence, I find myself propelled to saying that a brilliant mind exists. Hence, I believe in the presence of God." [64]

---

[63] "Chapter 7: *Oller and Omdahl.*" Moreland, J. P. The Creation Hypothesis: Scientific.

[64] *Darwin's Autobiography* - London Edition: Collins 1958 - pp. 92, 93.

Chaos Theory had proven that coincidence does not exist, but instead, all incidents in this universe, no matter how small, result from extremely accurate rules that we do not acknowledge.

Darwin's theory is a system made up of three elements:

> Mutual origin: It means that all living things, plants, and animals developed from one source, which is the unicellular organism. After that, they are in trouble with the lack of transitional organisms. Transitional organisms are rings that are supposed to exist as a result of transitioning from an organism to another. Darwin didn't involve a development series that contained sufficient transitional organisms in the fossil record. Darwin set a supposition representing the first cell that had a mutual origin. His "tree trunk" was where its branches represented the organisms that developed from this cell; he named it "Life Tree". But James Valentine did another study about this theory or the supposition set by Darwin, which says: "Many of the Life Tree's branches that Darwin adopted are obstructed, which means that finding ancestors for those organisms is impossible."

> Random mutations: It means the progression from one organism to another in a more complex way that occurred due to unexpected changes in the genetic code of the organism, and that it should've been prolonged, but Darwin added that without this trait, his theory becomes unacceptable. Evolutionary scientist Stephen Gould surprised Darwin's followers with his extensive research results.

The results showed that the fossil record does not reveal prolonged evolution, but has two primary characteristics which have undermined the theory:

- Sudden completed appearance.
- Stability and recession.

➢ Natural selection: It is a mechanism that passes from beneficial, random mutations to the second generations, and then it is preserved. This hypothesis lacks evidence, as science cannot prove the randomness of conversions, and hence the statement of randomness becomes a philosophical rather than a scientific concept.

Science provides convincing evidence for the concept of evolution from a common origin, which was mentioned in the Holy Quran.

…And made from water every living thing? Then will they not believe? [65]

God Almighty created living creatures that are intelligent and innate to suit the surrounding environment. They can develop in size, shape, or length. For example, sheep in cold countries have specific conditions and skins that protect them from the cold, and wool increases or decreases depending on the weather; it is different in other countries. Forms and types differ according to the environment. Humans differ in their colors, characteristics, tongues, and shapes, as no human being is like the other. They only remain human beings who do not change into a type of animal.

---

[65] (Qur'an 21 30).

The Almighty said:

And of His signs is the creation of the heavens and the earth and the diversity of your languages and your colors. Indeed, in that are signs for those of knowledge. [66]

God has created every [living] creature from water. And of them are those that move on their bellies, and of them are those that walk on two legs, and of them are those that walk on four. God creates what He wills. Indeed, God is over all things competent. [67]

The theory of evolution, which intends to deny the Creator's existence, states the common ancestry in the genesis of all living and plant organisms and that it has developed from a single origin, a single-celled organism. It also says that the first cell's formation resulted from amino acids gathering in water, which formed the first structure, DNA, which carries an organism's genetic traits. By combining these amino acids, the living cell's first structure was created. As a result of various environmental and external factors, these cells proliferated, which formed the first sperm, developed into a leech, and developed into an embryo. As we notice, these stages are very similar to human creation steps in the mother's womb. However, living organisms stop growth, and the organism is formed according to their DNA carried genetic characteristics. For example, frogs complete their growth and remain frogs. Likewise, every living organism completes its development according to its genetic features.

Even if we include the subject of genetic mutations and their effect on genetic characteristics in the emergence of new living creatures, this does not contradict the Creator's Ability and Will. However, atheists say: This

---

[66] (Qur'an 30: 22).
[67] (Qur'an 24: 45).

is done randomly. In contrast, we see that the theory confirms that these developmental stages cannot take place and proceed except with the intent and management of an expert. Thus, it is possible to adopt guided evolution, or divine development, which agrees with biological evolution and rejects randomness. Also, it is possible to accept that there must be a wise and capable expert behind evolution. We can accept evolution, but we reject Darwinism entirely.

Here, the great paleontologist and biologist Stephen Gull expresses the dilemma of Darwin's henchmen sarcastically. He says: "Either one of my fellow halves are stupid, or Darwinism is full of concepts that go along with religion."

The Holy Qur'an corrects the concept of evolution by narrating the story of Adam's creation:

Has there [not] come upon man a period of time when he was not a thing [even] mentioned? [68]

The creation of Adam was from clay:

And certainly, did We create man from an extract of clay. [69]

Who perfected everything which He created and began the creation of man from clay. [70]

Indeed, the example of Jesus to God is like that of Adam. He created Him from dust; then He said to him, Be, and he was.[71]

Honoring Adam, the father of human beings:

---

[68] (Qur'an 76:1).

[69] (Qur'an 23: 12).

[70] (Qur'an 32: 7).

[71] (Qur'an 3: 59).

[Allah] said, O Iblees (Lucifer), what prevented you from prostrating to that which I created with My hands? Were you arrogant [then], or were you [already] among the haughty? [72] Honoring Adam, the father of humankind, was not only for being created independently from clay, but he was created by the Lord of the World's hands, as indicated in the noble verse. Also, honoring Adam was about God requesting the angels to prostrate to him as obedience.

And [mention] when We said to the angels, prostrate before Adam; so, they prostrated, except for Iblees. He refused and was arrogant and became of the disbelievers. [73]

Creating Adam's offspring:

Then He made his posterity out of the extract of a liquid disdained.[74]

Then We placed him as a sperm–drop in a firm lodging. Then We made the sperm–drop into a clinging clot, and We made the clot into a lump [of flesh], and We made [from] the lump, bones, and We covered the bones with flesh; then We developed him into another creation. So blessed is God, the best of creators.[75]

And it is He who has created from water a human being and made him [a relative by] lineage and marriage. And ever is your Lord competent [concerning creation]. [76]

---

[72] (Qur'an 38: 75).

[73] (Qur'an. 2: 34).

[74] (Qur'an 32: 8).

[75] (Qur'an 23: 13- 14).

[76] (Qur'an 25: 54).

Honoring Adam's offspring:

And We have certainly honored the children of Adam and carried them on the land and sea and provided for them of the good things and preferred them over much of what We have created, with [definite] preference. [77]

Here we notice the similarity in the emergence stages of Adam's offspring (degrading water, sperm, leeches, embryos, etc.) with what was mentioned in the evolution theory in the emergence of living organisms and the methods of their reproduction.

[He is] Creator of the heavens and the earth. He has made for you from yourselves, mates, and among the cattle, mates; He multiplies you thereby. There is nothing like unto Him, and He is the Hearing, the Seeing. [78]

God made the descendants of Adam start from degrading water to signify the unity of the source of creation, along with the Creator's Oneness. He also distinguished Adam from other creatures by creating him independently to honor the human being and to achieve the Lord of the World's wisdom in making him a successor on earth. Also, the creation of Adam without a father or mother is also to indicate the ability to create Jesus, peace be upon him to be a miracle of ability and a sign for people.

Surely, in the sight of God, the similitude of the creation of Jesus is as the creation of Adam whom He created out of dust, and then said: 'Be', and he was. [79]

---

[77] (Qur'an 17: 70).
[78] (Qur'an 42:11).
[79] (Qur'an 3:59).

That's what atheists try to deny by adopting the theory of evolution is evidence against them.

Survival of the fittest:

I had a conversation with an atheist and a supporter of Darwin's theory; he defended it staunchly. He was also one of the most vigorous defenders of homosexuality.

I told him: You are one of the advocates of homosexuality and a supporter of Darwin's theory. Darwin's theory talks about natural selection. Natural selection is a mechanism in which beneficial random mutations are passed on to the following generations, and later they are preserved. But organisms that contain unbeneficial fungi die, perish and extinct. Darwin's theory says that survival is for the fittest of life. Of course, we also know that male and female marriage is one of the beneficial things because they produce future generations that can rebuild the earth. You say that the existence of homosexuals on the planet is a natural thing. You say that they are just natural desires and inclinations which are not odd.

I added: Isn't that against Darwin's theory? Darwin's theory states that natural selection helps with the survival of what's beneficial and fit from random mutations. So, what is useful in homosexuals' behavior?!

Of course, he had no answer!

Instinctive religion:

There is a beautiful story about my meeting with two visitors from Mexico. They had frightening looks, along with tattoos on their bodies and hands. Also, they had piercings all over their ears and other parts of their faces. I was hesitated to talk to them about Islam, but I accepted to be their company because they did not speak English. Some of my colleagues also accompanied me, so I intended to finish that tour quickly.

I started talking about how Muslims believe in One God who is the Creator, God of Moses, Jesus, and Abraham. I knew previously that they were from Mexico, so I assumed that most Mexicans are Christians who know about Moses, Jesus and Abraham, peace be upon them.

I told them: The Creator God is one. He has no son, and nothing is like him. God created Adam without a father or mother and created the Prophet Jesus without a father. He sent one message with the prophets; the one message says that there is one Creator that we should worship as the prophets worshipped this Creator. For example, Noah's people worshipped idols, and those idols were symbols of righteous people. Still, they elevated the status of these symbols to the point that they worshipped them. The nation of Jesus worshipped Jesus and raised his status to the level of divinity. For this reason, God Almighty used to send the prophets from time to time to remind people to worship God alone and return to righteousness. For example, in Abraham's time, Abraham's followers always had to worship God alone and testify that there is no god but One God and that Abraham is the Messenger of God. God also sent Moses to confirm Abraham's message. Abraham's followers had to accept the new Prophet and testify that there is no god but One God and that Moses and Abraham are messengers of God. After that, when Jesus came to confirm the Moses' message, Moses' followers had to believe in Jesus. They then had to accept his message, testify that there is no god but One God and that Jesus, Moses and Abraham are God's messengers. Eventually, Muhammad came to confirm the prophets' messages, the ones that came before him. Both Jesus and Moses' followers had to accept the new Prophet. They also had to testify that there is no god but One God and that Muhammad, Jesus, Moses, and Abraham are messengers of God, peace be upon them all.

I was surprised that the two visitors started crying heavily! The two men of great size, muscles, and length, whom I was terrified from, suddenly showed me a terrible scene of crying! So, I asked them the reason for their crying, and they answered me. They were talking at the same time as children out of their passion and enthusiasm.

With bitterness, they complained to me: We were very certain from a young age that the Creator is One and Only, and that He has no son, and we did not accept that Jesus Christ was God or a son of a God, and the Trinity was for us meaningless, aimless and with no explanation. They added that they had rejected it and left all atheism theories and random biological evolution. They also mentioned that they wandered around the earth and resorted to drugs and atrocious behaviors despite their deep inner belief in God The Almighty's existence.

They added: We thought that there is no religion on the earth that says that there is no god but One God. We believed that Muslims worship Muhammad, Christians worship Jesus, and Buddhists worship Buddha. We thought that we were crazy and unnatural, as what we find in the religions on earth does not match what we had in our hearts, so we resorted to nightclubs.

They said that they lived a very miserable life and that they never enjoyed that empty life.

I said to them: Of course, this religion exists, which is the origin of religions; this is the true religion, and it is the one religion for all, that there is no god but God, and that Muhammad is the Messenger of God. I told them that every Muslim must bear witness that there is no god but One God (Allah) and that Muhammad is the Messenger of God, and that Jesus is the Messenger of God. Then, the time for noon prayer came, and the mosque's prayer caller started calling to prayer with a beautiful voice, so they wept even more and cried more with the prayer call sound. I stopped talking to listen to the prayer call. After the prayer caller finished, I asked them: Did you understand what the caller has just said?

They said: No.

I said to them: The caller said: I bear witness that there is no god but God, and that Muhammad is the Messenger of God. We always say that Muhammad is the last messenger of God, so with it, we accept Jesus, Moses, and all of God's prophets.

They said: Can we say as he said?

I told them: If you say it, it will be the first step in accepting this religion.

They said: Yes, we accept. Then the two Mexicans uttered the testimony of faith in a beautiful atmosphere of tears and joy. I even cried.

That was the proof of common sense that God installed in people.

Conclusion:

We can get the conclusion in these amazing words:

Scholar Ibn-Taymia said: "The essence of monotheism is to worship God alone, not anyone but Him, fear not anyone but Him, trust not anyone but Him, and religion is for Him only, not for anyone of the creatures."

They Denied What is Beyond Their Knowledge

He is with you wherever you are:

I had a conversation once with my driver in Nigeria, who was a religious catholic. He said that even though he believes that Jesus is the son of God, he refuges only to God never to Jesus. He told me about an incident that had happened to him in the past. One day he was weeping and praying to God: Oh God! I never ask and pray to anyone except you! You know that I'm willing to marry and marriage is a huge responsibility. My future wife will be pregnant one day and will need me to drive her to the hospital to give birth to my child. I will need a car then, so God, please give me a car of my own. He said he was desperate and cried abundantly. He then said that a few weeks later, a wealthy man in his neighborhood to whom he used to do some paid errands told him that he had bought a small car to his wife as a present but refused it because it was small. So, the rich man wanted to give my driver that car, because he was furious with his wife.

My driver said: You would never imagine how happy I was, but my happiness with the fact that God had responded to my prayers was more than my satisfaction with the car.

I remembered the verse: **He is with you wherever you are,**[80] and I said to myself: how great you are Allah! If this is your action with whom claims a son to you, then how would your action be with whom says: **He begets not, nor was He born. There is none like unto Him**. I was delighted indeed.

---

[80] (Qur'an 57:4).

I recall the boredom I used to feel while travelling with my husband and his efforts in helping me accommodate to living in these different countries. I remember that he one day invited his Armenian friend and his wife for dinner in a beautiful restaurant. He hoped I would get to know his wife and maybe that would decrease my homesickness.

The modesty and angelic features of the wife attracted my attention so much. I felt innocence and faith glowing out of her.

I was happy to know her, especially after telling me that she is a Spanish teacher and wants to learn Arabic. We agreed that I'd daily teach her Arabic for an hour and she would speak Spanish with me for an hour in return, because I didn't want to forget that language.

We used to meet in a small restaurant in the compound we both lived in. Everything was going on smoothly till one day she surprised me by asking about the meaning of the term "Ahamdu Allah" that Muslims say. I answered: Muslims thank their Creator for the good and bad. They know that whatever good happens to them is from God, and whatever bad is from themselves, meaning that they need to repent and ask for forgiveness.

So – much to my surprise – she said: God does not exist. You are fooling yourselves. Life will perish, and we will all be nothing.

I was shocked, not because this was my first time to encounter an atheist. I have had many debates with atheists, but I never expected such modesty and innocence to behold such a black heart that doesn't know the Creator (Allah).

She added: I have postgraduate studies in physics and my father is a physician. He has always warned me of such nonsense. I can almost hear his voice saying: Take care because they will try to fool you!

I told her: Then who do you turn to when even your father can't help you? She said: I don't need anyone. I depend on myself, and I don't need any claimed god to help me.

So, I told her: I'm astonished by your thoughts. How could your way of thinking be right? Let's say you are sick with influenza; you might not even be able to reach a glass of water! What did physics tell you?!

Physics told you that there are sound waves that you must believe in even if you can't see them. It told you that there are ultraviolet waves that again, you must believe in even if you can't see them.

It told you that light is out of time and that the connected particles, when separated over great distances, continue to interact instantaneously. Physics convinced you that there are other worlds and you believed all this even without seeing it.

The materialistic world told you to believe in things that do not exist like the mirage. You believed in all this and then at the time of death neither physics nor chemistry will help you because they promised you nothingness.

You accept to believe that light is out of time, yet you refuse to believe that the Creator doesn't abide by the laws of time or space. He is before everything and after everything, and none of His creations can encompass His knowledge.

You believe that the connected particles when separated over great distances, continue to interact instantaneously. Yet, you refuse the idea that The Creator is continuously with His creations with His knowledge. God can be omnipresent; present with everyone simultaneously.

You believe you have sense without seeing it, but won't believe in God unless you see Him.

You refuse to believe in Paradise and Hell yet believe in multiple universes you have never seen.

Then I continued: Some believers also have postgraduate studies in physics and chemistry, yet believe that a Great Creator has created these universal laws. The science that your father believes in has discovered laws that have been created by God. Science hasn't made these laws. Scientists won't find anything to study without these laws created by God. On the other hand, believers will benefit from their faith in life and the Hereafter. Inform your father what I have told in your next visit to him and ask him: Who believes in nonsense now?!

She responded: This isn't nonsense. Science says that we came here as a result of some irrational, blind, and random events. According to science, this universe is moving towards destruction and will suffer from "Thermal Death". Human life will be destroyed before thermal death. The sun will finally purify the earth, then death and nothingness will come.

I told her: Then, according to your theory, if this life is a ship that will inevitably drown with its passengers, what is the point of having a means of comfort on this ship?

Where is the way?

I continued my conversation with this Armenian lady saying: You claim that everything doesn't have a definite meaning, which means we are free to find a purpose for ourselves to acquire a good life. Denying our existence's objective is a way of fooling ourselves because it's as if we are saying: Let's pretend that we have an objective in this life. We would become like children who play games pretending to be doctors, nurses, or parents. We will not achieve true happiness unless we realize the objective of our existence in this life.

She replied: I'm happy just the way I am.

I told her: What's the definition of true, purposeful happiness? Imagine you found yourself on a train without your will, but in the first-class section with the most luxurious means of comfort. Would you be satisfied on this trip if you had no answers to questions like: How did I come aboard on this train? What is the purpose of the trip? Where am I going? If these questions remained unanswered, how could you feel delighted? Even if you enjoyed the means of comfort available, you still wouldn't achieve true, meaningful happiness. Would the appetizing meal be enough to make you forget about these questions?

This kind of happiness will be fake and temporary and will only be achieved by deliberately ignoring these questions. It's like the fake pleasure of consuming alcohol which leads to destruction.

It was only then that I surprisingly found a change in the tone of her voice. She said: Very well! Whether God truly exists or not makes no difference because I'm a good wife, I treat everyone with respect, and I hurt no one. So why would He punish me?!

At this point, I remembered the verse:

And they attribute to Allah (God) that which they dislike [i.e., daughters], and their tongues assert the lie that they will have the best [from Him]. Assuredly, they will have the Fire, and they will be [therein] neglected. [81]

---

[81] (Qur'an 16:62).

And:

And I do not believe that the Hour of Resurrection will ever come. Anyhow if ever I am returned to my Lord, I will get even a grander place than this. [82]

So, I told her: What's the point of your relationship with everything around you when you have no connection with the Creator from the first place? Would you accept your relationship with your father whom you consider your role model to be the worst relationship in your life? Would your father accept that and reward you for it?!

Is it not the heaven with horoscopes and the earth with broad passes evidence of the Omniscient the All– Aware?!

The Islamic scholar Ibn–Taymia says: "How could we ask for evidence of whom is the evidence of everything?"

He frequently used this saying: "If daylight needed proof, nothing would be valid in the minds!"

The Qur'an lists evidences on the existence of Allah (the Creator).

Evidence of creation:

The creation of the universe from nothing is evidence on the existence of the Creator.

Indeed, in the creation of the heavens and the earth and the alternation of the night and the day are signs for those of understanding. [83]

Evidence of obligation:

If we say that everything has a source, and this source has a source and if we keep up this pattern, each source is causatively coming from a previous

---

[82] (Qur'an 18:36).
[83] (Qur'an 3:190).

source, then the pattern will perpetually carry on. Therefore, logically this pattern must come to an end or instead to a beginning. It must reach a source that has no basis. That's what we call the ' Primary Source.' The primary source must have existed before the beginning of time, because if it came into existence after the start of time, then that source itself must have had a start, there must be something that preceded its existence. The primary source must have preceded time and space. Without the sun, the moon, the planets, the stars, there would be no night or day; there would be no hours, days or months. Therefore, time and space must have come into existence simultaneously, and that is what science has proven.

An atheist asked me one day a question. He wondered: If Allah is the Creator, then who created Allah?

I replied: I'll ask you a simple question. If you answer it, you will find the answer to your question.

He said: Fine.

I said: What is the smell of red?

He answered: There is no answer to this question because red isn't classified as one that could be smelled.

So, I said: Thank you. So yes, everything has a reason for its existence, but the Creator does not have that reason simply because the Creator is not classified as one of the things that could be created. God is before everything else.

For Example:

The manufacturing company of a television set or refrigerator puts rules and instructions for using these devices in a manual explaining how to use these devices. The user must follow these instructions to use these devices successfully. On the other hand, the company is not subjected to these instructions.

God has created Causality Law, but we cannot consider Him subjected to this law He has created. He made time, yet He isn't subjected to it. He does not undergo the stages of time that we do. He does not get tired. He does not need to set Himself in a material form or to come down on earth. That is why we could never see Him in this life. We are trapped in time and space. For example, a person who is sitting in a room cannot see beyond that room unless he/she leaves it.

So, he asked me: Why doesn't He come down to earth in any form?

I said: I'll give you an example just to make the idea understandable, otherwise to Him belongs the highest attribute. When you use an electronic device, you control it from outside, yet you do not enter it by any means. He laughed and said that's correct.

Evidence of perfection and order:

This means that the astonishingly accurate construction of this universe and its laws are evidence of God's existence.

[And] who created seven heavens in layers. You do not see in the creation of the Most Merciful any inconsistency. So, return [your] vision [to the sky]; do you see any breaks? [84]

Indeed, all things We created with predestination. [85]

Evidence of care:

This universe has been very precisely created to suit human life, resulting from the most beautiful and merciful godly attributes.

---

[84] (Qur'an 67:3).
[85] (Qur'an 54:49).

It is Allah (God) who created the heavens and the earth and sent down rain from the sky and produced thereby some fruits as provision for you and subjected for you, the ships to sail through the sea by His command and subjected for you the rivers. [86]

Evidence of harness:

This is related to the godly attributes of Majesty and Ability.

And the grazing livestock He has created for you; in them is warmth and [numerous] benefits, and from them you eat, and for you in them is [the enjoyment of] beauty when you bring them in [for the evening] and when you send them out [to pasture], And they carry your loads to a land you could not have reached except with difficulty to yourselves. Indeed, your Lord is Kind and Merciful, and [He created] the horses, mules, and donkeys for you to ride and [as] adornment. And He creates that which you do not know. [87]

Evidence of customization:

All that we see in this universe could have been in many forms, but God Almighty chose the best.

And have you seen the water that you drink? Is it you who brought it down from the clouds, or is it We who bring it down? If We willed, We could make it bitter, so why are you not grateful? [88]

Have you not considered your Lord – how He extends the shadow, and if He willed, He could have made it stationary? Then We made the sun for it an indication. [89]

---

[86] (Qur'an 14:32).

[87] (Qur'an 16: 5-8).

[88] (Qur'an 56:68-70).

[89] (Qur'an 25:45).

Where have we come from?

The Qur'an mentions several prospects of how the universe might have been created.

Or were they created by nothing, or were they the creators [of themselves]? Or did they create the heavens and the earth? Rather, they are not certain, or have they the depositories [containing the provision] of your Lord? Or are they the controllers [of them]? [90]

Or were they created by nothing:

This contradicts many of the laws of nature we observe around us. As a simple example, to say that Egypt's pyramids have been created by nothing, is enough to abolish this prospect.

Or were they the creators [of themselves]?

Was the universe able to create itself? The term "creation" indicates something that didn't exist then came into existence. Subjectivism Creation is totally logically impossible because this means that something existed and didn't exist at the same time. This is impossible! To say that the human being created himself means that he existed before he was created!

If people are asked who created you, they would reply by saying: My parents are the reason for my existence in this life. It's evident from this reply that it's just an attempt to find a way out of this dilemma. People by nature do not want to think deeply into matters or strive hard. They know that their parents will die, then generations will come after them and give the same reply while they know that they had no role in the creation of their children. So, the actual question is: Who brought the humankind into existence?

---

[90] (Qur'an 52:35-37).

An atheist replied to this issue once that subjectivism creation could be found in single-celled organisms, known in biology as a sexual reproduction. As usual, my reply to such ideas is: We must first assume that the first cell already existed, and if we considered this then this is not subjectivism creation, it is a way of reproduction. The product will be the offspring of one living organism, and it will inherit that parent's genetic material alone.

Or did they create the heavens and the earth?

No living being ever claimed to have created the heavens and earth except the owner of the creation and matters alone. It is only Him (God) who has revealed this truth when He sent His messengers to humanity. The truth is that it is Him who is the Creator, Innovator, and Owner of the heavens and earth and what is in between with no partner or son.

Say, [O Muhammad], "Invoke those you claim [as deities] besides God (Allah)." They do not possess an atom's weight [of ability] in the heavens or on the earth, and they do not have therein any partnership [with Him], nor is there for Him from among them any assistant. [91]

We could give an example: If a bag was found with no owner, only one person would come and claim to be the bag's owner and provide evidence by stating its contents. So according to human civil laws, this person alone is the owner of the bag until someone else comes to claim it.

The existence of a creator:

All this leads us to an inevitable conclusion that there is a creator without denial. The strange thing is that the human being always tries to assume

---

[91] (Qur'an 34:22).

possibilities other than this one. It is as if this possibility is unbelievably imaginary or unverifiable. If we stand a sincere pause that is fair and with scientific insight, we will reach the fact that we can never fully comprehend the Creator. For it is He who has created the whole universe, so definitely He is beyond human perception. As a result, it's logical to assume that it is not easy to be sure about the existence of this invisible metaphysical power. This power must reveal itself in a way it sees comprehensive to human cognition. The human being must reach the conviction that this metaphysical power is an existing reality and that this last possibility is the only explanation left to this universe's existence.

So, flee to God. Indeed, I am to you from Him a clear warner.[92]

If we are looking for eternal bliss and happiness, we must believe and submit to the existence of God, the Creator and Innovator.

Why Are We Here?

I recall meeting an English lady in Nigeria. She asked me: Why did God create us?

I replied: Imagine yourself a wealthy and generous person, what would you have done?

She said: I would have invited my friends to food and drink.

So, I told her: Such human attributes are just a tiny part of God's characteristics. God has the most Majestic and Beautiful attributes, and is the most Merciful and Compassionate. He is the Provider and the Generous. He has created us to have mercy on us and to give us happiness. All human attributes are derived from His attributes.

---

[92] (Qur'an 51:50).

He created us and gave us the ability to choose. So, either we choose the path of submission and obedience or select the way of rebellious disobedience.

She asked: Why didn't He force us to worship Him?

I answered: He could have forced us to worship and obey Him, but compulsion will not achieve the objective of creating the human being.

Divine wisdom is that Adam peace be upon him was created and distinguished with knowledge.

And He taught Adam the names of all things; then He asked the angels: Tell me the names of these if ye are right. [93]

Then gave Adam the ability to choose.

We said: "O Adam! dwell thou and thy wife in the Garden; and eat of the bountiful things therein as (where and when) ye will; but approach not this tree, or ye run into harm and transgression." [94]

Then opened the door of repentance for him because the ability to choose must lead to slipping into mistakes and error.

Then learnt Adam from his Lord words of inspiration, and his Lord Turned towards him; for He is Oft–Returning, Most Merciful. [95]

All of this is to make him ready to be an inheritor of the earth (ruling on earth).

And [mention, O Muhammad], when your Lord said to the angels, "Indeed, I will make upon the earth a successive authority." They said, "Will You place upon it one who causes corruption therein and

---

[93] (Qur'an 2:31).

[94] (Qur'an 2:35).

[95] (Qur'an 2:37).

sheds blood, while we declare Your praise and sanctify You?" God said, "Indeed, I know that which you do not know. [96]

Having a will and ability to choose is a blessing if it was used correctly. Yet it will be a curse if it was falsely manipulated and directed towards corrupt goals.

Dangers, sedition, and self-struggle undoubtedly surround the ability to choose. This, without doubt, is much more honorable and magnifying to Man than despicable submission leading to fake happiness.

Not equal are those of the believers who sit (at home), except those who are disabled (by injury or are blind or lame), and those who strive hard and fight in the Cause of God with their wealth and their lives. God has preferred in grades those who strive hard and fight with their wealth and their lives above those who sit (at home). Unto each, God has promised good (Paradise), but God has preferred those who strive hard and fight, above those who sit (at home) by a huge reward. [97]

Otherwise, what is the benefit of having reward and punishment if there was no free choice that deserves judgement?

But with all this, the actual space of choice given to human in this life is limited. God will judge us only on the matters that He gave us the freedom of choice in. We have no choice in the community we have been brought up in, nor in our parents, look and color.

---

[96] (Qur'an 2:30).
[97] (Qur'an 4:95).

The honor of worship rather than the humility of sin:

Worshipping God isn't limited only to praying and fasting. Worshipping also includes loving, obeying, and knowing Him. Worshipping God must be our ultimate objective. It frees us from being enslaved to the society.

Full submission to God alone maintains the person's dignity and keeps him/her from humiliations to others. Whoever desires glory will find it in approaching The Lord of the Worlds by right words and doing good deeds. **Whoever desires honor [through power] – then to God belongs all honor. To Him ascends good speech, and righteous work raises it. But they who plot evil deeds will have a severe punishment, and the plotting of those – it will perish.** [98]

The more a person approaches his Lord with humility, the more highness he will achieve.

I recall now words that I frequently say: "Oh my Lord! How glorious it is for me to be your slave! How proud I am that You are my Lord!"

The Prophet Muhammad peace be upon him said:

And know that if the nation were to gather to benefit you with anything, they would not benefit you except with what Allah had already prescribed for you. And if they were to gather to harm you with anything, they would not harm you except with what Allah had already prescribed against you. The pens have been lifted, and the pages have dried. [99]

It is untrue what some think that the believer is enchained with the acts of worship. A person's heart needs to be attached to an objective he/she is seeking.

---

[98] (Qur'an 35:10).
[99] (Sahih Al-Tirmizi).

Indeed, if we don't worship our Creator, we will end up worshipping something else. The human heart will either be attached to an earthly materialistic matter that he/she is striving to reach or attached to the Creator. Hence, our desires might enslave us without realizing it. On the other hand, being attached to God Almighty and the hereafter frees us from being enslaved to others. Our Creator and has the right to be resorted and refuged to.

Many people get attracted to fame and fashion. Also, social media attracts people excessively and exaggeratedly. It has a significant role in broadcasting concepts that call for focusing on inferior matters and distracting people away from priorities. All this leads to a troubled, unhappy life filled with suffering.

Also, some social standards and family pressures force us to considerate inherited traditions that drive us away from our role in this life and our duty towards religion.

For example, a mother will feed her children in all cases whether she is a believer or a non-believer. But only the believer renews her intentions and gives away the good deeds she is doing to God. She awaits the reward only from Him. In this way, she will never get disappointed if she didn't find gratitude from her children. She awaits her reward from her Creator. As a result, we see a woman who will never be disappointed by being let down and will never fear her boss or fear from being bullied. This is because she said with a loud voice: My whole life is for God!

When I said these words to a Portuguese atheist with the PhD in philosophy, she said: You are lucky with this faith and way of thinking. I have not found this beauty in philosophy books, but I have found it with you Muslims.

Conclusion:

We conclude that we do not have an option in this life other than accepting God's call with faith and submission. In this way, we win the best of this life and the Hereafter. Or we could be satisfied just by this life, and then it will destroy us, and we will be doomed to Hell.

Science and Faith

None is the victor but God:

In our visit to Alhambra Palace in Granada, we found a phrase engraved on the walls which says: "**None is the victor but Allah (The One True God)**". My eyes burst into tears because the breeze of the Muslims' glorious was around everywhere. I imagined yore days when Muslim scientists used to teach the Arabs and the western world medicine, pharmacy, geometry, astronomy, and poetry. Muslims had also established the first university all over Europe in Spain. Still in my imagination, I also experienced the days of Abdul-Rahman Ad-Dakhil [100], whose army girded Italy and France. I even imagined the days of Al-Mutassim[101], who set a whole army to defend a Muslim woman whose garment was raised by a Roman man after she cried "O Mutassim help"! I was surprised by the claim made by some people that abiding by the teachings of our religion holds us back. My wandering got distracted when the Spanish tour guide said: the phrase engraved on the wall means " **None is the victor but Allah**", in Arabic. If we have any Arabs here, let them emphasize that in a loud voice. I then shouted: Yes, none is the victor but Allah, and my heart jumped from joy.

---

[100] Abd al-Rahman "the Entrant" (731–788) was the founder of a **Muslim** dynasty that ruled the greater part of **Iberia** for nearly three centuries (including the succeeding **Caliphate of Córdoba**).

[101] The last Abbasid caliph in Baghdad; (October 796 – 5 January 842), better known by his **regnal name** al-**Mutassim** bi'llah, "he who seeks refuge in God"), was the eighth **Abbasid caliph**, ruling from 833 until his death in 842.

The famous German writer, Sigrid Hunke, the author of the book "God's Sun over the Occident"[102] published in 1960, reproduced an essential and funny text. It discusses a situation that imitates the reality of many Muslims today.

The speaker that talked in the text was the bishop of Cordoba (Alvaro), which was during the era of the flourishing of Islamic culture.

He complained that many of his Christian brethren read the legends of Arab, and studied the writings of Muslim philosophers and scholars. It wasn't to refute them, instead, it was to learn Arabic and to be able to argue eloquently proficiently, and with fine gustation. He said:

"Where, nowadays, is that un-specialized Christian who reads Latin interpretations of the Bible? Who amongst them, even studies the four Bibles? What a pity! The Christian young men knew nothing but Arabic language and literature! They profoundly studied Arabic references, exerting all their efforts, spending large sums of money to buy them, and compiling huge libraries. They told everyone that the Arabic literature is worthy of respect and admiration at that time, to the point that if anyone tried to convince them to plea with the Christian books, they would declare that these books never grab their attention. What a misfortune! Christians have forgotten their mother tongue; you would rarely find one in a thousand who could write a simple correct letter in Latin. Vice versa happened concerning Arabic, whether phrasing, writing, and composing. Some of them might even excel in competing with the Arabs themselves."

---

[102] She also wrote: (God is not like this). It is a book in which she defends Muslims, Islamic civilization, and Islamic history.

Muslim scientists' discoveries were the accredited ones during the middle centuries. Muslim scientists used to worship God (Allah) and draw nearer to Him with their knowledge, without any signs of contradiction between religion and science. Yet, most of them were scholars in their faith, as well as being scientists.

The Muslim scientists put an experimental, materialistic, and rational approach for research. It was different from the Greek practice, as they also put an independent scientific theory for knowledge.

Some great scientists won the Noble prize in medicine and physics without viewing any opposition between science and religion even in the modern age.

The religion vs science conflict never appeared across history, even in Judaism. For many ages, the dominance was always given to religion. The scientific development was slowly moving forward according to necessities only, or perhaps it was mixed with legendries and paganism.

However, this conflict appeared in the era of church domination, after nine centuries of Christianity's appearance.

The issue of religion vs science conflict was declared during the European boom era, and the firm stands of scientists were then against the church control.

Humans developed atheism in various forms, but the people of the previous scriptures declared it. This is because God's complicated distorted concept was put in these books; it opposes the simple concept that God has put naturally in people's hearts.

One of the reasons that encouraged people to Atheism and the demand of replacing religion with science was the unacceptable commands from both religious representatives and institutes that aimed at earning worldly and political benefits.

The world then suffered from deterioration in the moral, humanistic values, and intellect due to this struggle between religion and science.

Science in Qur'an:

God has mentioned many verses in the Noble Qur'an, which encourage stimulating the human mind, alerting senses, contemplation, and meditation.

Have they not considered how God begins creation and then repeats it? Indeed that, for God, is easy. Say, [O Muhammad], Travel through the land and observe how He began creation. Then God will produce the final creation. Indeed God, over all things, is competent. [103]

Indeed, in the creation of the heavens and the earth and the alternation of the night and the day are signs for those of understanding. Who remember God while standing or sitting or [lying] on their sides and give thought to the creation of the heavens and the earth, [saying], Our Lord, You did not create this aimlessly; exalted are You [above such a thing]; then protect us from the punishment of the Fire. [104]

---

[103] (Qur'an 29:19-20).
[104] (Qur'an 3:190-191).

The first verses that were revealed have spoken on science generally, and the creation of the human being in particular. This excellent blending in the integration between science and faith is manifestly shown in many verses.

Recite in the name of your Lord who created (1) Created man from a clinging substance (2) Recite, and your Lord is the most Generous (3) Who taught by the pen (4) Taught man that which he knew not. [105]

We find here that the verses referred to looking at and contemplating the rain, along with the different colors of fruits, mountains, people, and animals, including a clear indication of the universality of science and knowledge in all its specialties, which made religion and science two integral parts.

Have you not seen that God sends down water from the sky? With it We produce fruits of various colors. And in the mountains are streaks of white and red—varying in their hue—and pitch–black. Likewise, human beings, animals, and livestock come in various colors. Only those fear God, from among His servants, who have knowledge. Indeed, God is Exalted in Might and Forgiving. [106]

---

[105] (Qur'an 96:1-5).
[106] (Qur'an 35: 27-28).

Why is the need for religion?

Hans Schwarz, the Professor of Theology, said: "Although science is critical, it can be used as a tool for destruction just as it is used in construction. As then, comes the role of faith, clarifying that the practical experiment cannot have all the answers."

He also said: "Faith and knowledge need each other, and scientists should admit that they often use faith to be able to understand the deep relations between the natural phenomena they observe."

Schwarz also viewed that scientists do not have all the facts and answers as they claim. The inquiries they face every day are the best evidence to that, especially those investigating the origin of life. One day, they would reach a conclusion, but it gets contradicted by somebody on another day.

Questioning the origin of our life and the purpose of living is one thing that science cannot answer. Instead, it has given the turn to metaphysics to provide the answer.

The Hiroshima accident and other disasters that occurred because of the scientific inventions have caused science to lose its innocence.

Karl Jaspers, the philosopher, along with others, have called science as a superstition.

We can conclude that it is impossible to answer the questions on the origin, purpose, and ethics of life and maintain scientific development, except by achieving conformity between science and religion.

Atheism of the gaps, not God of the gaps:

I had a conversation with a Russian atheist who asked me many questions.

One of which was: Can the Creator create a big rock that He cannot lift?

I was astonished by his question. The first time I read about atheists asking those types of questions was the day before I had this conversation with him[107], so it was an extraordinary coincidence.

However, whether my answer was yes or no to his question, it would show that the Creator is not Omnipotent (may He be Exalted to that).

I told him: Well, can you draw me a circular triangle?

He directly answered: You are manipulating with speech.

I told him: It was you who manipulated, not me. Your question has no meaning; it doesn't make sense. The One Unique Creator does not do whatever doesn't befit Him, may He be Exalted to that. Then I gave him a simple example to just clarify the idea for him.

I told him: Any priest or religious person does not go out naked in the street, despite his ability to do that, but he cannot go out in front of people that way such an action is not suitable for his religious rank.

God has the best example. He can do anything, but He only does what befits His Majesty and Glory.

He said: God does not exist; science is the only way to truth.

I proceeded: This statement is not a scientific release that is based on evidence and experimental observations. Thus, we cannot accept it as a fact. The truth is that we know things do not immerge without a cause, not to

---

[107] *The Myth of Atheism.* Dr. Amr Sharif. Edition 2014 AD.

mention this vast populated universe and the creatures there that own an intangible sense and obey the non–materialistic mathematical theories.

He said: You! The believers adopt the "god of the gaps" principle[108]. When you fail to provide a scientifical explanation to anything, you present the deity as a cover to your ignorance and mental stupidity. At the same time, you cite this ignorance as an evidence on the existence of your god, i.e. whenever you find a gap in science, you attribute it to the deity.

I told him: Is referring to the plane manufacturer when misunderstanding the motor's mechanism considered a gap in our intellect? Despite that the plane manufacturer has no existence in any of the steps involved in operating the engine, he is still responsible for the mechanisms we know.

Science concluded that the universe evolved from nonexistence, while the same science taught us that matter does not perish and is not immerged from nonexistence, which troubled scientists. If the matter was not immerged from nonexistence, how come that the whole universe evolved from nonexistence? Here comes the role of religion that explains what science failed in explaining.

Our Deity is not a "god of the gaps" that evolved from ignorance, but He is the cause of every mechanism discovered by science.

I proceeded: You are the ones adopting the "atheism of the gaps" principle. You use your inability or lack of desire to observe the universal laws' origin as an evidence that this origin does not exist. This is an enormous gap of consciousness and logic, isn't that the "atheism of the gaps"?

---

[108] This theory points to another attempt by some Catholic theologians to reconcile the organization's scale of history with some state beliefs.

I continued: To explain the existence of a limited materialistic universe, we need an independent eternal source that is not subjected to matter. Only science can study sensible or visual things, and this means the things of limited physical properties. Hence, we cannot, in any means, explain the existence of the universe by science alone.

Nature, with all its properties, is nothing but one of the facts of the universe. It is not an explanation of the existence of the universe. All the laws discovered are not a disclaimer to the Inventor's presence; instead, it is a declaration to His creation.

For example, someone can monthly deposit a sum of money in a savings bank, then he'd go to the bank to receive the money he put with the profits at the end of the year. The accountant then tells him that the multiplication law that they used in calculating the sum was the one which generated the money for him.

If this person didn't deposit his money, his balance would have been zero. Therefore, claiming that the laws of physics are the ones that originated the universe is the real foolishness. Theories and laws only describe the path of the things precisely, but they cannot develop anything from nonexistence. The laws of motion can only describe the basketball path, but it is the hands of the player that moves the ball. Accordingly, laws need a form of existence that is influenced by a specific power, in a particular place and time. Therefore, without these elements, these laws are useless; instead, they will never exist.

Religion provides us with what science cannot offer:

Learning science can help Humans create a rocket, but it cannot help with letting them taste the beauty of an art painting or value things. Science cannot help humans with acknowledging the evil and good. We know from science that a bullet can kill, but it cannot help us realize that it is wrong to use it for killing others.

Albert Einstein, the famous physicist, said: "Science can never be a source for morals, there is no doubt that there are morals for science, but we cannot talk about the scientific principles for morals, as it's a failure. Every attempt in trying to submit morals to the laws of science and equations will surely fail."

Emmanuel Kant, the well-known German philosopher, said: "Ethical evidence for the existence of a deity has been established under justice. A good person should be rewarded, while a bad person should be punished, and this shall never take place except on the existence of a superior origin that reckons every person for his deeds. Also, the evidence is established in compliance with the capability to gather virtue and happiness, for they can only be gathered under who is Super Natural, which is All-knowledgeable, All-Powerful. This superior origin that overcomes nature represents the Deity."

The Russian atheist said: Okay, but for me, the existence of the benefits behind the deity's idea made humans falsely think of the god's presence to attain these benefits.

He proceeded: If the rainbow is a reflection of sunrays on the rain, it is wrong to say that our benefit in enjoying the rainbow scene urges us to think of a creator's existence. The discovery of science about the mechanism that showed the rainbow refuted a creator's existence.

I told him: Let's say you were walking in the street and lost your cellular phone, then you found a public telephone, and you wanted to use it to call your wife. Will using your cellphone while discovering the mechanism of its operation form be an evidence of a manufacturer's nonexistence to that phone? Or is that public phone a real existence that has an actual manufacturer? The presence of benefit does not disclaim the existence of the manufacturer. Instead, it supports it.

Enjoying the beautiful rainbow scene, and discovering the mechanism that shows the bow does not disclaim the Creator's existence who created the sun and sent down the rain.

He said: The atheist doesn't harm others, and doesn't encourage anyone to do evil deeds as some do in the name of religion.

I told him: Religion calls to abide by good deeds and avoiding bad deeds. Thus, some Muslims' bad manners are attributable to their culture or religious illiteracy, as well as being apart from the true religion. Haven't you heard of the worldly attempts to establish communalism that lead to killing millions of Muslims and Christians? How can you say that the refutation of deity doesn't urge a person to do evil deeds?

One of the communist philosophers said: "We thought we could be better without a deity, and that we can maintain humanity, but we were very wrong, for we destroyed the concept of god as well as destroyed the society itself."

He said: Describe the Creator to me.

I said: I shall give you an example just to clarify. First, I want you to describe for me an intangible thing such as an "idea". Give me its weight in grams, length in centimeters, chemical construction, color, pressure, shape, and figure.

He said: Of course, it is impossible.

I told him: To describe an intangible thing, we should use terms and descriptions that differ a lot from the words we use in science, let alone describing the Creator of the whole universe.

He said: I feel that the idea of faith resembles bedtime stories or beautiful visions that only release the person's distress, nothing else.

I told him: These beautiful visions are way better than the nightmare of atheism that you are living in. Be with your One Unique Creator Who provides life and death, and mind nothing else.

He said: The doctor provides life and death when he decides either to treat or neglect his patient; hence, when the killer holds back from killing his victim, he would have provided him life.

I then mentioned this verse to him:

Have you not considered the one who argued with Abraham about his Lord [merely] because God had given him kingship? When Abraham said, "My Lord is the one who gives life and causes death," he said, "I give life and cause death." Abraham said, "Indeed, God brings up the sun from the east, so bring it up from the west." So,

the disbeliever was overwhelmed [by astonishment], and God does not guide the wrongdoing people. [109]

I told him commenting: Do you know what the punishment of God to this man was? God has sent to him one of the weakest and tiniest creatures, a mosquito, that entered his nose, reached his brain, and made him die. It was to prove that no matter how much a person is powerful and tyrant, he remains incapable of protecting himself from the tiniest creatures of God.

The Russian atheist proceeded: But the Creator had to ask for my opinion before creating me! How come that the Creator forces someone to a life that he does not want to live?

I told him: If God wants to take His creations' opinion in creating them, they must exist from the first place. How can humans have an opinion while they are in nothingness? The issue here is the issue of existence and non-existence. The human attachment to life and his fear for this life is the most significant evidence of his satisfaction with this blessing.

The grace of life is a test for human beings to distinguish the wicked and indignant person from who is satisfied with his Lord, to possess the place of dignity in the Hereafter.

He said: You said that at the beginning of human creation, a covenant was made between the Creator and the humans who have testified for Him of Oneness and Lordship, but I do not remember that.

I said: Don't you have your eyes looking to the sky forcibly when you are subject to horror or fear?

---

[109] (Qur'an 2: 258).

Don't your hands rise without knowing to ask for help from this hidden power that exists in heaven?

He said: Yes.

I was starting to hear a tone of grief in his voice.

I told him: So, you remember, but in bad times. You are a believer in fact, but you must remember Him in good times and bad times so that you get to attain the perfect faith.

This Russian atheist surprised me when I told him that I was going to my office to bring him a copy of my book "The original concept of the God" by telling me that he had to leave the mosque instantly since the time specified for visiting the mosque was finished according to the program of the tourism office he was following. The tour guide was waiting for him in the mosque hall, but at a far corner. When I got the book and came back again, I entered the hall and he wasn't there, so I started looking for him everywhere. The tour guide told me he was there at another corner. When I looked at where he pointed, I found him getting up from a Muslim-like prostration position while weeping a lot. I was astonished, and then the tour guide told me joking: What have you done to the man?

I replied: I did nothing, he just asked me many questions and I answered him. So, the tour guide told me: The visitor told me in your absence that he was very impressed, and that he always wanted to be a believer, but he had many unanswered questions in his mind, and he finally found them. I then told the tour guide: Praise be to God, all that is attributable to the Guidance of God. God certainly knows that this person is a good man and that he is looking for the truth; therefore, He facilitated him to come to this place.

The proactive and teleological cause:

Abu Hamid Al-Ghazali [110] describes that existence (a book, for example) has four causes:

- The materialistic cause: The ink, and the paper from which the book was formulated.
- The explicit cause: The shape in which the book was formulated.
- The proactive cause: The compiler, the papermaker, and the printer operator.
- The teleological cause: The reason behind the compilation of the book.

However, the atheists ignored the teleological cause, considering that it is beyond the scientific scope since none can tell the reason for the invented thing except its inventor.

They also considered that believing in it is against science. Thus, everyone agreed to believe that the creation of the whole universe has no cause.

In fact, everything a person does regarding any activities and everything in the universe of incidents compiles both the mechanism and teleology.

For instance, when we drink a cup of water, we use the mechanism of holding the cup to drink and relieve our thirst.

Also, we use the plane using the mechanism of riding to reach a particular place.

---

[110] An Islamic scholar.

One day, an atheist told me: admitting the existence of a creator disables the sense and logic.

I told him: The role of the mind is to judge things and accredit them. Thus, the mind's inability to realize the purpose of human existence, for example, does not cancel its role, instead, it gives a chance for the religion to tell him about what the mind failed to realize, like informing him about his Creator, and the origin and purpose of life. Therefore, he then tends to understand, judge, and accredit this information. Accordingly, admitting the presence of a creator has disabled neither the sense nor the logic.

Ibn Al-Tufail [111] said in the story of Hay Ibn-Yaqzhan:[112]

"The mind, with its first innate ideas, can perceive the truth in relation to the first principles, and realize from them the existence of God. As for the mysteries of existence, creation, and the Creator, which are hidden from us by blocking the unseen, it is unable to realize their true nature, because the senses do not realize the purpose of things. We see that the mind can perceive the universal laws and derive the universals and consciousness by the causes if only freed from arrogance.

Moreover, the mind cannot reach the details and parts that the religion presents, which are considered a second-degree fact, and it should be accepted based on the big facts. Even the mind that is also capable of realizing God's existence is unable to discover His essence. I do not think that it has anything to do with the scientific research to continue with

---

[111] A philosopher and novelist.

[112] An Arabic philosophical novel and an allegorical tale.

persistence in searching for the essence of God. **There is nothing like unto Him**[113]. This is not only because the senses do not perceive it, but because no scientist can know everything about the reality of a single fly and its properties. How is he expected to know about God's essence? Does a human, who does not know the substance, does not know how he knows and does not know how to perceive it, desire to realize the truth of God?"

I remember a comment that an atheist said one day: science has reached the fact that the computer resembles the human mind and the reason for that is:

- First: All worldly things that have forms and systems can be emulated.
- Second: the brain consists of matter and system.
- Third: Accordingly, the brain can be emulated.
- Fourth: the brain is a computer.

I told him: You are just like the one who says that the computer realizes the information that's put in, or like a person who says that the TV can perceive whatever programs it presents.

The difference between both is the perception of the human mind and his feelings towards what he does.

From worshipping the universe to worshipping the Lord of the universe:

One of the manifestations of the controversy between religion and science in ancient Greece is that Greek prescriptions forbade studying astronomy, which hindered the scientific development because of worshipping the creations of the universe.

---

[113] (Qur'an 42:11).

The city–states system in Ancient Greece hastened the failure of ancient religion, for the rising certainty that the gods of the city were unable to protect them. People's faith in these deities and their blending with foreign traders spread doubts, myths, and illusions among the citizens. The legends of the ancient local gods continued among the naive peasants and city residents, at the time in which science reached its peak point.

Therefore, science in ancient Greece did not develop except after some of its free thinkers stopped sanctifying the universe's creations.

However, the mistake they made was when they considered atheism as a necessity for applying science.

The story of Prophet Abraham, peace be upon him, in the Qur'an teaches that giving up the worship of the universe does not mean refuting the existence of a creator to the universe. It is a call to worship the Lord of the universe. [114]

Thus, We showed Abraham the empire of the heavens and the earth, that he might be one of those with certainty. (75) When the night fell over him, he saw a planet. He said, "This is my lord." But when it set, he said, "I do not love those that set" (76) Then, when he saw the moon rising, he said, "This is my lord. "But when it set, he said, "If my Lord does not guide me, I will be one of the erring people." (77) Then, when he saw the sun rising, he said, "This is my lord, this is bigger." But when it set, he said, "O my people, I am innocent of your idolatry. (78) I have directed my attention towards

---

[114] *The Illusion of Atheism.* Dr. Amr Sharif.

Him Who created the heavens and the earth—a monotheist—and I am not of the idolaters."[115]

Why did we fall behind?

The Islamic civilization succeeded in showing the freedom of mind and intellect. Islam itself was responsible for establishing an international civilization shared by many people from different ethnic backgrounds, still, it also played a crucial role in developing the intellectual and cultural life in an unprecedented wide range. Eight hundred years ago, the Arabic language was the scientific and scholarly language that spread worldwide. Why, then, did we fall back now?

I was having a conversation with a Muslim friend whose daughter failed in the general secondary test. The girl was known for her negligence in education and study, also, this incident came across my friend's mother's severe illness. Due to the nature of her job, my friend was unable to stay with her mother to take care of her. Moreover, the girl's failure necessitated her to restudy the syllabus at home, so it was a good chance for the girl to stay with her grandmother since she could not join a college that year.

I was surprised when my friend kept telling people that God caused her daughter to fail to stay with her grandmother during her illness.

I told her then: This is strange, was God the cause of your daughter's failure or negligence in studying?

She answered: Haven't you seen how God facilitated that perfect timing for my daughter's failure with my mother's illness?

---

[115] (Qur'an 6: 75-79).

I told her: **And your Lord does injustice to no one** [116], God will not wrong your daughter to make things easy for you, with His predestined knowledge, God knew that your daughter is careless and that she will not pass the exam, but He did not force her to fail. If your daughter were diligent, God would have arranged other ways to care for your mother.

I then remembered one of my mother's stories that she told me when I was young, and I do not know its source, but it has many true aspects.

The story says: "In Andalusia, when the countries were under the ruling of Islam, one of the tyrant rulers wanted to conquer it, so he sent a spy to get him news about the armies and the capabilities they have. As soon as he entered one of the cities, he found a little boy at the town's edge. He was sitting under a tree crying, for he was used to striking two birds with one arrow, but that day he couldn't hit but one bird only, so he considered that as a failure because of a sin he made. The spy said talking to himself: if these were their kids, how would their men be like? The spy returned from the city to the ruler telling him: You will not be able to face those men, but wait until they get overwhelmed by sins and misdeeds so as you can be able to enter these countries."

It was Satan who caused them to slip because of some [blame] they had earned. [117]

The critical point here is that we do not fall behind because of sins only, but because of the insistence on denying our negligence and wrongs.

---

[116] (Qur'an 18:49).
[117] (Qur'an 3:155).

Overcoming our enemies and achieving success in life should be preceded by overcoming oneself, striving it to strengthen its faith, beware of sins, take the legitimate causes, confess the misdeeds, and always renew the repentance to achieve targeted goals.

Ibn Al-Qayyim said[118]: "Beware of yourself, you will never suffer any affliction except from it. Therefore, do not make peace with it. I swear to God that no one shall respect it until he abases it, and none shall honor it until he humiliates it, none shall reconcile it until he breaks it, and none shall comfort it until he exhausts it, and none shall assure it until he frightens it, and none shall rejoice it until he grieves it."

Conclusion:

We conclude that in the Islamic civilization, the so-called religion vs science conflict was not an issue, instead, some Muslim physicists, astronomers, and mathematics scientists considered themselves in a state of worship to God.

The West has developed in knowledge and science when they abandoned the false beliefs based on their distorted religion. Therefore, they succeeded when they neglected these novelties, started adopting science and logic, and stopped indulging in the occultations drawn from the clergy's thoughts.

Despite their turning to science in the right way, they lost their values, morals, and the purpose of their existence, by disregarding to adopt the true religion.

---

[118] An Islamic scholar.

For Arabs, it was the contrary; they fell behind when they left the true religion and turned to science in the wrong way when they blindly chased and imitated the western pattern of thinking.

If we have a real and robust urge to retrieve the past glories, we should correct this situation and rearrange our priorities. We have the right beliefs and religion that encourage science through the correct spiritual, reasonable, and logical means and refutes myths and novelties. Thus, we have the basis; it only lacks the structure to rebuild the civilization.

The Upright Religion

But those who believe, love God more:

During a visit to one of Hong Kong's distinguished attractions, we found people flocking to pray to Buddha statue and present offerings to it. I wondered how Gautama used the word "Buddha" in the context of the term "Prophet" which refers to a person who is enlightened by a divine revelation. He told his followers: "I am not the first Buddha and will not be the last". When the Buddhist feels a lot of fear, he resorts to the power in the sky to ask for help.[119]

In the middle of the crowd, while I was thinking about these people's beliefs, I heard my husband saying clearly and loudly: There is no God but Allah, I laughed and told him: Lower your voice, there are people around us. He said: Believe me, I cannot keep my voice down; I cannot control myself.

So, I said to myself: Glory be to God, who created and taught intact hearts His supplication and I remembered the verse: **But those who believe are stronger in love for God**[120], and I was so happy.

---

[119] Buddha Bible (page 217,218)

"Ananda told the blessed one: "Who will teach us when you go?" the blessed one answered: "I am not the first Buddha who came to earth and I will not be the last. In the right time another Buddha will appear in the world""

[120] (Qur'an 2:165)

He has commanded that you worship none but Him. This is the upright religion:

Looking at different cultures and civilizations, foreign languages, and beliefs, we find common grounds, concerning values, ethics, and human meanings, also, our problems, challenges and ambitions look a lot alike. People do not share only values, ethics, human purposes, and historical backgrounds, but the origin of religions and beliefs as well. We all meet at Adam; Adam indeed had one religion and one faith. But humans created the differences between religions and beliefs.

By looking deeply into peoples' beliefs, we discover that most nations with different religious symbols and inheritance, still believe that there is a Creator for the universe, and they seek refuge to him when facing hardships. This confirms that these religions and beliefs had historical origins that emanates from one original right religion, and what people currently have from the religious heritage contains "monotheism", which is the belief in One God and unifying Him in worship. There are many proofs in these religions, and their sacred books indicate that their roots and origins go back to the doctrine of "monotheism".

I remember when my son did voluntary work in his summer vacation where he spread the message of Islam. He was studying engineering at that time. He once told me that while he was talking with a Hindu, it occurred to him that he believes in One and Only God, but he turns to Him by supplication to others. The Hindu told him: We buy our gods according to our capabilities; whoever has money buys a golden god, and the poor buys a wooden god. My son was surprised, then asked him: When you are on a plane, and a problem happens, and after that, you discover that you are probably going to die, what do you do? He replied: We seek refuge to the

One God who is in the sky. My son told him: Why don't you seek refuge to Him every day so that your hearts are unified to what is best for you? When my son told me this story, I remembered Emran ibn Hossain's story, when Prophet Muhammad, peace be upon him, asked the father of Emran: How many gods are you worshipping today? He replied: seven, six on earth and one in the sky. The Prophet said: Which one of them do you adore and fear? He said: The one in the sky. Then the Prophet said to him: Leave the ones on earth and worship the one in the sky, so al Hossain accepted Islam.[121]

I was pleased and told my son: Glory to God, who guided you to this answer.

And when they board a ship, they supplicate Allah (the Creator), sincere to Him in religion. But when He delivers them to the land, at once they associate others with Him.[122]

...He has commanded that you worship not except Him. That is the upright religion, but most of the people do not know.[123]

I will not forget a Hindu visitor's answer when I asked her about why she was feeling scared while talking to her about the original concept of God. She said: I am afraid to discuss the issue with you because you might be a god yourself. You have a lot of knowledge. God can come in the form of human or maybe an animal to teach us a particular lesson; perhaps He showed up in your form.

---

[121] (Sahih Al-Tirmizi).

[122] (Qur'an 29:65).

[123] (Qur'an 12:40).

Then I had mixed feelings between wanting to laugh, saddened about her way of thinking, and astonished from the condition those people have reached.

I told her: how strange is this! I can't imagine my father or my husband in the form of an animal or any other creature. How can you accept this image for God, the Creator, may God be exalted above that?

I now remember the story of a Hindu visitor who came with his daughter and her husband, who were Muslims. The daughter's eager tears wishing that her father would embrace Islam are still in my memory.

He had already accepted an offer from me to embrace Islam when I answered a question he was always thinking of. He said: I am convinced with Islam, but I feel that when I become a Muslim, this action will bear a lot of disrespect and disaffection to my parents who passed away.

I told him: Have you forgotten the right of your Creator, who created you, portrayed you and honored you, gave you money and kids? If your parents have thrown themselves in water to drown, would you throw yourself with them? Your future is with your Creator, not with your parents. If your parents had the chance to return to life, they would have advised you with Islam. Before he pronounced Shahada (first step to embrace Islam), I emphasized the importance of believing in the resurrection day, leaving the concept of reincarnation; this is one of the essential points that we should concentrate on.

He asked: why?

I told him: No school or university administration accepts that anyone else but its students to complete the exam for themselves when the time of the exam is over. Life is your exam paper.

If we look at the harmony between human bodies and their souls, we would conclude that it is impossible to make these souls live in animal bodies. They cannot wander between plants and insects, not even in human beings.

God distinguished human with mind, knowledge and made him a successor in the earth, differentiated him, honored him, and elevated him above most of His creatures. God will never humiliate human beings. Day of Judgment, heavens [Paradise] and Hellfire represent the Creator's Justice when sins and good deeds of humans are weighed.

Then shall anyone who has done an atom's weight of good, see it and anyone who has done an atom's weight of evil, shall see it. [124]

Among the beautiful stories that one of our distinguished scholars told us was about a Hindu travelling for the first time in his life. He put his small god in his luggage with the rest of his stuff. When the plane landed, he unfortunately lost his bag. He went to the airport's lost and found desk to report about the incident. When they asked him about what was in the bag, he was ashamed to tell them that his god was inside. This embarrassing situation was a turning point in his search for truth and understanding the fatal mistake he was making all his life by worshipping what does not harm or benefit, other than Allah (The Creator). He embraced Islam; he then knew that losing his bag that day, was good luck not bad luck as he thought in the beginning.

Your God is One God:

Since human appeared on earth, since Adam's era, God, the Lord of the universe sent messengers. He chose the most pious and devoted person in his people to be a prophet and judge between them, to remind them with

---

[124] (Qur'an 99:8-9).

sincere servitude to the One and Only God. Whenever people twist the message of previous messengers, deviate from the right path and worship others, God would send a new messenger to lead people and bring them back to the right direction. These messengers would direct them again to worship Him alone.

The Creator sent one clear, simple message to all nations and one way of salvation. The message is: Believing in One God, worshipping Him alone. The messenger's existence among his people was considered as a lamp that enlightens the way to his followers. The messenger clarified for them the meaning of achieving the salvation, by following the messenger's teachings and his acts in worshipping God alone, not as some wrongly understand and make their messenger a mediator between them and God.

As many prophets and messengers that God sent to different nations, were mentioned in the Qur'an (such as Jesus, Moses, Abraham, Noah, David. Salomon, Ismael, Isaac, Joseph, etc....), others weren't. Therefore, the possibility that other famous religious teachers such as the Hindu Lords Rama, Krishna, and Gautama Buddha were prophets of God cannot be outrightly negated. But these people used these symbols for polytheism.

While some people are arguing that God did not send them a messenger or a prophet as he sent Prophet Muhammad to Arabs, the Holy Qur'an asserts the opposite of this as God said:

And We have already sent messengers before you. Among them are those [whose stories] We have related to you, and among them are those [whose stories] We have not related to you. And it was not for any messenger to bring a sign [or verse] except by permission of

God. So, when the command of God comes, it will be concluded in truth, and the falsifiers will thereupon lose [all]. [125]

He also said:

Indeed, We have sent you with the truth as a bringer of good tidings and a warner. And there was no nation but that there had passed within it a warner. [126]

Here, the greatness of Islam prevails in its simplicity and inclusivity. The term "Islam" is not connected with any person or place, or a particular group, but it reflects a relationship with God Almighty.

I remember when I was the only Muslim among all my classmates in a French class. The French teacher, who was a catholic, told me: I love Islam. I said: why?

He said: Muslims worship one God, they have one sacred book, and they pray towards one direction (Qibla). I admire this religion a lot.

I was then so pleased and proud of this great religion. That moment was my starting point to dedicate my time and effort to study the right way to present Islam. I wanted to change the typical dialogues between advocates that drive away from Islam rather than attract. Islam is the religion of natural disposition, comprehensive and straightforward, but is presented in a complicated way, almost wrong. I liked a saying that I once heard which said: Islam is a good product, but whoever does the marketing for this product is a failure.

During a visit of an Argentinian to our center, he surprised me by saying: I only have five minutes here, and before I go, I want in only three minutes

---

[125] (Qur'an 40:78).
[126] (Qur'an 35:24).

to know the difference between a Muslim and a Christian, so that I have time to take some photos of the mosque.

I said to myself: What should I say in these three minutes. I was confused for a while, but I felt a sudden power to answer the Argentinian swiftly.

I told him: Do you have in Argentina among Christians, someone raised in a Christian family and got baptized and when he grew up, he said: I am not convinced that God has a son, for me, He is one. Jesus is only a Prophet, and I resort to God directly in supplication, and I don't resort to Jesus?

He said: There are many, and I am one of them.

I said: So, you are Muslim without knowing it.

He seemed astonished and said: Amazing! so am I a Muslim?

I said: Yes, but you must accept Muhammad peace be upon him as the last Messenger from God because you heard about him from me here.

He said: yes, I accept. When I entered this center, my maximum hope was to know the difference between a Muslim and a Christian, but I wasn't expecting to get out of this place as a Muslim. Thank you for enlightening my path.

I told him: Praise and thanks to God alone who guided us to the true religion.

Logic comes from God, and complications come from humans:

I was once making a German language presentation about Islam to many Germans who were visiting our center. One of them asked me: If Islam is that simple and logical as you are saying, why do Muslims cause all these political problems?

His question was in front of the group, and I had to deal with it so that his attack would not ruin the calm dialogue.

I told him immediately: For your information, I will die alone. I will be resurrected alone. I will meet my Creator alone, without my family and money.

I shall meet God with answers to three questions: who is your God, your religion, and who is your messenger? God will be waiting for my response which is: "Allah" the Creator is my God; my religion is believing in Him and worshipping Him alone without any mediator; my Prophet is Muhammad the last messenger. By recognizing Muhammad as his final messenger, I have realized all messengers who were before him, and this is a must and obligation to every Muslim.

The Messenger has believed in what was revealed to him from his Lord, and [so have] the believers. All of them have believed in God and His angels and His books and His messengers, [saying], "We make no distinction between any of His messengers." And they say, "We hear and we obey. [We seek] Your forgiveness, our Lord, and to You is the [final] destination.[127]

Say, [O believers], "We have believed in God and what has been revealed to us and what has been revealed to Abraham and Ishmael and Isaac and Jacob and the Descendants and what was given to Moses and Jesus and what was given to the prophets from their Lord. We make no distinction between any of them, and we are Muslims [in submission] to Him."[128]

I told him: You too, every person on earth, will meet God alone, life is short, death is coming for us suddenly. When will we learn to differentiate

---

[127] (Qur'an 2:285).
[128] (Qur'an 2:130).

between political problems and religion? Isn't it time for us to know how to decide our priorities?

The man calmed down, and the group applauded.

After that, I told them: I want to ask you a question. It is known that every nation and people have habits, traditions, whims, and novelties.

I continued: How can a simple person like me here, or another in China, Germany, South America, or Africa, primarily differentiate between the simple religion of God, and the traditions and whims of the place where he is, before reading any religious book?

They tried to guess, and after they failed to give me the right answer, I told them: You all know something called the common sense. So, everything logical is from God, and everything complicated is from humans.

They all laughed hard, and some of them applauded again.

I told them: For example, if a religious scholar whether Muslim, Christian, Hindu or from any other religion told you that the universe has a Creator, One and Only, without any partner. He doesn't come to earth in the form of humans or animals, nor a stone or an idol, that we must worship Him alone, resort to Him alone in hard times, this is the religion of God.

If a religious scholar, Muslim, Christian or Hindu, told you that God incarnates in any form, we must worship and resort to Him through a person, prophet, priest, idol, or saint, this comes from humans, don't listen to him.

I continued: For instance, it is enough to visit India, and say between the crowds, the Creator is One. They would then reply in harmony, yes, the Creator is One. I told the group: and this is what is written in their books.[129]

---

[129] (chandogya Upanishad 6:1-2).

"He is one god without another"

Vedas svetasvatara Upanishad 9 :6,4:20,4:19

But they disagree, fight, could even slaughter each other, over one point which is the form and shape that God comes through to earth. For instance, the Christian Indian says: God is one, but He is incarnated in the trinity (the Father, the Son and the Holy Spirit). The Hindu Indian says: God is one but he comes in the form of an animal or a human or an idol.

I told them: If you think carefully, you will find that all problems and differences between religious sects, religions themselves, exist because of the mediators that humans put between them and their Creator. For instance, Catholic and Protestants denominations, and Hindu sects all disagree about communicating with God, not on the concept that God Himself exists.

If they all worship the God directly, they would be united.

Say (O Muhammad): O people of the Scripture (Jews and Christians): Come to a word that is just between us and you, that we worship none but God, and that we associate no partners with Him, and that none of us shall take others as lords besides God (the Creator). Then, if they turn away, say: Bear witness that we are Muslims. [130]

"God no fathers or master).

"He is invisible, no one sees him with his eyes"

"No one is like him"

Pajur veda (9 :40).

The wrongdoers enter, the who worship natural assets (air, water, fire.etc.), they are filled with darkness ,those who worship Sambhuti (things made by hand such as idol, stone, etc.)

In Christianity (2,6).

In Matthew's bible (4:10).

Then Jesus said to him, "Get behind me, Satan! For it is written, 'You shall worship the Lord your God, and you shall serve him only.'"

Book of exodus (20:3-5).

3- You shall have no other gods before Me.

4-You shall not make for yourself an idol of any kind or an image of anything in the heavens above, on the earth beneath, or in the waters below.

5-You shall not bow down to them or worship them; for I, the LORD your God, am a jealous God, visiting the iniquity of the fathers on their children to the third and fourth generations of those who hate Me.

[130] (Qur'an 3:64).

I continued: In addition to this, you must know that the religion of God is clear and logical, no mysteries in it. If I want to convince you that Prophet Muhammad is god whom you must worship, I should put so much effort to convince you, and you will never be convinced.

You might ask me how is Muhammad a god while he eats and drinks like us? I would say that you are not convinced because it is a mysterious concept and riddle; you will understand it when you meet God. This example proves that God's right religion must be free of mysteries; mysteries only come from humans.

I added: The religion of God is also free of charge. Everyone has the freedom to pray and worship in the houses of God without paying any subscription to get a membership. Humans create the rule of having to register and pay money in any place of worship.

But if any religious scholar told me that I should pay charity directly to people to help them, then the rule comes from the religion of God.

In God's religion, people are equal, like the teeth of a comb. There is no difference between Arab or foreigner, white or black, only by piousness.

If you were told that any mosque, church, or temple is for whites only while black people have a different place, then this is a rule created by humans.

I told them: Honoring women and raising their status is an order from God, but oppressing them is what humans chose to do.

One of them asked: Then why is the Afghani Muslim woman oppressed?

I told him: Do you think that Buddhist or Christian women in Afghanistan live in paradise?

If the Muslim woman in Afghanistan is oppressed, so is the Hindu, Buddhist, and Christian woman; this is people's culture; it has nothing to do with the true religion of God.

I added: the right religion of God is always compatible and in harmony with natural disposition. For instance, any smoker or alcoholic asks his kids to stay away from smoking and alcohol, because he is deeply convinced about the danger they cause to health and community.

When the religion forbids alcohol, for instance, this is an order from God. But if the religion forbids milk, it is not logical; everyone knows that milk is good for health. His mercy and kindness in His creation allowed us to eat good things and prohibited us from eating bad things.

Another example, head cover for women and decency for men and women are an order from God, but the details of colors and designs are from humans. The rural atheist Chinese woman and the Swiss Christian rural woman are both committed to covering their heads, based on that decency is a natural disposition.

This is how we can differentiate between right and wrong before we read any religious book.

Terrorism, for instance, is common in different forms in the world, among sects of all religions. I lived long in Africa, and I know that there are Christian sects that kill and practice horrific forms of oppression and violence in the name of religion and the name of God. They represent 4% of the world's Christian population. While who performs terrorism in the name of Islam represent 0.01% of the Muslim population. Terrorism is not limited to this, but is also common among Buddhist, Hindus, and other religions.

We can never accept that the media highlights bad examples of Muslims and good examples of non-Muslims. It is unacceptable that they call the Muslim who kills others a terrorist while calling the non-Muslim who kills others mentally ill.

I talked to a French journalist about the same issue: In media, you play a dangerous role in misreporting Islam's image through your continuous persistence in publishing these bad examples of Muslims.

He said: Excuse me, but we only publish the truth, not fake news.

I said: I don't claim that your news is fake, I'm saying that when you allocate an article in your news magazines to talk about bad examples of Muslims, you should give another part to talk about others. When you call the Muslim killer a terrorist, you should also call the non–Muslim killer a terrorist.

He said: A lot of what you are saying is correct.

Set your face steadily to the true religion:

Say, Come, I will recite what your Lord has prohibited to you. [He commands] that you not associate anything with Him, and to parents, good treatment, and do not kill your children out of poverty; We will provide for you and them. And do not approach immoralities – what is apparent of them and what is concealed. And do not kill the soul which God has forbidden [to be killed] except by [legal] right. This has He instructed you that you may use reason.[131]

And do not approach the orphan's property except in a way that is best until he reaches maturity. And give full measure and weight in justice. We do not charge any soul except [with that within] its capacity. And when you testify, be just, even if [it concerns] a near relative. And the covenant of God fulfill. This has He instructed you that you may remember.[132]

---

[131] (Qur'an 6:151).
[132] (Qur'an 6:152).

Religion is a set of relations, ethics and values that bond a human with his Creator, and the community around him.

- First: A part concerning the relationship with the Lord of the universe (the Creator).
- Second: A part concerning organizing human relationships.

The previous Quranic verses' commandments stressed on preserving rights, especially the right of the Creator by devoting bondage to Him. This is the point that covers the relationship between a human and his Creator.

God also commanded that the right of parents remains preserved by being benevolent to them and protecting the rights of children in having a decent life. He prohibited getting near evil deeds, as well as killing a human soul for no legal right. Also, we were commanded by God to preserve the money of orphan, be just when weighing, just when talking and acting, and fulfilling commitments, primarily the commitment with the Lord of the universe.

These commandments exist in other religions worldwide, but through my conversations with non-Muslims, I surprisingly found out that they remember all commandments except the first one. When I ask them to mention these commandments, they most often begin from the third commandment. Their excuse is that they always forget the first and second commandments. The first and second commandments state the importance of worshipping God alone (Monotheism), and staying away from polytheism. This is proof that ignoring these commandments is done intentionally through religious scholars and foundations, to gain mundane and political benefits.

As for the rest of the moral international commitments and laws, we can summarize them as follows:

- The set of instructive moral principles that restrict human behavior can be pointed to as the human or human monitor's inner conscious. This conscious or monitor is reinforced through the raising up and education, fed by information, and culture from the environment surrounding human.

- These principles are natural disposition and immaterial; they cannot be explained or clarified to people. The regulations shouldn't be imposed by force, because they are part of a human's innate behavior. Therefore, people are aware of these ethical values in an instinct and natural way. For instance, to be true and honest are natural characteristics and virtues, while lying and dishonesty are disregarded characteristics by nature. One can easily violate or exceed these rules and moral orders because they are not materialistic or tangible. That's why the civilized community had to impose social restrictions for accountability through the system of reward and penalty. Anyone who tries to undermine these values must be held accountable and prosecuted.

- These moral orders are social commitments that we can't disagree on or can become the subject of a general referendum. They are social facts that the community cannot live without in their content and meaning. Parental disrespect or lying is always considered awful behavior; it cannot be justified as honesty and respect.

Applying these moral values as social uprights doesn't mean that lewdness and evil do not exist in this world.

Religion is realistic and practical. It doesn't contain illusions, nor it assumes idealism. It acknowledges the existence of good and evil as it acknowledges the reality of life and death.

Every soul shall have a taste of death: and We test you by evil and by good by way of trial. to Us you shall be back.[133]

All these directives and moral principles are firmly linked, and form a comprehensive network of connections and bonds. They do not allow disintegration or division, because they represent a straight, one path that can't be segmented.

And, [moreover], this is My path, which is straight, so follow it; and do not follow [other] ways, for you will be separated from His way. This has He instructed you that you may become righteous.[134]

Abiding by these moral principles does not demand power or skills from individuals. Believing in the Creator, following ethical recommendations do not require sharp intelligence or unique capabilities. A person does not need to be exceptionally talented or creative to know that killing others is not right, and averting this habit is rooted in human nature. The pillars of Islam and its recommendations can't bear interpretation or half solutions.

O you who have believed, fear God as He should be feared and do not die except as Muslims [in submission to Him].[135]

Ethics can be considered a spiritual and social law that lays down on the base of the relationships among members of the human race. There is no doubt that it differentiates humans from animals, and it is valid regardless of the economic pattern of the society.

---

[133] (Qur'an 21:35).
[134] (Qur'an 6:153).
[135] (Qur'an 3:102).

Their validity distinguishes religious ethics on the international level. These ethics are different from habits and traditions (customs). Judgments, ethics, and values are detailed rules and specific, fixed laws; they exist since Prophet Noah's era. We share many different cultures globally and abide by them, regardless of the nature of the economic system or social environment.

They are considered the common human factor, that unifies culture, political systems, ethnicity, level, and race. It directly affects the individual's social behavior when adding jurisdiction and legal character to constitution articles or local laws. It is worth mentioning that religions also called for considering customs (the prevention of vice and promotion of virtue). Their respect of traditions and habits of the society does not contradict general values and ethics, which most people are used to and have been implementing, from any saying or deed, which doesn't contradict the code of valued religion.

… And We will bring you, [O Muhammad], as a witness over your nation. And We have sent down to you the Book as clarification for all things and as guidance and mercy and good tidings for the Muslims. [136]

An atheist once asked me about the importance of abiding by international ethics under the umbrella of religion. His opinion was that it is enough that people treat each other with good manners, without believing in God, if life's goal is developing the earth. Many atheists are fully committed to good manners and are trying hard to construct the earth.

---

[136] (Qur'an 16:89).

I told him: developing the earth and good manners are not the goals of religion, but they are tools! The purpose of religion is to let a person know his God, origin, path, and destiny.

The good ending and destiny only occur when you acknowledge your Creator through developing the earth and good manners. The deeds of the servant should seek the satisfaction of Almighty God.

Say, I am only a man like you, to whom has been revealed that your god is one God. So, whoever would hope for the meeting with his Lord – let him do righteous work and not associate in the worship of his Lord anyone.[137]

Conclusion:

We conclude that:

The correct religion is: Believing that the universe has one Creator, who is Allah the One and Only, the religion of God must be one, easy, simple, and straightforward, compatible with human disposition, valid for every time and place.

It is:

- The oneness: Believing that there is no god but Allah, without any partners or son, He is the Creator, the provider to the whole universe.
- The servitude: To worship God alone, never associate anyone or anything with Him.
- Believing in messengers: Following messengers (Abraham, Moises, Jesus, etc.) and believing in what they brought (in that era). (The messengers prophesied the coming of last Prophet– Muhammad, and

---

[137] (Qur'an 18:110).

urged their followers to believe in him and follow him if they reach his time).[138]

-   Ethics: Doing good deeds and avoiding evil deeds.

Say, My Lord has guided me to a straight path, an upright religion, the creed of Abraham the Monotheist, who was not a polytheist.[139]

---

[138] The original concept of God. Faten Sabri. Www. fatensabri.com

[139] (Qur'an 6 :161).

A Moderate Nation

Do not forget your portion of the present world!

During a visit to China, we visited "Window of the World", a public park established on enormous land areas with monolithic figures of the most distinguished world sites. You find for example, in one corner a model of the Eiffel Tower, a model of Big Ben in another, along with the Egyptian Pyramids, the Niagara Falls, etc. In this park, you get a chance to taste Latin food, wear East Asian costumes, and live African traditions. It's a breath-taking place.

I was amazed by the place. My children were having fun, and my husband was taking photos. In the middle of my amazement, I recalled a frequent question that came to my mind when I was young. How could we balance between enjoying the pleasures of life and getting to know different cultures, while at the same time winning eternal happiness? Then I remembered the Qur'anic verse: **But seek, through that which God has given you, the home of the Hereafter; and [yet], do not forget your portion of the present world. And do good as God has done good to you**[140]. I got very happy afterwards.

---

[140] (Qur'an 28 :77).

The Austrian philosopher Leopold Weiss, who converted from Judaism to Islam and changed his name to Muhammad Al Assad, said in his book (Islam at the Crossroads): "Our travel through this world is necessary, positive part in God's plan. Therefore, human life is of tremendous value, but we must never forget that it is purely instrumental. There is no place in Islam to maximize the material side as it is in the modern West, which says: "My kingdom is of this world alone", nor is the contempt for life that is being spoken by Christianity: "My kingdom is not of this world". Islam goes the middle way. The Qur'an teaches us to say: **Our Lord! Give us in this world that which is good and in the Hereafter that which is good.**[141] Thus, a full appreciation of this world and whatever it offers is not necessarily a handicap for our spiritual endeavors. Material prosperity is desirable, though not a goal.

Every individual Muslim must regard himself as personally responsible for all happenings around him and strive for establishing the good and abolishing the wrong at every time and in every direction.

A result for this attitude is to be found in the Qur'anic verse: **You are indeed the best community that has ever been brought forth for [the good of] mankind: you enjoin the doing of what is right and forbid the doing of what is wrong.**[142]"

The Austrian philosopher continued: "The concern for the spread of Islam was not prompted by the love of domination; it had nothing to do with economic or national self-aggrandizement or with the greed to increase Muslim comforts at other people's cost.

---

[141](Qur'an 2:201).
[142] (Qur'an 3:110).

It has never meant the coercion of non-believers into the religion of Islam. It has only meant as it means today, the construction of a global framework for the best possible spiritual development of Man. According to the teachings of Islam, acknowledging morals automatically enforces responsibility to work according to these morals. A mere Platonic discernment between right and wrong, without the urge to promote right and to destroy wrong, is gross immorality. Morality lives and dies with the human endeavor to establish its victory upon the earth."

The presence of contradictions in some religious concepts in other religions is one of the reasons that lead to aversion of religion and drives people towards science alone.

One of the main features that drives people towards religion is its balance and moderation, which are apparent in Islam.

The problem in other religions which have been distorted from the correct religion is that they are either:

- purely spiritual and call their followers to monasticism and isolation.
- Totally materialistic.

Do not exceed the limits in your religion:

Extremism, fanaticism, and inflexibility are mere features that have been forbidden in the true religion. In various verses, the Qur'an has called for kindness, tolerance in treatment, mercy, and forgiveness.

So, by mercy from God, [O Muhammad], you were lenient with them. And if you had been rude [in speech] and harsh in heart, they would have disbanded from about you. So, pardon them and ask forgiveness for them and consult them in the matter. And when you

have decided, then rely upon God. Indeed, God loves those who rely [upon Him].[143]

Invite to the way of your Lord with wisdom and good instruction, and argue with them in a way that is best. Indeed, your Lord is most knowing of who has strayed from His way, and He is most knowing of who is [rightly] guided.[144]

The fact that everything is permissible is a principle in religion, though there are some enumerated prohibitions that are clearly mentioned in the Holy Qur'an which no one disputes.

O children of Adam, take your adornment [i.e., wear your clothing] at every mosque, and eat and drink, but be not excessive. Indeed, He likes not those who commit excess, Say, "Who has forbidden the adornment of [i.e., from] God which He has produced for His servants and the good [lawful] things of provision?" Say, "They are for those who believed during the life of this world, exclusively [for them] on the Day of Resurrection." Thus, do We detail the verses for a people who know, Say, "My Lord has only forbidden immoralities – what is apparent of them and what is concealed – and sin, and oppression without right, and that you associate with God that for which He has not sent down authority, and that you say about God that which you do not know. [145]

The religion has considered radicalism and inflexibility without authentic proof as a satanic action that the religion revolts.

---

[143] (Qur'an 3 :159).

[144] (Qur'an 16 :125).

[145] (Qur'an 7 : 31-33).

O mankind! Eat of that which is lawful and good on the earth, and follow not the footsteps of Satan. Verily, he is to you an open enemy, He (Satan) commands you only what is evil and sinful, and that you should say against God what you know not. [146]

Verily, I will mislead them, and surely, I will arouse in them false desires; and certainly, I will order them to slit the ears of cattle, and indeed I will order them to change the nature created by God. And whoever takes Satan as a protector instead of God, has surely suffered a manifest loss. [147]

God intends for you ease:

Originally, religion comes to ease a lot of restrictions that people impose on themselves. During pre-Islam ignorance, there were some highly detested practices such as female infanticide, permitting certain types of foods for males while forbidding them on females, prohibiting females from the inheritance. Also, fornication, drinking alcoholic beverages, eating the money of orphans, eating the dead, usury, etc.

We find as well in some people's legislation and rules that have been falsely related to religion to force them upon people. This has deviated people from differentiating between the correct religion that meets their innate needs, and the traditions and customs inherited from ancestors, leading people to replace religion with science.

The correct religion relieves people's suffering and puts rules and legislation that aims to ease their lives.

---

[146] (Qur'an 2 :168-169).

[147] (Qur'an 4 :119).

God intends for you ease, and He does not want to make things difficult for you. [148]

God wishes to lighten (the burden) for you and man was created weak. [149]

…and do not kill yourselves (nor kill one another). Surely, God is Most Merciful to you. [150]

…and do not throw yourselves into destruction, and do good. Truly, God loves the good–doers. [151]

The Prophet peace be upon him said:

Facilitate things to people (concerning religious matters), and do not make it hard for them and give them good tidings and do not make them run away. [152]

During the Prophet's time, three men talked among themselves about worship, where one of them said: I will offer the prayer throughout the night forever. The other said: I will fast throughout the year. The third said: I will keep away from women and will not marry forever. Prophet Muhammad came to them and said:

Are you the same people who said, so–and–so? By God, I am more submissive to God and more afraid of Him than you; yet I fast and break my fast, I do sleep, and I also marry women. So, he who does not follow my religious tradition is not from me (not one of my followers). [153]

---

[148] (Qur'an 2 :185).
[149] (Qur'an 4 :28).
[150] (Qur'an 4 :29).
[151] (Qur'an 2:195).
[152] (Sahih Al-Bukhari).
[153] (Sahih Al-Bukhari).

And We have not sent you, [O Muhammad], except as a mercy to the worlds.[154]

The Prophet, peace be upon him, said to Abdullah Ibn Amr:

O Abdullah! I have been informed that you fast during the day and offer prayers all night. Abdullah replied: Yes, O Allah's messenger! The Prophet said: Don't do that; fast for few days and then give it up for few days, offer prayers and sleep at night, as your body has a right on you, and your wife has a right on you, and your guest has a right on you.[155]

Balance in giving rights:

I recall a funny conversation with a Latin lady who asked me: Is a Muslim woman allowed to wear earrings like other women? I laughed and replied: A Muslim woman is a human who doesn't differ from any woman, but she understands and knows her rights and obligations and how to arrange her priorities. She can deal with such matters with great moderation in a way the Latin and western woman cannot.

She said: What do you mean?

I replied: The Muslim woman has understood the meaning of the term "privacy" well. So, while she loves her father, brother, son, and husband, she has realized that each type of love is distinguished from the other.

She realized that her love for each of them requires her to give each their suitable rights, so, her father requires honor and respect, while her son requires breeding and care. She knows when and how to show her beauty, and she doesn't appear the same way for all.

---

[154] (Qur'an 21:107).

[155] (Sahih Al-Bukhari).

I continued: The Muslim woman is free. She has refused to surrender to the whims of others and fashion. She wears what she likes and pleases her Creator. Can't you see how the western woman has become a captive of fashion?! Suppose style came out this season for women to wear tight pants. In that case, all women will automatically wear them even if the pants aren't suitable for their figure or aren't comfortable wearing them.

I continued: Doesn't it scare you how the woman has turned into commodity?! There is almost no commercial without a half-naked woman; this gives an indirect message of the deteriorating value of the woman in this age.

By covering up her beauty, it's the woman who is sending a message to the world. A statement that she is a human with value honored by God. People dealing with her must judge her according to her knowledge, beliefs, and ideas, not according to her physical appearance.

She said: That's strange! This is what is called etiquette.

I told her: Yes! The Muslim woman has understood human nature and has understood that she needs to cover up her body from strangers to keep herself and the society from hurt. I don't think you could deny that all women who are used to showing off their bodies wish that all women are wearing the head cover when they get old.

She said: That's 100% correct!

Then I asked her: Have you read about women's death and distortion rates during plastic surgeries? What do you think forced the woman to go through this suffering? It's this beauty competition that has been forced upon her instead of an intellectual one, and that has made her lose her true value in society and lose her life.

She said: This is a strange philosophy that I have never heard before.

Then she said: Ok well, has Islam given the woman equality with men?

I replied: The Muslim woman is looking for justice, not equality.

Equality with the man has made her lose a lot of her power and value.

She asked: How is that?

I answered: Imagine buying shirts for two of your children who are five and eighteen years old. Equality by buying them the same size would make one of them suffer from not having a shirt that fits him, while justice is that you must purchase a shirt for each one of them but a suitable one, for both to be happy.

I continued: The woman in this age is striving to prove she can achieve all that the man can do, but actually, she is losing her uniqueness and distinguished qualities. God has created her to be able to do what men can't do. It has been proven that birth pain is one of the most severe types of pains, so, religion honored and compensated her in return by relieving her from the burden of providing living expenses or sharing her private wealth with the man, unlike what happens in western societies. As for men, God has not given them the ability to tolerate the pain of giving birth but had given him the ability to climb mountains, for example.

She said: But I like to climb mountains and I could do it just like men.

I told her: Yes, maybe you can climb a mountain and work hard, but still it's you who will give birth and nurse because men couldn't do that in all cases. Therefore, you will have a double burden that you could have avoided.

There is something that a lot of people don't realize. If a Muslim woman chose to demand her rights in the United Nations while giving up her rights in Islam, she would lose a lot, because her rights are more in Islam.

Islam achieves the integration between man and woman in a way that grants happiness for all.

The favor of Islamic civilization:

A Columbian visitor and her work colleague told me one day that they strongly need to worship the one God, but they do not want to let go of the Virgin Mary in their prayers because they do not want to underestimate her rights.

I told them: A Muslim could achieve the balance in worship without underestimating the prophet or the prophet's mother.

They asked: How?

I answered: A Muslim loves his Creator and gives Him His right in worshipping Him alone. Love for the prophet is by following the way revealed to him by God, and that is by worshipping the One God but not worshipping the prophet himself.

I then asked them: What statements can you not give up in your prayers that include mentioning the Virgin Mary?

The first one replied: God bless Mary and help her.

I told her: That's true. We say: May God bless the Prophet Muhammad and bless Jesus and Mary as well.

The other one said: We also say: Oh, Mary, help me and bless me.

I said: This is incorrect.

They said: What's the difference?

I answered: In the first prayer we are asking for Mary, while in the second we are asking from her. We are only allowed to ask from God. Therefore, you could say the first prayer but should stop the second.

They were thrilled because they found out that worshipping God directly won't make them lose their love to Virgin Mary, and they converted to Islam at once.

We find that many nations and civilizations have failed to achieve this balance. While Christianity has exaggerated in loving Jesus and his mother by making them Gods, we find out that Moses's followers rejected Jesus as a messenger of God.

Islam has achieved the required balance by believing in both Jesus and Moses and granting them the respect and appreciation they deserve.

The needed balance is achieved by following their right message in worshipping the One God just like how all prophets and messengers worshipped the Him.

The Islamic civilization has dealt with the Creator well, and put the relation between Him and His creations in its correct standard. In contrast, other human civilizations have mistreated the way they dealt with their Creator. Some people have worshipped others apart from Him. Other people disbelieved in Him. They have dealt in ways far from what He deserves in Glory and Grace.

A true Muslim doesn't mix between matters. He knows how to establish a balance between ideologies and sciences, along with differentiating between:

- Civilization elements, which are represented in the ideological and mental evidence, morals, and ethics.
- Civil elements, which are represented in scientific discoveries and industrial achievements.

A Muslim deal with them in a framework of faith and morals.

- ➤ The Greek civilization believed in God, but denied His oneness and described Him as a god who does not benefit or harm.
- ➤ The Persian civilization before Islam worshipped the sun, prostrated to fire, and sainted it.
- ➤ Hindus stopped worshipping the Creator and worshipped created gods, which are incarnated in the trinity that is composed of the three gods: Brahma the creator, Vishnu who preserves the universe and Shiva who destroys the universe.
- ➤ Buddhism denied the Creator and worshipped a created god (Buddha).
- ➤ The Sabian civilization were people of the book (have divine revelation), but then denied their Lord and worshipped the stars and planets, except for some Muslim monotheistic groups that are mentioned in the Qur'an.
- ➤ The civilization of the pharaohs had peaked in monotheism during the time of king Akhenaten. Yet, civilization still symbolized God in some of His creations like the sun, which was the main symbol of God for them. After that, disbelieving in God also reached its peak in the time of Moses, peace be upon him, when the Pharaoh claimed to be God and the only legislator.
- ➤ The Arabic civilization stopped worshipping God, and worshipped idols instead.
- ➤ Christianity denied the oneness of God, and worshipped Jesus, peace be upon him, along with his mother. They believed in the trinity represented in three coeternal consubstantial persons or hypostases, which are the Father, the Son, and the Holy Spirit.

- The Roman civilization denied the Creator before Christianity and gave partners to Him in Christianity by worshipping idols and symbols of power.
- The Jewish civilization rejected God and chose a god of its own. They also worshipped the calf and gave the Creator human attributes in their book.

While these civilizations have decayed, the previously explained Christian and Jewish turned into an atheist, communistic and capitalistic civilizations. These two civilizations dealt with God and life based on an ideological and intellectual context that is considered backwards-minded, brutal, and characterized with immortality. Though they have reached the peak in civil, industrial, and scientific developments, which are not the basis for assessing a nation's development.

The correct civil development standards that should be used to assess nations depend on mental evidence, and how these nations deal with God, life, Man, and the universe. A proper civil development should lead to God's correct way and His relationship with His creations, which puts this relation in its appropriate level. We conclude that the Islamic civilization is the only truly developed civilization, because it merely achieved this required balance.

Islam is a Religion and a State:

Capitalism has given Man a free-living method and has claimed that following this path will lead to happiness and satisfaction. But what happened is that Man found himself deteriorating in a society classified by class. People either live in extravagant wealth established by unfairness to others, or in poverty and suffering for those who are morally committed.

Communism, on the other hand, cancelled all social classes and tried to establish firm principles, but this caused more poverty and pain, leading to societies that are more revolutionary than others.

As for Islam, it has achieved moderation. It is a moderate nation that has offered humanity a great balanced doctrine praised even by the enemies of Islam. But unfortunately, there are Muslims who haven't followed Islamic morals properly.

A French diplomat asked me one day about what is considered a contradiction:

He said: I couldn't understand how could Islam, according to your explanation, be so reasonable at a time when Muslims are living in such randomness which has driven them away from morals and ethics. Isn't this a contradiction?!

I replied: Where is the contradiction? If your driver made an accident with your luxurious car due to his ignorance of driving rules, would that affect the fact that your vehicle is originally luxurious?

His fellow, who was French with Arab origins, instantly said: Yes, a loser Muslim represents himself. Many people noticed that many non-Muslims behave with Islamic behavior, which led to a saying: We find Islam without Muslims.

Joseph Franz Schacht, a German researcher in Arabic and Islamic studies, had extremist thoughts yet still managed to tell the truth regarding his assessment about Islam.

He said: "One of the outstanding features of Islam is that it's a religion and state. The Sharia law (Islamic law) and the Islamic jurisprudence are characterized by their clear and strong influence on the legal culture that exceeded or contacted it.

Their domination is stronger than the states. There have been different types of conflicts between religion and the state throughout history. In Christianity, the conflict was over political power, in which the church had an organized, graduated, and coherent institution that had a head leader. The church law was one of its political weapons. As for Islam, the case was totally different than the church's case. Islamic law never depended on such organized power. Thus, there has never been a real test for the power between religion and the state. The principle stating that Islam must organize the legal aspects in Muslims' lives has been kept strong and dominant, with no one defying it."

One of Schacht's thoughts was: "The civil law is one of the most important gains that Islam has given to the civilized world. This is what is called "Sharia". It is entirely different than all other laws. Islamic sharia is what clearly distinguishes the Islamic way of life. What distinguishes it is that it looks at all human behavior and their relation amongst each other, including the obligatory duties, the desirable, the left out, the hated, or the forbidden."

He also said: "The Islamic legislation has affected all branches of law with the Christians and Jews who lived in Islamic states and have seen the mercy along with forgiveness of the Islamic sharia. The Jew Mousa Ibn-Maimonides (601 Hijri – 1204 AD) was affected by the Islamic compositions while putting the legal materials in Mishnah Torah, an action which no Jew has done before. Also, Jacobins and Monophysites and Nestorians weren't reluctant to take from the Islamic legislation."

In his book "observations into the Islamic History", the Dutch historian Reinhart Dozy said: "Most Christians in the East followed different doctrines.

They suffered immensely from persecution under the Constantinople governments, still, when Islam came with its brotherhood rules and forgiveness, they were left to choose their religion and were protected and treated with equality. After being exhausted by Roman taxes, they were obligated only to pay the "Jizya"[156] which doesn't exhaust anyone."

The state in Islam is not a "religious" state, understood in earlier Western thought.

In Islam, there is a cancellation of any infallibility or holiness to humans. It's a state which has a primary target of serving the people. Islamic legislation doesn't contradict novelty and civilization. It should be a source of pride in our civilized position in history.

A French atheist asked me one day: Why not separate religion from the state, and let human thoughts and their points of view be included in references, similar to western societies? Along with completely separating religion and people's lives, similar to how it was implemented in French society.

I replied, smiling: You mean references depending on the human's whims and mood swings? We need godly legislation that suits humans in all their cases and doesn't change because of inconsistent human thoughts and mood swings, similar to what happened when usury and homosexuality were allowed. We need legislation that isn't put by the people in power to be a burden on the weak like in Capitalism, nor do we need Communism that opposes the innate human need for possession.

---

[156] It is a type of a (Poll Tax), imposed on non-Muslim citizens of an Islamic state, for which their lives, progeny, possessions, are protected by the State, and they are entitled to practice their religion without any interference by anyone not from their faith, and they are guaranteed to settle their intracommunity disputes according to their own traditions and laws - not according to Sharia- and they are exempted from military service while being entitled to full protection from alien enemies.

I continued: The French experiment resulted from the dominance and alliance between the church and the state over the people's minds and destiny in the Middle Ages. The Islamic world hasn't faced this problem at all due to its logical and applicable system.

He said: You don't acknowledge democracy then.

I said: We have what's better than democracy. We have Consultancy.

He asked: What's the difference?

I answered: Democracy is when you consider all family members' opinion no matter their age or how badly their experience would affect the family. During decision making, both views of a kindergarten child and a wise older person would be equal. On the other hand, the consultancy system depends on experienced members' opinions; they get to decide what is beneficial and what isn't.

I added: The difference between the two systems is noticeable. A piece of valid evidence that proves the deficiency found in the democratic system is that some countries have given legitimacy to practices that oppose human nature, customs, traditions, and religion, such as homosexuality, fornication, usury, and other abhorrent practices just because such practices have been voted for by the majority.

With many voices calling for moral decay, democracy has helped by participating in creating immoral societies.

I continued: The difference between the Islamic Consultancy system and Western Democracy is the source of sovereignty in legislation.

In Democracy, the power starts from the people and nation.

As for the Islamic Consultancy system, power starts from the Creator. It's not the result of human thoughts. Humans can just build upon the godly legislation.

Also, they have the right to jurisprudence in whatever's not included in heavenly legislation, as long as it's within the religious framework of what's permitted and forbidden.

He said: The Islamic legislative system is unique. Even though it's a religious system, it doesn't contradict reason in any way. It's an organized, coherent doctrine; its various branches are coherent with one another, but I'm against the punishing penalties in the Qur'an.

I said: These penalties have been put as a deterrent, and to punish those who intend to corrupt the community. As evidence to this, these penalties aren't implemented on unintended killing or stealing during a famine and extreme need. It's to protect society, and some are already in French law such as the death penalty.

He asked: Is there truly a death penalty in French law?

I replied: Yes, as well as in many postural law systems in other countries. Imagine that you went home and found your whole family murdered by a person. Then that person was arrested and put in prison for a specific period eating and enjoying the prison facilities you are funding through the taxes you are paying.

How would you tolerate this?! You will probably either end up going insane or falling into an addiction to forget your pain. If this same situation happened in a country practicing the Islamic legislations, the case would be completely different. The murderer will be brought in front of the family of the murdered. They will decide whether to take revenge through retribution, which is justice itself, or to take the "Deyaa", which is the money that the murderer must pay on intentional killing to the family of the murdered, or to give pardon, which is much favored as mentioned in the Qur'an.

…But if you pardon (them) and overlook, and forgive (their faults), then verily God is Oft–Forgiving, Most Merciful. [157]

I continued: There are 6348 verses in the Qur'an, while the verses of penalties are no more than ten, and have been put by the One Who is Wise and Well-acquainted with all things. Would you leave reading, enjoying, and practicing this system you consider unique, just because you don't know the wisdom of ten verses?!

The balance in the economy:

I remember a Latin person interested in economics, once asked me about the difference between the economic system in Islam, capitalism, and socialism.

I replied: Concerning the freedom of ownership, the private property is the main principle in capitalism, while in socialism, public property is the main principle.

In Islam, several types of ownership are allowed:

- The Public Property, which is publicly owned by Muslims, rich lands, for example.
- The State Property, which is owned by the state, like for example, natural wealth, that includes forests and minerals.
- The Private Property, which is acquired only through investment work, in a way that does not threaten the public welfare.

He asked: What about the free economy?

I replied: In capitalism, the free economy has no boundaries. Socialism, on the other hand, completely confiscates free economy.

---

[157] (Qur'an 64:14).

In Islam, the free economy is acknowledged, but is limited within certain boundaries:

> ➢ Self-determination, which emerges from the depths of oneself based on Islamic education, and the spread of Islamic concepts in society.
> ➢ Objective determination, which are legislations that forbid certain practices such as usury, gambling, cheating, etc.

He said: Religion is like a drug that oppressed and impoverished people to accept suffering and unfairness. Then, they are left to dream about paradise to give the rich people a chance to acquire wealth; this has resulted in the poverty of Muslims and other religious nations.

I told him: Never have societies suffered from poverty and social unfairness because of being religiously faithful or lacking in their resources. It was because of people distancing away from religion and unfair resource distribution.

Extreme poverty is only the result of outrageous wealth. In capitalism, it is claimed that natural resources are unable to meet humans' renewable needs; while in socialism, people believe that there is a contradiction existing between the forces of production and distribution relations.

In Islam, it has been clarified that God has created plenty of natural resources that entirely satisfy human needs without running out. The problem lies in the human misuse of these resources and inequality in distribution.

I added: The real drug addiction in societies is atheism, not religion.

He said: Why?

I replied: Because atheism calls its followers to pure materialism. It causes them to exclude their relation with the Creator by relinquishing duties and responsibilities. It calls for enjoying only the current moment, regardless of the consequences, so, they behave as they wish, believing that there are no sanctions, no resurrection, and no judgement.

Isn't this the correct description of an addict?

He said: Yes, that's true.

He then asked: How did Islam achieve social balance?

I answered: One of the general concepts in Islam is that wealth belongs to the Creator. We are only in a subordinate position in our control over this wealth. Islam has forbidden wealth to be only exchanged between the rich. Islam has prohibited treasuring wealth without giving out a small portion to the poor and needy from the person's savings "Zakat". This act of worship helps the person overcome being tight-fisted; it helps them become generous and giving.

And what God restored to His Messenger from the people of the towns – it is for God and for the Messenger and for [his] near relatives and orphans and the needy and the [stranded] traveler – so that it will not be a perpetual distribution among the rich from among you. And whatever the Messenger has given you – take; and what he has forbidden you – refrain from. And fear God; indeed, God is severe in penalty. [158]

Believe in God and His Messenger and spend out of that in which He has made you successive inheritors. For those who have believed among you and spent, there will be a great reward. [159]

---

[158] (Qur'an 59:7).
[159] (Qur'an 57:7).

…And those who hoard gold and silver and spend it not in the way of God – give them tidings of a painful punishment. [160]

Also, Islam encourages hardworking for those who are capable.

It is He Who made the earth subservient to you. So, traverse in its tracks and partake of the sustenance He has provided. To Him will you be resurrected. [161]

Islam has forbidden extravagance. It calls for setting the standards of living at a moderate level; this does not mean that the concept of richness in Islam is limited only to the vital needs. Still, it also includes the possession of food, a home, clothing, the ability to marry, perform the pilgrimage, and to give out charity.

And [they are] those who, when they spend, do so not excessively or sparingly but are ever, between that, [justly] moderate. [162]

The poor, from an Islamic perspective, is whoever's incapable of achieving the vital needs. These needs are determined according to the living standards in the country that the person is living in. So, if it's normal for every family to own a separate home in a certain country, then the family that is incapable of this is considered poor. Thus, the law of balance is based on the ability to satisfy every individual's needs according to what's known in the community at that time.

Islam ensures meeting the needs of every individual in society; this is achieved through public interdependence. The Muslims are considered brothers; helping each other and meeting each other's needs is obligatory.

---

[160] (Qur'an 9:34).
[161] (Qur'an 67:15).
[162] (Qur'an 25:67).

The Prophet, Muhammad peace be upon him, said:

The Muslim is the brother of the Muslim, he doesn't oppress him and doesn't put him into ruin, and whoever is concerned for the needs of his brother, God is concerned for his needs, and whoever relieves a Muslim of a burden, God will relieve him of a burden from the burdens of the Day of Judgement and whoever covers (the faults of) a Muslim, God will cover (his faults) on the Day of Judgement.[163]

I recall a beautiful incident with a Colombian visitor. She came to the center with her teenage children and friend. Unfortunately, they arrived late when the working hours were about to end, so I couldn't answer all her questions. I explained what I could within 15 minutes.

I had the feeling that she was hiding something. She came back the next morning with her children only without her friend.

She said: I insist on continuing our conversation because I have some questions keeping me from converting to Islam for years. I want answers to these questions.

I responded: Ask all you wish. I have the whole day to answer your questions.

She said: I met a Muslim friend while travelling with my husband. This friend told me that Muslims don't need to go to doctors when they get sick because they just pray to God to get well. I wasn't convinced at all, and that was one of the points that kept me away from accepting this religion. I believe we must follow the underlying causes.

---

[163] (Sahih Al-Bukhari).

I told her: That's true. Concerning this point, you, unfortunately, know about Islam more than that Muslim. She needs someone to explain to her her religion. She hasn't given you the correct information. Islam is a realistic religion.

God Almighty ordered us to rely on Him, and trust His wisdom, but He also forbade us from full dependency without depending on the causes. Reliance includes determination while exerting effort and applying the reasons, then surrendering afterwards to the wisdom of God.

The Prophet Muhammad, peace be upon him, told someone who wanted to leave his camel without being tied, thinking that this is reasonable reliance on God:

Tie your camel, then trust God[164]; this is the correct balance.

She was delighted with my explanation.

We spent the whole day together, answering her questions. She talked about a time six years ago when her husband, who had no religion, converted to Islam.

He didn't have any religious interests; he said that he found answers to all his questions in Islam. He invited her to join Islam, but she was reluctant because she still had many questions. Thanks to God, she said that our conversation provided her with answers to all questions.

Conclusion:

We conclude that Islam looks at life as it should be. People are looking for a balanced religion that meets their spiritual needs, a religion that is indispensable and at the same time doesn't marginalize their worldly needs.

---

[164] (Sahih Al- Tirmizi).

The religion calls for moderation, which is the concept that has been strictly stressed in the final heavenly religion. This heavenly religion was sent through the final messenger Muhammad, peace be upon him, who came to correct the errors previous nations have made, leading to the distortion of the religion concept by putting it in a spiritual path only. This has resulted in superstitions that have entirely driven people away from religion.

Also, religion has been manipulated to achieve personal objectives by being used as an instrument to pressure the people. This has led to many people following secularism, which is a total separation between religion and the state.

Islam has succeeded as a ruling system and a living method, while capitalism and communism have failed. But atheists and agnostics are increasing because many Muslims stray away from their religion; they also fail in spreading the correct Islamic concept. Humanity has started to lose faith in all creed due to the corruption of the religious concepts that are being introduced. Nevertheless, no oriental researcher, no matter what his opinion in Islam is, hasn't admitted that Islam is a Religion and State.

My Lord is Merciful and Compassionate

We feed you only for the countenance of God:

In the first two years of our stay in Lagos, Nigeria, we lived in hotel apartments so that it would be easy for us to look for a suitable house near the kids' schools. Usually, after I returned from any trip, I was keen to bring simple presents for all janitors and workers, and share with them food and drinks. At that time, spreading the word of Islam (da'wa) was not in my mind; my intention was only to get close to God by giving gifts.

When we decided to leave that place to move on to the new house, we were surprised that everyone in the was crying! The driver told us that they have never met a Muslim family of such high manners who spread the spirit of love and fraternity and wanted to reward us. After hearing that from the driver, I had two thoughts. Should I feel good that we made their hearts happy? Or should I feel sad about the condition that the Muslims are in that gave the people of that country such a bad impression about Muslim people in general?!

I told the driver that we already got our reward which was their happiness, and I then remembered the verse: **We only feed you for the sake of God. We want from you neither compensation, nor gratitude**[165], so I got relieved.

---

[165] (Qur'an 76: 9).

My mercy encompasses all things:

I remember the story of my French language teacher. She was an African from a country called Benin which was adjacent to Lagos where we stayed. After the lecture, I told her that I needed a housemaid who could speak French, for my kids and I could practice the French language with her.

I was surprised when she replied to me: I am ready to work for you!

I told her: You are my teacher, and you have my all respect!

She said: You are very kind, but I am really in need of this job. You know that I come from Benin adjacent to this city, and I need a place to stay.

I will clean the house for you at morning, and work in the center at evening. Also, I noticed that you are very friendly even though your Holy Book (Qur'an) never talked about love, nor even about the love of the Creator to His servants. How can He love them while He tests them and restricts His provision?!

I replied to her: Regarding the place you need to stay in, you are welcome with no job and for free. We already have an annex for the workers, and you can share the dorms with them. Regarding what you've said about the Qur'an, have you ever read the Qur'an?

She replied: No, but I have heard about it.

I told her: If you read the Qur'an, you will see what is mentioned in it about the mercy and love God has for His servants.

But God's love to His servants is different from the love humans have with each other because love in humans' case is a need that the loving person seeks and finds in the beloved, but God does not need us, humans. Hence, His love for us is out of generosity, kindness, and mercy. The love coming from the Powerful to the powerless; coming from the Free of need to the needy.

The love coming from the Competent and Mighty to the helpless; coming from the Most Great to the humble. The love which comes with sagacity and wisdom.

She asked: How come?

I replied: Wouldn't you bring your child to the operation room to have his/her stomach opened? Wouldn't you fully trust the doctor's insight, his love to your baby, and his consideration to save him/her from the illness?

She replied: How come He loves His creations while He limits their freedom and doesn't permit them to do whatever they like to do?

Have you never heard about individualism?

Have you ever heard about this evolving concept, which means that the individual's decisions should be based on their benefits and pleasures? The individual is the focus of attention, so the individual's interests should be above the nation's considerations and above the society's and religion's effects. Besides, people should not be prohibited to gender transition; they should be able to do whatever they like to do and wear and behave in public in the way they want to, as the street is everyone's.

I said: Do you allow your children to do whatever they wish because you love them? Would you let your little son to jump out of the window or to play with an electric cord?

I also told her: Your statement where you said that the street is everyone's is correct, but your understanding of it is wrong. If you were living with a group of people in the same house, would you ever accept one of the house members to urinate in the hall, on the same concept that the house belongs to everyone? Would you ever accept living in this house with no laws and rules to govern it?

A human who has complete freedom becomes an ugly being, as it has been unquestionably proven that the human is unable to handle this kind of freedom.

Individualism can never take the place of collectivism regardless of the individual's power or influence. Community members are classes that cannot survive without each other and can never be independent. Some of them are soldiers, doctors, nurses, and judges. How can any of them outweigh their benefit and personal interest over others to achieve their happiness and be the focus of attention?

She said: How can we achieve happiness then?

I replied: the meaning of happiness in individualism is victory, domination, and the possession of technology. However, in Islam, true happiness is a content heart, a successful marriage, a spacious house, a good neighbor, and a comfortable vehicle, with sharing and cooperation.

Although the Islamic Civilization was formed by a mixture of different people and tribes, it produced accountability and reward systems, along with duties and rights. The person is punished for his crimes, but he is also rewarded in other cases. Islam liberated the individual from his previous prejudices and led him to his pure inner-self to live like an honest, social civil who lives in a community, respects its laws, and appreciates his intellectual potential along with his ability to coexist beautifully with others. A nation that aspires to progress and builds a higher goal emerges from the concept of a single identity. Everyone has their ideas and capabilities, but applying these ideas requires teamwork, and thus everyone is equal with whatever they present. Therefore, Islam has presented the perfect relationship of the individual with his society.

I proceeded: The individual is only a small and integral part of society; this makes a peaceful and secure society because if the balance between classes is disturbed, conflicts will arise, and it will lead to dissatisfaction in society. Money is no longer the highest standard that distinguishes its owner from others, nor the power or leadership of the world is recognized because of money.

The leader in the Islamic government is not evaluated by the money he possesses, still, by the knowledge, morals, and justice he has, and these were the qualities with which they were able to advance and achieve victories one after the other.

Prophet Muhammad, peace be upon him, said:

The example of the believers regarding mutual love, affection, and fellow-feeling, consists of one body; when any limb of it aches, the whole-body aches, because of sleeplessness and fever. [166]

She said: Individuality is directly related to homosexuality, so why do you not like homosexuals? As I know, it is a natural genetic issue, and we must respect it.

I said to her: Would you respect a thief's tendency to steal? It is an inclination too, but in both cases, it is an abnormal proclivity. It's against the human instinct, and aggression against nature; it should be rectified.

God created the human and guided him on the right path. He also gave him free will to choose between the path of righteousness and the way of evil.

And We showed him the two ways.

167

---

[166] (Narrated by Muslim).
[167] (Qur'an: 90-10).

Therefore, we find that homosexuality was rarely seen in the societies which prohibit it. At the same time, the percentage of homosexuals is high in the ambient which permits and encourages such a behavior.

The surrounding ambient and teachings determine the probability of one to be homosexual.

God glory be to Him said about the people of Prophet Lot, peace be upon him:

And Lot, when he said to his people, "Do you commit lewdness no people anywhere have ever committed before you?" "You lust after men rather than women. You are an excessive people." And his people's only answer was to say, "Expel them from your town; they are purist people."[168]

This verse assures that homosexuality is neither inherited nor relates to genetic code composition, for the people of Prophet Lot were the first to innovate such an obscenity; this is in line with an eminent scientific study which ensures that homosexuality has nothing to do with inherited genes.[169]

The identity of a human being is continually changing. For example, it could change according to their watched channels, used technologies, or the liking for a soccer team, as globalization made him or her so complicated. A betrayer is now portrayed as someone with a point of view. A homosexual is described as a normal-behaving person, who thoroughly enjoys legal rights that enabled him or her to participate in public debates.

---

[168] (Qur'an: 7: 80-82).
[169] https://www.nature.com
https://kaheel7.net/?p=15851

Also, it is assumed that we must advocate him or her and strengthen ties too.

Superiority now is for the technology holder. Hence, if a homosexual has the power sources (technology), he or she will surely pass his convictions; this caused spoilage in the relation of the human being, society, and the Creator.

By a direct correlation among individualism and homosexuality, human nature, which human beings belong to, is dispersed, and the family's concepts were dropped.[170]

Then, the westerns started setting up resolutions to get rid of individualism; this is because keeping this perception will undoubtedly cause the loss of the accomplishments modern man has achieved, the same way it will cause the failure of the notion of Family. So, till now, the Westerns have been suffering from a population decrease, which has led to attracting immigrants.

Believing in God and respecting the Divine laws He created for us, as well as the determination to following His instructions and avoiding wrong deeds, is the way to happiness in the worldly life and the hereafter.

And never has the gift of your Lord been restricted:

My teacher ended her conversation by telling me: How do non-religious countries develop and religious countries go down although God loves the latter (religious countries)?

I said: Does the school headmaster reward his son who failed with a success certificate because he is his son?

---

[170] From the article on the concept of absolute individuality and the individual in the nation, written by: Marwan Sabah, Al-Watan newspaper.

Some rules and norms must be followed, and on that basis of these sets, we define who succeeds and who fails.

However, this does not affect the fact that the headmaster loves his son more than anyone else. Indeed, he (the son) is who carries his name (headmaster) and will be his only heir.

I also told her: The universe is just like a school; it has its laws and norms. The disbelievers achieved the materialistic and technological progress because they applied the universal laws and the Divine norms to establish good political systems and robust educational and pedagogical systems with methodological standards. This materialistic progress is only for those who apply the Divine norms and the universal laws; this proves that the worldly success doesn't favor a white or a black; "justice" is one of God's names and injustice is one of the ugliest acts God warned us, humans, from committing, but a disbeliever still won't be given the reward of the Hereafter which is only for God's servants and lovers.

The Messenger of God, peace be upon him, said:

God does not wrong a believer a good deed as he is given blessing for it in this world and will be rewarded for it in the Hereafter. But the disbeliever is given in the world the reward for good deeds he has performed and when he comes to the Hereafter, there is no good deeds for which he can be rewarded.[171]

God Almighty gives them what they deserve in this world, considering what they have of goodness and what they exert of justice.

---

[171] (True hadith).

God, glory be to Him, may support a nation of disbelievers over a Muslim nation as a punishment for its sins, just like what happened in the battle of Uhud.

And God had certainly fulfilled His promise to you when you were killing the enemy by His permission until [the time] when you lost courage and fell to disputing about the order [given by the Prophet] and disobeyed after He had shown you that which you love. Among you are some who desire this world, and among you are some who desire the Hereafter. Then he turned you back from them [defeated] that He might test you. [172]

The Messenger of God said:

God Almighty shared out your character between you as He divided provision between you. God Almighty bestows wealth on those He loves and those He does not love. He only gives faith to those He loves. [173]

She replied: Well, if I believe in Him right now, will He make me wealthy and give me a house?

I said: If your father didn't make you wealthy or give you a house, would you deny his existence?

God is waiting for us:

There is a beautiful story about a group of Chinese atheists who were wondering about God's mercy. One of them asked: How come the Creator gives us instincts, then after that, He asks us not to use them?

---

[172] (Qur'an 3: 152).
[173] (True hadith).

How come He gives us money, and after that, He asks us to lose it by giving it to charities? How come He gives us time and then He asks us to waste it in worship? Isn't that a proof of His cruelty?

I replied to him: That means you believe in Him, but you just question whether He is merciful or not?

He said: No, I don't believe in Him because He is cruel.

I said to him: Your assumption that He is cruel is just itself evidence that He exists. Sorry, but you are contradicting yourself. God is above from being unjust or evil. He is the Merciful Compassionate; His mercy is the absolute mercy. Anyways, the cruelty you assume is not evidence against God's existence, but it's against whether He is merciful or not.

I also told him: When you wish to release your instincts, you tend to be a slave to them (instincts). Yet, God wants you to become a master over them. He wants you to be a reasonable, wise person who manages his instincts. At the same time, you are not supposed to restrict them. It is better to direct them towards upgrading your soul and elevating yourself.

I asked him: Do you have children?

He said: Yes.

I said: If you obligate your children to devote some time to study to have an honorable intellectual rank in the future, while the children's desire is just to play, are you considered an oppressive father?

I was sincerely astonished, seeing the group fly from excitement about my response.

Then, one of them asked me: What can we do now, considering that we have been distanced from God a lot? Will He forgive us if we came back? We have offended Him a lot.

I told him: You just offended yourselves. God, the Almighty does not need us, but we need Him. Anyway, what would you do if your disobedient son stayed away from you? Would you make him feel ashamed? Would you ask him to shoot himself?

He replied: I would keep waiting for him to come back, and pardon him if he came.

I told him: So, God is waiting for you now.

He burst into excitement and chanted loudly: God is waiting for us. He chanted again. Then everyone turned to each other saying: God is waiting for us.

God's messenger, Muhammad, peace be upon him said:

God is more pleased with the repentance of His servant than anyone of you who loses his riding beast in a barren land while it was carrying his food and drink. He despairs of ever finding it, so he comes to a tree and lies down in its shade, having given up all hope of finding his beast that he rides, then whilst he is there like that, suddenly he sees it standing near him, so he takes hold of its reins and because of his great joy he says, 'O God, You, are my slave, and I am Your Lord!' — i.e., he makes a mistake because of his great joy. [174]

I also remember a personal experience I had with a famous Indian actor who has converted to Hinduism so far and his team from work. We discussed the mercy of God and His affection towards His servants.

---

[174] (Narrated by Bukhari).

One of them asked: How come God sometimes depicts Himself as the Forgiving and the Merciful, yet He becomes the Severely Punishing?

I replied: God is forgiving and merciful with those whose sins are committed without persistence because of their weak human character. He is also forgiving for the sins that do not intend to defy the Creator (Allah). Indeed, the Almighty destroys the one who defies Him and denies His existence; He also destroys the one who draws Him in the form of an idol or an animal. I was then inappropriately interrupted by the actor.

He said: These are minor issues that God doesn't care about.

I told him: If you insult an animal, no one can blame you, but if you insult your parents, you'll be reprimanded severely.

Don't look how small the sin is but look to the greatness of whom you disobeyed.

Then follow me so that God will love you:

I had one of the most challenging experiences with two Christian South African siblings, and the brother's wife, who was a Buddhist Thai. The woman and her brother were white South Africans, and they were remarkably tall and massive, while the brother's wife was very short and tiny. I was confused at first by the differences in the heights, the body frames, and the visitors' beliefs.

I was supposed to start my conversation with them by a short presentation about Islam.

Instead, I was surprised with the fluency of non-stop talking by the South African woman; she barely gave me a chance to utter one word. She kept saying: "God is love. God loves you. God died for you."

I then held myself up and said to her: Alright. I'm ready to embrace Christianity if you answered my questions.

The visitor cheered up, and she went to bring her sister-in-law to let her listen to our conversation; she was in another corner of the Mosque, taking pictures. I understood that the South African lady had been trying to convince her Buddhist sister-in-law to convert to Christianity since a long time, and she thought that if I accept converting to Christianity, it would be a motivation for her sister-in-law to do the same.

In the presence of her sister in-law, the visitor said to me: Well, I'm ready, tell me your questions.

I said to her: You said that God loves me and that He died to forgive my sins.

She said: Yes, that's right.

I asked:

- Would the love I have for my son make me kill myself to forgive his sins?

- With all His love for me, is God unable to forgive me if I just repent and turned back to Him?

- Can the love God has for me make Him punish me for a sin committed by someone else (Adam's sin), and then grant me salvation just if I believed in the death of another person on a cross (Jesus), not for my good deeds?

- Was God with all His love to Jesus unable to protect him from killing and crucifixion?

- How come God may die when He is Ever-living and does not die in your creed? Isn't this a contradiction?

- According to what you believe, when God died for three days, who was managing the universe in His claimed absence? Who gave the provisions, lives and caused death?

- God is Omnipotent, does it suit His majesty to be fixed to a wooden beam, and to be tortured to death as you claim, especially that the crucified person is considered cursed in your book?
- In which chapter in your book did Jesus say that he is God?
- When Jesus cried and prayed to God for help when they wanted to crucify him, did he pray to himself?

Exalted is God, God the Almighty is High above what they say.

And [for] their saying, "Indeed, we have killed the Messiah, Jesus the son of Mary, the messenger of God." And they did not kill him, nor did they crucify him; but [another] was made to resemble him to them. And indeed, those who differ over it are in doubt about it. They have no knowledge of it except the following of assumption. And they did not kill him, for certain. Rather, God raised him to Himself. And ever is Allah (God) Exalted in Might and Wise. [175]

God is Perfect; He does not need to die for us. He gives life and death, so He did not die, nor was He resurrected. He saved His Prophet Jesus and protected him as He helps and protects His chosen believers.

Then We will save Our messengers and those who have believed. Thus, it is an obligation upon Us that We save the believers. [176]

As I was asking my questions, I noticed her confusion, fret, and peeping gazes to her sister-in-law, and I felt that she got worried from the influence of my talk on her sister-in-law. So, she told me that she is in a hurry, and without replying to any of my questions she said to me: I liked your dress so much, then she hugged me tightly to the point that I was frightened.

---

[175] (Qur'an 4: 157-158).
[176] (Qur'an 10: 103).

She then grabbed her sister in law's hand and left the Mosque right away!

I also remember facing a similar situation with a religious Christian, a French man.

He said to me: God loves you, He died for you.

I asked him: Who told you that? God Himself or Jesus?

He replied: Saint Paul did. He was a smart and educated man. His educational level was the same level as a person who holds three doctorates in our time.

I said: What is the relation between Paul's educational level and the Divine Revelation?

He told me: He saw a vision telling him that the Almighty God died for us.

I told him: The Divine Revelation comes from God, including the revelation descending with the Divine Messages. On the other hand, it's the devilish revelation that comes in the form of dreams to humans. He laughed at my response.

I proceeded: Human knowledge is a human production that is subjected to correctness and error. It includes scientific achievement or inspiring literature, and it has nothing to do with Divine Revelation. I do not have much information on this point, but I am shocked from a person who leaves the right message of the Messiah which is a Divine Revelation and goes for a vision of a person who had never met the Messiah during his life such as Paul, and that is just because he is educated! This is insensible and is in all means opposing to both instinct and rationale. Paul was one of the Messiah's worst enemies who tried to destroy his religion, kill him, and torment his followers.

I continued: For me, as a person who loves the Messiah, I must believe in his message.

In your book, the Messiah said: God is only One God. [177]

Saint Paul said: God is three in one. [178]

In your book, the Messiah said: I ascend onto my Father, and your Father, and to my God, and your God.[179]

Paul said: The Messiah is the only begotten son of God.[180]

In your book, the Messiah said: I do nothing of myself.[181]

Paul said: Jesus is omnipotent.[182]

In your book, the Messiah said: My Father is greater than I.[183]

Paul said: God, in all things may be glorified through Jesus Christ.[184]

So please tell me, whom shall I believe now the Messiah or Paul?

The French visitor said: You know all that and you claimed that you don't have any information!! Would you allow me to take some photos because I have a necessary appointment to go to?

I told him: Please do!

What can God gain by your punishment, if you are grateful and you believe?

I have witnessed the most wonderful story in my life, which is about an American and a Japanese. I was so exhausted after a busy day.

---

[177] (Mark 12:29).

[178] (Corinthians 12:3-6).

[179] (John 17:20).

[180] (Galatians 4: 4,5).

[181] (John 30:5).

[182] (John 5:15).

[183] (John 28:14).

[184] (Hebrews 3:1).

I had been informed that an American and a Japanese visitor were waiting for me. I doubted they were friends, but then I was surprised that they didn't know each other. They met each other in the center's waiting room; I invited them inside. Despite my exhaustion, I approved the visit.

The American kept asking questions always, a question after another. The Japanese spoke English fluently, but he was just listening carefully and didn't interrupt us. However, the American didn't give up asking questions abnormally, which made me doubt that he wanted to attack Islam and didn't ask to benefit from the information.

He requested that he wanted to learn and memorize chapter number (1) of the Qur'an (the opening), and he memorized it. Then, he asked to learn chapter number (112) (sincerity), and learn how to practice praying during his visit. That took him around three hours. Although I was exhausted, God provided me with patience. I understood that the American was an atheist and didn't have any religion from the questions he asked. Indeed, Christians don't attack God.

One of the questions he asked was: Why doesn't God admit the pretension that Jesus is His son? Does He feel jealous of Jesus?

I replied: If you send me a package with the postman, and I spread among the public that the postman was your son, would you accept that?

He said: No.

I said: Is it because you feel jealous of him?

He said: No, simply because he is not my son.

I said: So, you accept something for your Creator what you don't accept to yourself.

He asked: Why does God punish with the Hellfire?

I told him: What do you expect from God to do with those who tortured children with chemical weapons, as an example, to let them go to Paradise directly?

I told him: Also, someone who disowned his mother and father, humiliated them, and kicked them out of the house to the street, as another example. How do you feel towards this man?

He said: I feel great wrath.

I said: If I told you I would let him in my house, feed him, praise him for this (wrong) deed, would you value my act? Would you accept it?

He said: No.

I said: What do you expect from God to do with the one who denies the existence of his Creator and disbelieves in Him?

Whoever is being punished in the Hellfire seems to be put in the right position.

It is a just judgment that Hellfire is their final abiding place. It will be like placing a thing in its rightful element. They do not deserve the beauty and peacefulness of Paradise as they disdained peace while on earth.

..And even if they were sent back, they would revert to what they were forbidden. They are liars. [185]

This means that their sin is not limited in time, but it is an eternal merit.

On the Day when God will resurrect them altogether—they will swear to Him, as they swear to you, thinking that they are upon something. Indeed, they themselves are the liars. [186]

---

[185] (Qur'an 6: 28).

[186] (Qur'an 58 :18).

So, they also face God with false swears on the Day of Judgement.

But the ones who deny Our verses and are arrogant toward them – those are the companions of the Fire; they will abide therein eternally.[187]

Evil comes from envious and jealous people. It is fair that the Hellfire will be their reward, which copes with their nature (evil).

The attribute of justice that God has requires that He should be vengeful alongside His mercy. In Christianity, God is only love, and in Judaism He is rage. In Islam, He is Just and Merciful, and He has all ideal names, which are qualities of Beauty and Grace.

I said furthermore: Practically, in life, we use fire to isolate impurities from a purified substance like silver and gold. God the Almighty, the Ideal, uses the Hellfire to purify His servants from sins and evils, and finally, those who have one atom of belief are released from it (the Hellfire) by Mercy of God.

He said: I want a tangible argument proving God's existence.

I told him: You are asking for the weakest argument. We see the rainbow and the mirage, and we believe they exist, but they don't have any tangible existence! Moreover, we believe in the presence of the law of gravity without seeing it because science has proven it.

The sights do not apprehend Him, yet He apprehends the sights, and He is the All-attentive, the All-aware.[188]

Merely, thinking that you can grasp God's total perception is a symptom of ignorance about Him. The car may guide you to the sea, but it doesn't let you go into it.

---

[187] (Qur'an 7:36).
[188] (Qur'an 6: 103).

For example, if I asked you how much the seawater is by liter and you answered with any number, you would be considered ignorant. If you responded by saying: "I don't know" you would be all-knowing. The only path to know God is His signs in the world and His verses in His book, The Qur'an[189].

He asked: Why do you not think that other gods give provisions and cure diseases?

I replied: Did anyone other than God claim to be the sustainer or the healer so that we would substantiate the validity or invalidity of their allegations?

You can even notice that all people direct to only One Truth and plead to only One God when facing trouble. Science proved that the entire universe consists of one matter, and proved the same building system of the universe by studying the universal aspects and phenomena and the similarity and symmetry in the universe.

For example, in families, when the father and mother argue over a life decision, they may lose their children and destroy their future. So, can you imagine what would happen if two or more gods are managing the universe?!

If there were in the heavens and earth gods besides God (Allah), they both would have been ruined. So exalted is God, Lord of the Throne, above what they describe. [190]

---

[189] From the sayings of Dr. Muhammad Rateb Nabulsi

[190] (Qur'an 21: 22).

He asked: Can that Creator give life to a dead body here before my eyes?

I replied: Surprisingly, you atheists repeat the same questions as if you all previously agreed on them, though I believe you are sure they are irrational and illogical.

I added: If God gives life to dead before your eyes, you won't be convinced, just like it happened in Moses' peace be upon his story, and like the other miracles of the other prophets they offered to their people. Their people were just accusing them that they were magicians!

Likewise, no messenger came to those before them, but they said, "a sorcerer or a madman." Did they recommend it to one another? In fact, they are rebellious people. [191]

And even if We were to send down angels unto them, and if the dead were to speak unto them and [even if] We were to assemble before them, face to face, all the things [that can prove the truth], they would still not believe unless God so willed But, [of this] most of them are entirely unaware. [192]

The American man added: How come the Creator may punish His servants with endless torture for a few sins they committed in a short life span?

I told him: Most crimes lead to a life-in-prison verdict. So, is there anyone who argues that the life- in-prison verdict is unfair because the criminal committed his/her crime within few minutes? Is a ten-year sentence unjust because the criminal looted money for just one year? Hence, legal penalties aren't related to the period of crime commitment; Instead, they're related to the magnitude and cruelty of the crime.

---

[191] (Qur'an 51: 52-53).
[192] (Qur'an 6: 111).

Then he asked: Why did God repeat the warning about hell? Doesn't that indicate His mercilessness and hatred towards us?

I told him: I exhaust my children by frequently alerting them that they must take care in their round trips whenever they travel or go to work. So, by doing that, do you consider me a harsh mother?! This is making things look upside down. You are turning mercy into harshness. God's alertness and warning for His worshipers is out of His mercy towards them. He guided them towards the path of salvation and promised to exchange their evil deeds into good deeds when they seek forgiveness.

...he who believed and did the right, will have his evil deeds expunged by God and admitted to gardens with rivers flowing by, and abide there perpetually. This will be the great achievement of success. [193]

Indeed, God is the Merciful:

The American man continued saying: Then, why did God order Prophet Abraham to slaughter his son, isn't that cruelty?

I replied: Did God order you to do this? If we suppose that there is a person who claimed himself to be the smartest person in the whole world, he should be subjected to the hardest tests to prove his claim correct. Abraham, peace be upon him, was a Prophet and Messenger who received the revelation from God, and he declared that his love to God was above his love to any other thing, so God tested him to prove the love that Prophet Abraham claimed to have.

---

[193] (Qur'an 64:9).

Keep in mind that it was reported at the time of Prophet Abraham that the habit of offering people their sons as a sacrifice to God was common. So, God aimed to end that old habit and to replace it with offering animals as a sacrifice instead of sons.

He said: Why does God keep repeating in the Qur'an that He loves the pious believers but doesn't like the disbelievers, aren't all of them His servants?

I told him: God guided all His servants to the path of salvation, and He emphasized that He disapproves the disbelief from His servants. God doesn't like the erratic behavior itself that humans may choose to adopt by his/her disbelief and corruption on earth.

If you disbelieve – indeed, God is Free from need of you. And He does not approve for His servant's disbelief. And if you are grateful, He approves it for you; and no bearer of burdens will bear the burden of another. Then to your Lord is your return, and He will inform you about what you used to do. Indeed, He is Knowing of that within the breasts. [194]

I added: What do you say about a father who repeatedly tells his sons: 'I am proud of all of you, no matter if you commit theft, murder, or corruption, you are just like any other pious and devoted son to me'? Simply, the most reasonable opinion about the father is that he is just like a devil who urges his sons to do evil deeds!

---

[194] (Qur'an 39: 7).

He said: But why does God keep reminding us in the Qur'an about the blessings He granted us with, when those blessings are merely nothing compared to what He owns. What is unique in this case?

I replied: God reminds us of the blessings He bestows on us to protect us from ourselves; we may show gratitude and thank someone else other than Him. If we don't worship Him, we would worship someone else. When I gain fortune or feel the euphoria of success and feel proud of my breakthroughs, I thank my own self unintentionally. It is as if I attribute my achievements to my own abilities which are already given to me by God. At that very moment, I would open the Qur'an to read the verse which says: **And my success is not but through God**[195], so that it opens my eyes and I thank God.

I added: If someone gave you a gift, would you feel happy for the gift itself or for its indication of that person's love to you?

The greatness of the gift is derived from its source/giver. If I gave you 100 dinar and the king gave you one dinar, you would be happier with the one dinar that the king gave to you more than the 100 dinars I gave you, and you would spread the news over social media.

The Japanese man listened without interfering throughout the three hours.

The American man then asked again: Isn't it considered harshness when God (Allah) accounts us for things He initially wrote for us?

I said: I will give you an example. Let's say that you want to buy something from the store, and decide to send your first son specifically to buy that thing.

---

[195] (Qur'an 11: 88).

It is because you previously know that your first son is wise. He will straight away go and purchase what you exactly want while you know that your other son will get busy playing with his friends and the money may be lost; this is an assumption which you built your judgments on.

I continued: Predestination does not contradict with freedom of choice as God predestines us based on His complete knowledge of what our preferences and intentions will be.

Our deeds are foreknown to God in His Record, but they are not preordained for us against our will. They are only preordained in His Prescience. In the same way, we may foresee in light of knowing our children's characters', they will make a wrong choice before they make it. We did not impose their choice upon them against their will, even though we may have expected that choice. God preordains the intentions and hearts of Man; if these are evil, Man will come to evil; if good, good will be his fate.

I also told him: Man, in his freedom, may act contrary to what satisfies God, but he cannot do anything in contradiction to His Will. God granted us the freedom to transgress against His wishes (we disobey Him) but He gave no one the freedom to transcend His Will.

He said: So why does God permit transgression of His orders?

I said to him: Sometimes my child, for example, insists on touching the fire and I say don't touch it, but at a certain point, when I find him stubborn, I let him touch it to learn from his experience. I know from my son's personality that he won't learn unless he tries. God is the All-Knowing.

His knowledge is perfect, while humans' knowledge maybe right or wrong.

Therefore, God knows the nature of His creation, and that they won't learn unless they try.

So, we find that some people face simple afflictions from God and some face difficult ones. This could be because that person won't return to God without trials and affliction. This is all based on the knowledge of God.

He said: Why does God compel us to believe?

I replied: Has God forced you to believe in Him? Here you are standing before me claiming that you don't believe in Him. Our experience further affirms the freedom that it is impossible under any pressure to compel the heart to accept anything it does not want to. We can force anyone through threats and force them to stay with us, but no pressure whatsoever can make them love us. God has safeguarded our hearts from all forms of compulsion and duress. Therefore, God judges according to the heart and rewards according to intention, which is visible to no-one but Him.

There was a surprise at the end of the visit; the American man asked me to take pictures inside the mosque. Meanwhile, the Japanese man came to me and said: I like this religion, what a great religion it is! I want to embrace this religion.

It was a fantastic surprise because he never had any reaction towards the previous conversation. He was just listening during the whole visit! The Japanese testified in front of the American there is no god but God, and Muhammad is the Messenger of God. The American congratulated him, and the Japanese asked me more details about practicing this religion. I gave him the Islamic Centre's phone number in Tokyo, and he promised me that he will continue in this path.

God will bring forth a people He will love and who will love Him:

Those [angels] who carry the Throne and those around it exalt [Allah] with praise of their Lord and believe in Him and ask forgiveness for those who have believed, [saying], "Our Lord, You have encompassed all things in mercy and knowledge, so forgive those who have repented and followed Your way and protect them from the punishment of Hellfire. [196]

God's love and mercy for His servants, manifests in creating them, honoring them, and guiding them to the right path.

And We have certainly established you upon the earth and made for you therein ways of livelihood. Little are you grateful. And We have certainly created you, [O Mankind], and given you [human] form. Then We said to the angels, "Prostrate to Adam"; so, they prostrated, except for Iblees (Lucifer). He was not of those who prostrated. [197]

One of the most delicate gestures in the Qur'an is God mentioning His love to His servants before mentioning the servants' love to Him. That's out of His great mercy on them.

…God will bring forth [in place of them] a people He will love and who will love Him. [198]

---

[196] (Qur'an 40: 7).

[197] (Qur'an 7: 10 - 11).

[198] (Qur'an 5: 54).

Also, one of the subtle gestures in the noble Qur'an is that God's mercy manifests even in the humans' afflictions of tests and trials.

Should I take other gods apart from Him, who would neither be able to intercede for me nor save me if the Most Gracious brings me harm? [199]

If "the Most Gracious" desires harm for a person, then this necessarily leads to the mercy and kindness of God. So, in this case, what seemed to be harmful, in fact, turns out to be merciful and good for the believer because "the Most Gracious" does not emanate from Him except mercy and kindness.

...but perhaps you hate a thing and it is good for you; and perhaps you love a thing and it is bad for you. And God Knows, while you know not. [200]

By the mercy of God, He distributed the livelihoods among human beings and made them the needs that one of them decides for the other to achieve cooperation among them in a way that benefits everyone. If each of them dispensed with one another, their interests would be disrupted.

By His mercy, He made the rich and poor among them, the honored and servile, along with the helpless and capable. Also, He kept the gate of Divine giving and open to compete in it and forever be attached to it.

Do they distribute the mercy of your Lord? It is We who have apportioned among them their livelihood in the life of this world and have raised some of them above others in degrees [of rank] that

---

[199] (Qur'an 36: 23).
[200] (Qur'an 2: 216).

they may make use of one another for service. But the mercy of your Lord is better than whatever they accumulate. [201]

God's mercy also manifests in His Sharia laws (provisions) and commandments, which are mere goodness and compassion to the creations regarding the providence of guidance and their religion's preservation. Also, regarding the protection of themselves, their bodies, their minds and thoughts, their honors and kinship, their offspring, and the conservation of their money and properties. All laws and rules related to those previously mentioned five essentials were merely sent as a mercy to people to safeguard and protect them from corruption and aggression, along with breaking the ice between people. Also, to keep them away from hardships and difficulties, and to preserve everyone's rights to be able to live in a healthy secure and happy society/environment, as the right of having a healthy society is one of the life rights pillars.

And when he goes away, he strives throughout the land to cause corruption therein and destroy crops and animals. And God does not like corruption. [202]

Conclusion:

The love of God for His servants is summarized in these beautiful words:
Ibn Al-Qayyim said[203]: "God inspired David peace be upon him saying: 'O David, if only the people who go astray from me know how much I wait for them to come back towards me, how kind I am to them, and how I long to them to give up their sins.

---

[201] (Qur'an 43: 32).

[202] (Qur'an 2: 205).

[203] Mentioning it only out of taking parable and moral from it.

If they just know about that all, they would die out of their love to me. O David, if this is the case of My Will for those who go away from me, what about for those who come towards me! '". [204]

---

[204] Rawda Al Muhibben (p. 438).

Muhammad: A Mercy to the Worlds

Indeed, you are of a great moral character:

I have always been contemplating the praise of Almighty God for the morals of his Messenger Muhammad (peace upon him). I was hoping that I could understand the magnificence of these morals; I wanted to understand the brilliance in this great Prophet's personality. Eventually, when my mother died, I felt extreme sorrow. It would've almost destroyed my life if it wasn't for God's mercy on me. Despite that I was already married, and did not need her care, missing her still made me lose the desire to talk to people. I felt that the whole world was tightening around me; it felt hard to lose the mother's love. I then remembered the Prophet Muhammad (peace be upon him), and how he lived as an orphan, moving from house to house, and how he lived missing his parents' love. Then I said to myself that these conditions in which the Prophet Muhammad lived have no way brought out a complex human being. Then I realized that he was different; when a person with this great personality comes out from these conditions, he is truly with unique ethics. I then remembered the verse: **And you are of great moral character**[205], and I calmed down.

---

[205] (Qur'an 68:4).

We do not differentiate between one of His messengers:

The British orientalist and archaeologist "Stanley Lee Paul" said: "Muhammed was compassionate and merciful. He visited the patient and the poor, answered the requests of the slaves, and sew up his clothes by himself. So, there is no doubt that he was a holy prophet. He was an orphan and indigent until he became a great leader."[206]

During my discussion with a group of different nationalities, cultures, and religions, I was talking about monotheism, the attributes of Divine Beauty and Majesty, and the importance of worshipping the Creator without a mediator. Someone from the group then interrupted me with a question.

He asked: Who is greatest, Christ or Muhammad?

I answered: Are you asking for a comparison between one god and another? Or for a comparison between a messenger and another? If you want to compare two gods, then there is no god but One God (the Creator), both Christ and Muhammad are messengers. However, if you're going to compare between one messenger and another, then we do not differentiate between one of God's messengers.

The Messenger has believed in what was revealed to him from his Lord and [so have] the believers. All of them have believed in God and His angels and His books and His messengers, [saying], "We make no distinction between any of His messengers." And they say, "We hear and we obey. [We seek] Your forgiveness, our Lord, and to you is the [final] destination. [207]

---

[206] Book – *Speeches & Table- talk of the Prophet Muhammad.*
[207] (Qur'an 2: 285).

The same group member asked: If you love Christ, why don't you celebrate his birth?

I asked him: Do you mean to celebrate the birth of Christ who is "the son of God" or "the Messenger of God"?

If you mean Christ's birth who is "son of God", your question is rejected because God neither begets nor is born, nor there's any equivalence to Him. Nevertheless, if you mean Christ who is "the messenger of God", we do not reject remembering or praising him on his birthday; we praise him all the time. Though it was proven he was not born in winter, but the controversy about determining his birthday does not affect the belief in anything.

He asked: Why don't you let your daughters marry Jews and Christians?

I answered: The Muslim husband respects the source of religion, the holy book, and believes in the messengers of his Christian or Jewish wife; that's how his faith is achieved. He allows her to practice her religion freely. On the other hand, the opposite is not valid. Whenever a Christian or Jew believes in the Prophet Muhammed, we would let our daughters marry them.

Islam completes faith. For example, if I want to convert to Christianity, I have to lose my faith in Muhammad and the Qur'an. I also have to lose my direct relationship with the Lord of the worlds, and I have to believe in the Trinity and resort to pastors and priests. If I want to convert to Judaism, I have to lose my faith in Christ and the correct Gospel.

I remember meeting with a large group from the state of Malta. I did a simple presentation about Islam, and then they all loudly said with one voice: So Muhammad is not your God!

I answered: No, Muhammad is a messenger of God. Unfortunately, this misconception is promoted by non-Muslims to justify the worship of Christ, Buddha and others.

Say, "I am only a man like you, to whom has been revealed that your god is one God. So whoever would hope for the meeting with his Lord – let him do righteous work and not associate in the worship of his Lord anyone." [208]

Whose description they find written in the Torah and the Gospel:

The American orientalist Senx said in his book "The Religion of the Arabs":

"Muhammad came five hundred and seventy years after Christ. His mission was to improve human minds by feeding it with the origins of morality, the belief in One God, and the belief of life after this life."

One day I had the most beautiful situation I experienced in my life; it was a difficult day because of the thousand visitors we had. On this day, a Latino man showed up among the crowded groups of visitors. He asked me in Spanish: Who is the Paraclete?

He said: I have been travelling the world with my wife and daughter searching for the truth. Moreover, I want to know who is the character that Christ talked about in the Bible.

"I still have many things to say to you, but you cannot bear them now. When the Spirit of truth (Paraclete) comes, he will guide you into all the truth, for he will not speak on his own authority, but whatever he hears he will speak, and he will declare to you the

---

[208] (Qur'an 18:110).

things that are to come. He will glorify me, for he will take what is mine and declare it to you."[209]

I answered him: The Paraclete is Muhammad (peace be upon him).

He asked: How is this?

I answered: Muslims don't believe that the Old Testament and the New Testaments are the words of God, but they believe that both have a valid source, which is the Torah and the Gospel (God's revelations to the prophets: Moses and Jesus Christ). Therefore, some parts of the Old Testament and the New Testament are from God, and other parts are not. Muslims believe that if this prophecy is true, then it is talking about the Prophet Muhammad. It talks about a prophet who comes after Christ goes, and he stays with his teachings forever.

Those who follow the Messenger, the unlettered prophet, whom they find written [i.e., described] in what they have of the Torah and the Gospel, who enjoins upon them what is right and prohibits them from what is wrong and makes lawful for them what is good and forbids them from what is evil and relieves them of their burden and the shackles which were upon them. So, they who have believed in him, honored him, supported him, and followed the light which was sent down with him – it is those who will be the successful.[210]

He said: But this character should not be human but rather a spirit. In Christianity, it refers to the third person in the Trinity, which is considered a god.

---

[209] (Gospel of John 15/26 - 16/12-14).
[210] (Qur'an 7: 157).

I told him: Go back to your book and check how many times the prophets were mentioned as "spirit". In the New Testament, the term "spirit" can be referred to a person, and according to history, many ancient Christians understood that the "Paraclete" was a man, not a spirit. Many men before the Prophet Muhammad claimed that they were the expected "paraclete". The Negus king of Abyssinia was Christian, and he was waiting for the coming of "paraclete".[211]

I added: The prophecy says that the Paraclete speaks what he hears. This is a description of a prophet not of God. The prophet speaks what he hears from God, and this is evidence that this prophecy does not refer to the third entity in the Trinity (as Christians believe), but rather it refers to a prophet sent by God.

He said: But the prophecy says that the Paraclete talks about upcoming events.

I told him: Yes, and this is what the Prophet Muhammad (peace be upon him) did. For example, the Roman's victory, after their defeat by the Persians, was mentioned in the Holy Book Qur'an.

I continued: This prophecy can't refer to the Holy Spirit because it says that the Paraclete will appear after Christ is gone. The Holy Spirit already exists, and according to your belief, it appeared to Mary before her pregnancy with Christ.[212]

The term "Paraclete" caused considerable controversy. The word "Paraklytos" in the Greek Bible was originally "Periklytos", and it was changed during the translation from Syriac to the Greek language.

---

[211] "Dear friends, do not believe every spirit, but test the spirits to see whether they are from God, because many false prophets have gone out into the world". (1John 4:1).

[212] (Luke 1:26-27). ".... The angel came to her and said, "Peace be with you! The Lord is with you and has greatly blessed you!"

"Paraclete" has two meanings in Greek-language.

1- Comforter, advocate and helper: Paraklytos (παρακλητος) as believed by Christians. This is based on pronunciation, which includes the "a" vowel sound.

2- Muhammad or Ahmed (the praised one): Periklytos (Περικλητος), as believed by Muslims. This pronunciation is without using the "a" vowel sound.

In addition to the fact that the second meaning has more evidence to support it, it has been proven that the Syriac language did not contain vowels until the fifth century. It consisted of consonants only, and vowels were introduced after the fifth century. However, both meanings apply to the Prophet Muhammad.[213]

He said: The prophecy says that he will convict the whole world[214], so how did Muhammad condemn the world?

I replied: Muhammad convicted the Jews because they didn't believe in Jesus as a Prophet sent from God. Also, he condemned the Christians because they adopted the Trinity's concept and considered Jesus as God, which is a sin as well because Jesus never claimed to be God or a begotten son of God. When Jesus referred to himself in the Bible as the Son of God, he made it clear that he is not the begotten son, but we are all sons of God metaphorically, in the sense that we are God's servants.

Then the visitor said: the Paraclete guides people to the truth and glorifies Jesus.

---

[213] *Eye on the Truth.* Faten Sabri.

[214] When he comes, he will prove the world to be in the wrong about sin and righteousness and judgment. (John 16:8).

I said to him: Prophet Muhammad reminded the world the pure faith (belief in one God and unify him in worship).

I also told him: No one glorified Jesus on earth as much as Prophet Muhammad (peace upon him) did:

- Prophet Muhammad said: "I am most worthy of Jesus, son of Mary among humankind in the world, and the next life. They said: o Messenger of God, how that? He replied: Prophets are brothers in faith, having different mothers, their religion is one, and there is no prophet between us (between Jesus and me)."

- The name of Jesus Christ is mentioned more than the name of Prophet Muhammad in the Qur'an (25 times vs 4).

- The mother of Jesus Christ, Mary, has been elevated over all women according to Qur'an.

- The Virgin Mary is the only woman mentioned by name in the Qur'an.

- The Qur'an has a full chapter named after the Virgin Mary. [215]

The visitor, his wife and daughter showed me happiness, and they said: It's enough for us to get this information from our long trip. We have found the truth; we thank God that He guided us to it after long time of hard work. We had a deep belief that there is no god, but One God (the Creator), and Christ is the Messenger of God. Now we will get out from here with a testimony that Muhammad is the Messenger of God.

---

[215] *Eye on the Truth*. Faten Sabri.

And [mention] when Jesus, the son of Mary, said, "O Children of Israel, indeed I am the messenger of God to you confirming what came before me of the Torah and bringing good tidings of a messenger to come after me, whose name is Aḥmad." But when he came to them with clear evidences, they said, "This is obvious magic." [216]

Those to whom We gave the Scripture know him as they know their own sons:

I had a discussion with a group of Canadian Jews, and after I talked about monotheism, someone asked me: Oh Muslims, why do you have a problem with us?

I answered him: A Muslim has no problem with anyone. Muslims believe in Jesus, Moses, and other prophets, and they worship God alone without an intermediary.

He said: I do not see any problem in Muhammed being a messenger.

I asked him: Is believing in him one of the pillars of your faith?

He answered: No

I said: Believing in Moses is one of the pillars of the Muslim faith.

He said: Muhammad was not mentioned in our books.

I told him: Then who does the paragraph talk about in the Old Testament?

Then the book will be given to the one who is unlettered, saying, 'Please read this'. And he will say, 'I cannot read.' [217]

---

[216] (Qur'an 61:6).
[217] (Isaiah 29:12).

Does this prophecy apply to anyone other than Muhammad, the unlettered Prophet?

Up until the birth of Jesus Christ (peace upon him), the Israelites were awaiting a prophet and the Christ to come.

Now this was John's testimony when the Jewish leaders[a] in Jerusalem sent priests and Levites to ask him who he was. He did not fail to confess, but confessed freely, "I am not the Messiah." They asked him, "Then who are you? Are you Elijah?" He said, "I am not." "Are you the Prophet?" He answered, "No."[218]

He said: I do not know; we are still waiting for Christ and the expected prophet.

He added: Muhammad copied his book from the Torah.

I asked him: Did the Jews claim this at the time of the revelation?

He answered: No.

I told him: If the Qur'an was copied from the books of Jews, they would be the fastest people in attributing it to themselves.

I also told him: Isn't our legislation such as prayer, pilgrimage and giving Alms different from yours? Then look at the testimony of non-Muslims which states that the Qur'an is distinguished from other books, it is without human intervention and contains scientific miracles. Therefore, when the one who has a creed acknowledges the validity of the creed that contradicts it, it is the greatest proof of its validity.

In fact, the existence of the similarities prove that it is only One Message and it should be One.

---

[218] (John 1: 19-21).

What the Prophet Muhammad brought is not evidence of his deception. God challenged the Arabs and non-Arabs to produce a literary work of a similar book as the Qur'an, but they were unable to do so despite their well-known eloquence and literary powers; the challenge remains.

He said: There is no scientific miracle in the Qur'an, but Muhammad copied this information from earlier civilizations.

I asked him: Was all the scientific information found in ancient civilizations right?

He said: No. Some are true, but there are many myths.

I asked him: How could that unlettered prophet, who grew up in a desolate desert, copy only these true information and leave the myths?

He asked: What do you think of Adam's first wife, whom he married before Eve?

Frankly, I could not help but laugh at this strange information, which I have never heard about in my life.

I said: This character has never been mentioned in Islam. But what does believing in the existence of this character add to your faith?

He said: Nothing.

I told him: Then think carefully about what else would be added to your faith, and would benefit you, which is the belief in the One and Only true God and worshiping Him alone, and the faith in all His prophets, including Jesus and Muhammad.

He asked: Why did Muhammad neglect Al-Aqsa Mosque (the Holy Mosque in Jerusalem), which was the Qiblah (the direction in which a Muslim turns to pray)?

I asked him: Why did the Samaritan Jews neglect the Qiblah (direction) of Al-Aqsa mosque in Jerusalem, and turn their Qiblah (the direction in which a Jew turns to pray) towards AL-TUR in Palestine?

I also told him: The fact that the Jews changed the direction of their prayers was not in terms of revelation and bless from God. There is no command in the Torah about turning the direction of the prayers towards the rock, so it is based on their choice. As for Christians, God did not command them in the Bible, or in others, to turn their direction of the prayers to the East at all.[219]

I continued: In fact, the Qur'an told us that the Holy Mosque in Mecca was the first mosque of worship appointed for humanity, and its structure was raised by the Prophet Ibrahim along with his son Ismail. It is well known that the temple in Jerusalem was built long after the Prophet Ibrahim, while the Holy Mosque was in Mecca before Ibrahim.

Indeed, the first House [of worship] established for mankind was that at Bakkah [i.e., Makkah] – blessed and a guidance for the worlds. [220]

The Kaaba[221] in the middle of the Holy Mosque has always been well known throughout history. People visit it every year, even from the farthest parts of the Arabian Peninsula, and its sanctity is respected from the entire Arabian Peninsula.

---

[219] http://www.aqsaonline.org/news.aspx?id=5664#_ftn6

[220] (Qur'an 3: 96).

[221] Kaaba is a cube shaped building covered with black cloth. It is an empty place with door but has no windows. A Muslim can pray inside in any direction, as it is in the middle of the universe.

It was mentioned in the Old Testament's prophecies: **Passing through the Bekaa Valley and making it a fountain.**[222]

The Arabs used to glorify the Holy Mosque at the age of ignorance. Upon the mission of the Prophet Muhammad, God made the direction of the prayers towards the farthest mosque in Jerusalem. Then God commanded him to change the direction from the farthest mosque in Jerusalem to the Holy Mosque in Mecca. The aim of the direction transformation was to extract people with good hearts who are loyal to God, and make their hearts get attached only to Him. It lasted until the Muslims submitted and turned their direction in prayer to Makkah at which the Messenger directed them.

Changing the direction of prayer was also a turning point and a sign of shifting the religious leadership to the Arabs after being taken away from the Children of Israel. This is because they have broken their covenants with the Lord of the worlds.

He said: I have to go now. In our faith, we do not shake hands with women because they are below men's level, but I will only shake your hand, as appreciation for your knowledge.

I told him: As for us, we do not shake hands with men, because we are as honourable as the Queens. Therefore, I will not shake hands with you. The Italian writer Dr. Laura Vicha Valeri says:

"In a wasteland, a valley without cultivation, and isolated from a civilized humanity, a fresh, flowy stream of water burst among the savages, heartless people who do not submit to Sultan and do not adhere to restriction.

---

[222] (Psalms 84).

That fountain is the religion of Islam that flowed abundantly. It took its way into the ground in a swarm, and it became a small river. It eventually turned into a great river; thousands of streams and rivers branched off from it quickly penetrating the country long and wide. Soon, people tasted this strange drink and recovered from their social diseases. The western men are about to be convinced that Muhammad's sincerity in his vocation was unquestionable. As a messenger calling to God, Muhammad was a merciful and soft-hearted man even with his enemies. Thus, two virtues, both of which are the greatest inconceivable by the human mind, were gathered in him, which are mercy and justice. We don't have to give examples of that, as it is easy to find many of them in the books about his life history."[223]

Even if I brought you proof manifest:

In my conversation with an atheist, he mocked the miracle of Israa and Mi 'raj (the night journey from the Holy Mosque in Mecca to the farthest mosque in Jerusalem then to Heaven). He wondered how the Messenger reached Jerusalem, ascended to heaven, and returned on the same night.

I told him: Today, what happened to me was even more extraordinary. While giving a lecture, I was present in more than twenty countries at the same time.

He laughed and said: You mean social media, of course.

I told him: Human technology delivered my voice and image to all parts of the world at the same moment. Couldn't the Creator of humanity be able to ascend His Prophet (the body and spirit) to the heavens 1400 years ago?

---

[223] *Beauties of Islam. Ahmad Alsayed.*

This journey happened according to Divine Power and Will, which is beyond our awareness. It differs from our human law; it considered signs and proofs of the Lord of the Worlds' Power. He is the One who enacted and developed these laws.

Ibn al-Qayyim said: "The journey of Israa and Mi 'raj was a new test for Muslims in their faith and certainty. It was an opportunity for the Prophet to see the wonders of Divine Power, to learn metaphysical beliefs, and to honour the invocation of God in a place that no humans have ever reached. It was also an opportunity for him to be a reason in reducing his sorrows and worries, renewing his determination to continue his call to worship One God, and confront the harm of his people.

There has certainly been for you in the Messenger of God an excellent pattern:

Gandhi, the famous Indian leader, spoke to "yang India" newspaper about the Prophet Muhammad's characteristics. He said:

"I wanted to know the characteristics of the man who, without any conflict, possesses the hearts of millions of people. I became convinced that the sword was not how Islam gained its status, still, rather it was through the simplicity of the Messenger with his accuracy and sincerity in promises, his dedication, and loyalty to his friends and followers, along with his courage and absolute confidence in his Lord and his message. These are the qualities that paved the way and bypassed the difficulties, not the sword. After I finished reading the second part of the life of the Prophet, I found myself sorry that there was no more to learn about his great life."

I had a dialogue with a Christian from Cameron and his British girlfriend. While I was saying there is no god but One God, he interrupted me by saying:

Why did Muhammad harass a little girl?

I asked him: Can I understand from your interrupting that you agree there is no god to be worshipped but God, and your problem now is with the details of the Messenger's life?

He said: No, no, I disagree, Christ is also god.

I told him: Why don't you discuss the same point with me, which I am talking about then?

He said: Do not answer my question with a question. Why did your messenger harass a girl?

I asked him: Who told you this?

He said: The Book of Bukhari[224] that you believe in.

I told him: Did Mrs Aisha ever complain?

Didn't you read in Bukhari about Mrs Aisha's strong love for the Messenger (peace be upon him)? Does the girl love a harasser?

Didn't you read in Bukhari that it is marriage and not harassment?

How old was Mary when she gave birth to Christ according to your faith? how old was she when she was engaged to a 90 – year – old man before she became pregnant with Christ? Isn't this age close to the age of Aisha when she married the Messenger?

---

[224] Sahih Al-Bukhari is the authentic, abridged, chain-supported collection regarding matters pertaining to the final Messenger of God Muhammad, his traditions, and his times.

I continued: It's strange that the Prophet's enemies accused him of the most heinous acts at the time. They said he was a poet and a madman. But this story doesn't matter; no one ever mentioned it, except you now. So this story is either a natural thing that people used to do at that time, where history tells us stories of the marriage of kings at a young age, such as the story of the Queen of England Isabella in the eleventh century who married at the age of eight and many others[225], or it didn't happen the way you perceive it.

He asked: Why did Muhammad marry nine women, even though it was forbidden for his companions? By specifying that they can only marry four women?

I asked: Why, according to your claim, you accuse God's prophets of fornication as mentioned in your book? Even though the accusement is far from them.

He answered: To teach us that fornication is forbidden.

I told him: Wondrous! You believe that the prophets of God committed major sins of fornication, killing and drinking wine under the pretext of teaching their followers the right or wrong. You condemn the Messenger's legal marriage by order of God to teach Muslims the lessons. During his life and before his prophecy, the Messenger remained in his marriage for 25 years without marrying another woman, and his wife was 15 years older than him. Then, the Messenger married more than once after his mission as an order from God.

---

[225] http://muslimvilla.smfforfree.com/index.php...
https://liguopedia.wordpress.com/.../19/agnes-de-france/...

When the verse of determining marriage by only four was revealed, the Messenger had more than four women, but because they are considered as mothers of the believers, they cannot marry anyone else if he divorced them.

He asked: Why did Muhammad fight his enemies? Christ was not a fighter, but rather a lover of his enemies.

I told him: Why then did you believe in Moses when he was a fighter, and you believed in David when he was a fighter?

Moses and Muhammad assumed political and secular affairs, and each of them migrated from the pagan community. So Moses migrated from Egypt with his people, and Muhammad migrated to Yathrib[226]. Before that, his followers migrated to Abyssinia to run away from the political and military influence in the country from which they fled with their religion. The difference is that Jesus was sent to non–pagans "the Jews" (unlike Moses and Muhammad, their environments are pagan: Egypt and the Arab countries), which made their circumstances more difficult. The change entrusted to Moses and Muhammads' call is radical and comprehensive, and a massive shift from paganism to monotheism.

I continued: The number of victims in wars that took place during the Messenger's time does not exceed one thousand people; their purpose was for self–defence, and response to aggression, or insurance of religion. But look at the number of victims that occurred due to wars waged in the name of religion in other religions, they were in millions.

---

[226] A city located in the Hejaz region of western Saudi Arabia, about 100 miles (160 km) inland from the Red Sea and 275 miles from Mecca by road. The city is where Prophet Muhammad established the Islamic community.

He said: The invasions of your Messenger were looting.

I told him: The Prophet continued to call people to Islam in Mecca for 13 years, and tolerated the Quraish people's persecution. He had no spoils or lootings, and what was taken from the spoils later was either money from the people of war that the Muslims take so that the enemy cannot fight them or recover the funds of immigrants that was taken from them by force. This differs from the pillaging that results in the loss of innocent souls, such as women and children. The Messenger distributed the spoils for those who converted to Islam to bring their hearts together, and for a non–Muslim to make them love Islam. He also called for forgiveness and restitution of rights to their owners, as well as preferring them over themselves in food and clothing.

He said: The angels who came down to help the Muslims in the battle of Badr were weak, and they did not kill all polytheists at that time.

I told him: Then you believe in the descent of the angels.

He said: No, but I will share with you the opinion.

I told him with a smile: The meaning of descending angels in the Battle of Badr is to stabilize the believers' hearts in the battle and teach them that God helps those who seek refuge and trust in Him. Also, God did not want all the polytheists to be killed, knowing that some of them would convert to Islam later.

He said: Why didn't the angels descend in the battle of Uhud?

I told him: The lesson here is different, and it is about the importance of taking into account the materialistic causes for victory and the importance of obeying the leader.

He said: Isn't the massacre of the Jews (Banu Qurayza), and the panalty on banditry brutality?

I told him: What is the punishment of the traitors and the covenants' breakers according to the laws of the United Nations today? Just imagine a group determined to kill you all and take your money? What would you do with them?

The Jews of Banu Qurayza broke the covenant and allied themselves with the polytheists to eliminate the Muslims, but their attempts were finally in vain, where the punishment for treason and breaking vows was applied on them, which was mentioned in their law (the law of Moses) completely, when the Messenger of God allowed them to choose the one who governs their affairs, who is one of the Messenger's companions, and they were sentenced to punishment contained in their Sharia law (legislation).

He said: Islam spread by the sword and did not spread by peace.

I told him: First of all, the word sword was not mentioned in the Noble Qur'an even once. Muslims ruled India for an extended period, and they did not kill Hindus or Christians. Also, Muslims did not force anyone to convert to Islam. Didn't the Jews and Christians live in Andalusia under Islam's ruling while practicing their beliefs and enjoying their rights?

The countries in which the history of Islam have not witnessed wars are where most Muslims reside, such as Indonesia, India, China and others.

Suddenly, the questioner surprised me by saying: I am only a prophet, and I have been testing you.

I smiled and told him: We were honoured by your presence; unfortunately, I did not know that. I will call a colleague of mine here at the centre, and he will complete the dialogue with you.

I couldn't complete my dialogue with him because I was exhausted, and I realized that he was manipulative.

My colleague came and said: Welcome, Sir, how can I help you?

He said: I am a prophet, and I can predict your future now.

My colleague told him: Why the future? We are in the present; today I am suffering from some pain, so tell me please what I'm suffering from since the morning.

He said: No, no. Things don't go like this.

He asked him: So how does it go?

He said: I have to leave the place right away, thank you for having us.

Italian writer Dr Laura Vicha Valery also says:

"It's enough to say that wars, which are the most basic necessities of human life, have become, thanks to Muhammad, less brutal and cruel, as he was asking his soldiers not to kill an old man, a woman, or a child, and they would not demolish homes that were not taken as military strongholds, nor did they destroy the causes of life, nor they touch the fruit on the trees and palms."[227]

We have sent you with the truth as a bringer of good tidings and a warner:

Edward Montet, Director of the University of Geneva, said in a lecture: "Islam is a rapidly spreading religion that spreads on its own without any encouragement offered by organized centres, because every Muslim is a preacher by his nature. The Muslim is very faithful, and the intensity of his faith seizes his heart and mind; this is an advantage in Islam that does not exist in other religions. For this reason, you can see a burning desire of a Muslim to preach his religion wherever he goes and transmits the severe contagion of faith to all of the pagans.

---

[227] *Beauties of Islam*. Ahmad Alasayed

The strong Islamic faith has the most outstanding merit in this rapid spread. In addition to faith, Islam is compatible with social and economic conditions. The Muslim has a fantastic ability to adapt according to the environment and make the environment adapt according to what this vital religion requires."[228]

I had a dialogue with priests from the Orthodox Church in Ethiopia.

One of them said: Why should the apostate be killed in Islam while claiming that Islam has guaranteed freedom of belief?

I said to him: Faith is a relationship between the human and his Lord. Whenever he wants to cut it, the decision is between him and God. If he wanted to speak out and take it as an excuse to fight Islam and distort its image, it is an axiom of human-made laws of war that it is imperative to kill him, and this is what no one disagrees about.

He said: Christ said that we should love our enemies. He also said that whoever slaps you on your right cheek, turn your left cheek to him. As for Muhammad, he fought his enemies.

I said to him: According to what is attributed to Jesus, peace be upon him, that whoever slaps you in your right cheek, turn your left cheek to him, we have no evidence to prove it to establish provisions on it. If this is true, it may mean forgiving the abuser, but not humiliation and submission. Didn't Jesus say: **"I did not come to bring peace to the earth; I did not come to bring peace, but a sword, fire and division?"** [229]

---

[228] The Park is a collection of masterful literature and eloquent wisdom. Suleiman bin Saleh Al-Karachi.
[229] (The Gospel of Matthew 10:34).

There are orders issued by Christ to his followers to not resist the enemies. If he ordered them to resist their oppressors, this would have eliminated his vocation from its inception. Therefore, if the saying: If anyone slaps you on the right cheek, offer the other is correct, it is not a general and absolute rule, but rather an expression of a method of work in exceptional circumstances. I do not think that Christ wastes people's rights, because beating is a case of aggression against others, resulting in retribution.

Prophet Muhammed's mercy (peace upon him) was manifested on the day he entered Mecca victoriously when he said: Today is the Day of Mercy. He forgave the Quraysh people, who spared no effort to harm Muslims, and he faced evil with good and bad treatment with fair treatment.

And not equal are the good deed and the bad. Repel [evil] by that [deed] which is better; and thereupon, the one whom between you and him is enmity [will become] as though he was a devoted friend. [230]

Among the characteristics of righteous people:

Who spend [in the cause of God] during ease and hardship and who restrain anger and who pardon the people – and God loves the doers of good. [231]

---

[230] (Qur'an 41:33).
[231] (Qur'an 3:134).

He said: Why did Jesus forgive the adulterer while Muhammad executed the penalty of adultery? [232]

I told him: There is a complete agreement between Judaism, Christianity and Islam to emphasis the punishment for the crime of adultery.

Also, in Christianity, Christ emphasized the meaning of adultery, and did not make it confined to an actual physical act, but instead transferred it to moral awareness [233]. Christianity has deprived adulterers of inheriting in the Kingdom of God, after which they have no choice but eternal torment in Hell[234]. The punishment for adulterers in this life is what the Law of Moses approves, which is stoning (murder by stone)[235]. As Biblical scholars admit, forgiveness for the adulterer, in reality, does not exist in the oldest versions of the Gospel of John, still, it was added to it later, and that what is determined by modern translations. Most importantly, Christ announced at the beginning of his vocation that he did not come to break Prophet Moses's law and the prophets before him. In addition, disappearance of heaven and earth was easier for him than to drop one point of Moses's law[236]. Hence, Christ cannot disrupt the Law of Moses by leaving the adulterous woman without punishment. [237] The penalty in Islam is held by the testimony of four witnesses, with the description of the adultery incident confirming that it occurred, not just the presence of a man with a woman in one place alone.

---

[232] (Leviticus 20: 10-18).
[233] (Matthew 5: 27—30).
[234] (Corinthians 6: 9-10).
[235] (John 8: 3-11).
[236] (Luke 16:17).
[237] https://www.alukah.net/sharia/0/82804/

If one of the witnesses retracts his testimony, applying the punishment should be stopped; this explains the scarcity of execution of prescribed penalty for adultery in Islamic law throughout history because it is not proven except this way. It is not only difficult, but it is almost impossible. Because this type of action is not done in public in general. The presence of four witnesses is almost impossible, and the punishment is not applied without the presence of the four witnesses or the recognition of the perpetrators, and this is also difficult to happen.

One of the general principles in Islam, about the execution of prescribed penalties on the crime, is that:

- ✓ Attentiveness must be taken, making excuses and avoid suspicions that make the judge's conscience uncomfortable with the execution of prescribed penalties; according to the saying of Prophet Muhammad: "Avoid the penalties which are based on suspicions."
- ✓ Whoever has sinned while only God knew about his sin and did not show his sin to people, there is no prescribed penalties on him; it is not Islam's ethic to spy on people's sins.
- ✓ In the case of executing prescribed penalty for adultery based on the confession of one of the sinners, and not based on the four witnesses' testimony, no prescribed penalty on the second party that did not confess his guilt.
  - **The repentance accepted by God is only for those who do wrong in ignorance [or carelessness] and then**

repent soon [after]. It is those to whom God will turn in forgiveness, and God is ever Knowing and Wise. [238]

- And whoever does a wrong or wrongs himself but then seeks forgiveness of God will find God Forgiving and Merciful. [239]

- And God wants to lighten for you [your difficulties]; and mankind was created weak. [240]

A woman, entirely by her choice, came to the Prophet (peace upon him) and admitted her adultery. She asked him to execute the prescribed penalty on her, and she was pregnant too. Then the Prophet of God called her guardian, and he said: Treat her good; this indicates the law's perfection and the perfection of the Creator's mercy with the creatures. The Messenger said to her: Go back until you give birth.

When she came back, he said to her: Go back until you wean your child. Based on her insistence to return to the Messenger after weaning the child, he executed the prescribed penalty on her and said: She repented, and if her repentance was distributed to seventy of the people of Medina, it will be enough for them.

The mercy of the Messenger (peace upon him), was manifested in this noble position.

---

[238] (Qur'an 4: 17).
[239] (Qur'an 4: 110).
[240] (Qur'an 4: 28).

I am the Messenger of God to you all:

There was a rare visit from three monks coming from a Buddhist temple in Thailand. They were accompanied by a diplomatic delegation from the Thai embassy. The monks were dressed in what is similar to Muslims pilgrimage clothes, but orange. We were instructed at the beginning of the visit that the monks do not shake hands with women. Also, when it came to taking the memorial photo with me inside the mosque as a tour supervisor, I was supposed to kneel with the embassy staff, while the monks remain standing, as they are considered for them in a higher position than everyone else.

I said to them: About shaking hands, I do not shake hands with men, but as for the photo, I will only be standing since I only kneel to God. If you don't like that, then I will come out of the picture. So they agreed, and the photo was taken for us. I was standing beside the monks at a distance, while the embassy crew sat on the ground.

One of the monks, who was the most fluent in English, asked me: What are your religion's teachings?

I told him: The teachings of our religion are similar to those of your religion, but we follow them fully, and you shortened them.

He said: How is that?

I told him: The commandments that you have regarding respect for human rights, including non-killing and respecting the rights of neighbour and kindness to the poor, are found in the teachings of every religion on earth, including Hinduism, Judaism and Christianity, and they are also in Islam.

However, the difference between Islam and other religions is that other religions marginalized and ignored the first commandment, yet kept the rest.

He asked: What is the first commandment?

I told him: The belief in One God, to whom all resorted in adversity.

He asked: Do you mean Gautama Buddha?

I told him: No. I mean the Only Truth and Power in the sky, the Creator of Buddha himself along with all human beings, to Whom all seek refuge when they exhaust all means to save them from crises.

I then said: When a strong fear of thunder happens, doesn't the Buddhist resort to the Power in the sky to seek protection?

He said: Yes. But what is the evidence that this was among the commandments that we follow?

I told him: The evidence is that you practice it unintentionally. Buddha taught you the religion of Islam by admitting that death is true and giving you a description of the eternal life in which there is neither death nor pain, which is what you call "Nirvana".

One of the famous scholars, Arthur Lily, says: "The following words were carved in stone: (What Buddha's disciples thought about God, the soul, and the future of man) **'We recognize and believe in God, who is a being worthy for this (faith).'**"[241]

---

[241] *"India in Primitive Christianity"*, page 85.

He said: But Buddha is a god.

I asked him: Does God say about Himself, I am not the first Buddha, and I will not be the last Buddha?[242]

Gautama Buddha did not demand any of his followers to worship him as a god or worship anything or any other person. Also, "Gautama" used the word "Buddha" in the context of the word "prophet," meaning a person who is enlightened by a divine revelation.

Buddha said: Everyone should believe in the next Prophet (Maitreya). [243]

The word "Maitreya" or "Meta" in the Balinese language and all the corresponding terms used in Burmese, Chinese, Tibetan and Japanese have the same meaning. It is the same word "Rahmat" in Arabic, which means "Mercy".[244] Where God Almighty referred in the Noble Qur'an to the Prophet Muhammad as a mercy to the worlds.

And We have not sent you, [O Muhammad], except as a mercy to the worlds.[245]

He said: Wondrous! Do you assert that Buddha was a messenger of God, who predicted the coming of your Prophet?

I told him: We can never be sure; the name of Buddha was never mentioned in the Noble Qur'an, but we see that there are striking similarities between religions; this does not exclude that its source is one, which is the Creator, and they differed due to human distortions.

---

[242] *Gospel of Buddha by Carus* pg.217 and 218 (from Ceylon sources).

[243] *"Arshagyanam"* (Page282).

[244] *Prophecy on The Coming of Prophet Muhammad in Other Scriptures* – Zakir Naik.
http://www.irfi.org/articles3/articles_4601_4700/prophecy%20on%20the%20coming%20of%20prophet%20muhammadhtml.htm

[245] (Qur'an 21:107).

The Qur'an repeatedly affirmed that God sent messengers and prophets to all nations to recall the worship of One Creator, and mentioned the names of some, and others did not.

He asked: Is there evidence of Muhammad's prophecy in the books of Hinduism too?

I told him: Yes.

It is Nirachanza or the praised person (Muhammad) that he is a Karama: Prince of Peace or Expatriate, and he is safe, even among a group of sixty thousand and ninety enemies. He rides the camel, and his chariot touches the sky.[246]

Nirachanza, "The man of praise", refers to the Prophet Muhammad. The actual meaning of the Arabic word "Muhammad" is: "the praiseworthy man." It is not known exactly how many enemies the Prophet Muhammad had at that time, but it has been proven that there were thousands.

When the Prophet Muhammad migrated from Mecca[247] to Yathrib[248], he went on the camel.

I also said: There are many others.[249]

Say, [O Muhammad], "O mankind, indeed I am the Messenger of God to you all, [from Him] to whom belongs the dominion of the heavens and the earth. There is no deity except Him; He gives life and causes death." So believe in God and His Messenger, the unlettered prophet, who believes in God and His words, and follow him that you may be guided. [250]

---

[246] *Prophecy on The Coming of Prophet Muhammad in Other Scriptures* – Zakir Naik.

[247] The city in which he was born, but had to leave due to his assassination plot.

[248] A city located in the Hejaz region of western **Saudi Arabia**, about 100 miles (160 km) inland from the **Red Sea** and 275 miles from **Mecca** by road. The city is where Prophet Muhammad established the Islamic community.

[249] *The original concept of God*. Faten Sabri.

[250] (Qur'an 7: 158).

The visit ended, and they requested copies of the Qur'an's translations in Thai language, and they thanked us very much.

Conclusion:

The conclusion is summarised in these words:

The English philosopher Thomas Carlyle (1881–1795) said: "It has become one of the greatest shame for any civilized individual of this age to listen to what he thinks that the religion of Islam is a lie, and that Muhammad is deceit. So we have to fight the rumours that have such silly and shameful sayings. The message that this messenger performed is still the enlightening lamp, for twelve centuries for about two hundred million people like us; God created them, He created us too. Have you ever seen that a false man can establish a religion and spread it? Wondering how the man who is a liar, cannot build a house of bricks. If he is not aware of the lime's properties, the plaster, the dust and what it's similar to, therefore, what was built was not a house, but a hill of rubble and a mixture of materials. Also, it was not worth staying on its pillars twelve centuries inhabited by two hundred million souls, but it is worthy of collapsing its pillars, so it will be destroyed as if it was not."[251]

---

[251] The Heroes. Thomas Carlyle. Translated by Muhammad Al sybaey.

Arguments Concerning the Truth

What is revealed to you from your Lord is the truth:

As a child, I have always been keen on knowing the right religion. Due to my mom's keen on watching the religious programs, I always asked her about that topic. I was born in Kuwait. As a society that receives expatriates from different countries, it contained other religions and cultures. I always pondered the adherence of each religion's followers in declaring that theirs was the true religion. I used to say to myself: The true religion ought to be one; What is this 'religion'? Why is Islam the accurate religion? With this question being asked a lot to my mother when I was in elementary school, she told me: Read; search and see for yourself that the true religion is the one that provides you with a direct relationship with your Creator.

Hence, I embarked on reading despite my young age, so that before I reached high school, I had had a crystal-clear picture about monotheism, and I felt immense energy to tell the world about this great treasure. I remembered the Noble Verse: **What is revealed to you from your Lord is the truth.**[252] I was delighted.

---

[252] (Qur'an 34:6).

And argue with them in a way that is best:

In an interview that was conducted by three journalists of Indian nationality, who according to my understanding came with a missionary campaign for Christianity, one of them said: The Messiah is God.

I told him: What is your evidence?

He said: Christ said in our book: Before Abraham was, I am.

I told him: Is this how God introduces himself, by saying that I was before so and so?

Indeed, I am Allah; There is no deity except Me, so worship Me and establish prayer for My remembrance.[253]

I asked him: How did God introduce himself to Moses? Did He not say: O Moses, that I am God, worship Me?

God spoke to Moses and said to him, "I'm the Lord".[254]

He faltered.

His colleague hastened to interject quoting: Christ said: "God and I are one?"

I replied: He also said: "The disciples and I are one." and "God and Christ and the disciples are one." Again, I repeat, is this how God introduces himself?

For example, let's say you come to my house in order to ask for my help, but you realize that I am not there. Then, my son tells you: My mother and I are one, how can I help you? God is the ideal. God and Christ have the same goal (for all people to enter the Heavens), but they do not have the same entity.

---

[253] (Qur'an 20:14).

[254] (Exodus 2:2)

He said: The Trinity's proof is that God in eternity and before He creates the universe had attributes. If he was only one, and not three in one, His attributes would be disrupted, so, he had to be three in one in order to be merciful, give sustenance, and interact through the three who are within Him.

I interjected because his comment angered me: I, for example, have the trait of being "a good speaker". Therefore, when I decide to be silent and not speak now, does this speaking trait break inside me?

Someone said: You are not only a good speaker, but also endowed with the ability of intuitive replying.

He went on saying: Who is Muhammad?

I said: He is a descendant of Ismail.

He said: But Ismail is not a legitimate son of Abraham.

I asked: Who said so?

So, after Abram had been living in Canaan ten years, Sarai his wife took her Egyptian slave Hagar and gave her to her husband to be his wife. [255]

This passage in the Old Testament indicates that Hagar was a legitimate wife of Abraham. The word Ismail means "God hears", for God responded to Abraham's supplications to be blessed by a son. God chose this name for Ismail. It was never mentioned in the Old Testament that Ismail was an illegitimate son.

---

[255] (Genesis 16:3).

You are now pregnant and you will give birth to a son. You shall name him Ishmael, for the Lord has heard of your misery.[256]

God has vowed to bless Ishmael and bring forth a great nation out of his descendants.

And as for Ishmael, I have heard thee: Behold, I have blessed him, and will make him fruitful, and will multiply him exceedingly; twelve princes shall he beget, and I will make him a great nation. [257]

He said: Please give me references to verify for myself.

Then said afterwards: God in your book changes His mind. He says: "There is no compulsion in religion," and on the other hand He says: "Fight those who do not believe in Allah or the Last Day". Do you deny the existence of Nasikh and Mansukh (abrogation) in your Book?

I was very impressed by the eloquence of his pronunciation of these two Arabic terms, even though our dialogue was in English.

I countered: There is no abrogation between these two verses. The first verse has a completely different topic; it establishes a great Islamic principle, which is to prevent religious coercion. Whereas the second verse deals with a specific topic, concerning those who repel off God's pathway, or those who prevent others from accepting the calling of Islam; in fact, there is no contradiction between the two verses.

But overall, the evolution of the legislations' provisions, a previous rule discontinuing, replacements of rules, reinstating a later provision, releasing the restricted, and restricting the released, are accustomed and familiar

---

[256] (Genesis 16:11).
[257] (Genesis 17:20).

things in previous covenants since Adam's era. Just as the marriage between brothers and sisters was judicious in the law of Adam, peace be upon him, then it became prohibited in all other covenants.

Likewise, permitting work on Saturdays was advantageous in the law of Abraham, peace be upon him, along with all other laws before him, only to become banned in the law of Moses.

Likewise, God Almighty had ordered the Israelites to kill themselves after worshipping the calf, and then this command was abrogated after that, and many other examples. Therefore, replacing one provision with another is commonplace in the same legislation (the message of the prophet), or between different legislations (messages of different prophets).

I added: The doctor who starts treating his patient with a particular drug and throughout therapy either increases or decreases the doses of the drug in a gradual treatment attempt, you consider him sage.

I continued: I am genuinely amazed by your question, for you have embraced the abrogation made by Saint Paul, which was not in only one commandment, instead he altered the whole creed from Monotheism to the Trinity, and made you violate God's eternal covenant with you to adhere to performing the right of circumcision as mentioned in your book.

He asked: You claim that God protected Christ from crucifixion and murder, so why did he not protect Muhammad from being killed when he died poisoned by a Jewish lady?

I answered: God protected His messenger from the poison of the Jews when the messenger was warned that the sheep was poisoned. He did not die from that poison; he lived nearly four years after the incident, completing his message and great victories.

God has protected him until the moment of his death. So, if his death was due to the effect of poison later on or from another cause, that doesn't make the Jews triumphant over him by murdering him to impede him from completing the mission he was sent for, instead, the Prophet's death was done by God's ordinance after he had finished conveying his message. Accordingly, the story does not refute his infallibility.

Someone said: Although, the Qur'an is in a high degree of order and accuracy; nonetheless, the disjointed and incomprehensible letters in it are evidence of deficiency and defect.

I retorted: You are like a person who sees a high building with a great degree of order and accuracy, then he sees several designs at an angle of the building that he sees as unnecessary, and says: 'I do not understand them, then that is a defect in the structure. Is your level of understanding and perception of things a measure of their quality?

Instead, we would say that whoever constructed that building with all its grandeur, precision and sophisticated systems cannot ignore these elements. He must have put them there for a good reason, which my ignorance of it does not negate its existence. It is peculiar that no one during the Qur'an's decent objected to these letters; they always praised its miracle and uniqueness even from its enemies.

He asked me: Why was the Qur'an revealed in Arabic?

I answered: In what language would you like it to be? You have thousands of languages and dialects in India, so which language would you prefer? If it was in one of these languages, you would have said why not the other.

I said further: God sends the holy books in the language of their people.

God Almighty chose His Messenger Muhammad to be the seal of all His messengers.

The language of the Qur'an was in the language of his people. God safeguarded it from distortion until the Judgment Day. Similarly, He chose -for example- the Aramaic for the book of the Messiah.

He countered: What is the story of collecting the Qur'an during Caliph Abu Bakr's era and its burning during the reign of Caliph Uthman?

I answered: The Messenger left the Qur'an documented and written in the hands of his companions to recite it and teach others. When Abu Bakr, may God be pleased with him, became the caliphate, he ordered the collection of these scrolls to be in one place and for reference.

Whereas during the reign of Uthman, may God be pleased with him, he ordered the burning of the copies and scrolls that were with the companions all over the counties and provided them with new copies identical to the original copy which was left by the Prophet Muhammad and collected by Abu Bakr.

He ensured that all the regions will refer to the same original and only copy that the Messenger has left. Thus, The Qur'an remained as it was without change or alteration ever since it has been inherited to Muslims throughout the ages for them to contemplate among themselves and recite in their prayers.

He said: The Qur'an says:

Your Lord is God; He who created the heavens and the earth in six stages, then established Himself on the Throne. He makes the night overtake the day, as it pursues it persistently; and the sun, and the moon, and the stars are governed by His command. His is

the creation, and His is the command. Blessed is God, Lord of all beings.[258]

Here, it says that God has created the heavens and the earth in six days, He said 'in six days' to teach the humans not to haste in getting things done, and this is comprehensible.

Yet here He says:

Do you reject the One who created the earth in two stages? And you attribute equals to Him? That is the Lord of the Universe. He placed stabilizers over it, and He blessed it, and He assigned its foods in four stages—equally for the seekers. Then He turned towards the sky, and it was smoke, and He said to it and to the earth, "Come, willingly or unwillingly." They said, "We come willingly." Then He completed them seven universes, in two Days. And He assigned to each universe its law. And We decorated the lower universe with lamps, and for protection. That is the design of the Almighty, the All-Knowing.[259]

Here, God has created the earth in two days, placed the stabilizers over it, and estimated the sustenance in four days, so the sum becomes six. Then He made the heavens in two days. Thus, the total is eight days. Is this not a contradiction in the Qur'an?

I responded: If I told you that I travelled from Paris to London in ten days, and to Chicago in fifteen days, then this means that I completed my journey in fifteen days, and this is what is meant by this verse.

---

[258] (Qur'an 7:54).
[259] (Qur'an 41:9-12).

The questioner said: You Muslims live in broadly scattered groups because you do not have a religious leader like the Pope of the Vatican to govern you.

I said: How did the Vatican help Christianity? Was the Vatican able to unify the Christian sects? The rift is increasing.

His colleague said: We will leave now, but we have meetings to come.

Who argues in God without knowledge:

One day in Africa, I attended a language class where I was the only Muslim among everyone.

The language teacher asked me a surprising question: Do you pray five times a day? You pray at five in the morning? Isn't this weird?

I had prior knowledge that this professor is employed on a part-time contract, which means that he'll be paid only if he gave the class, so, I told him: If this lesson was at five in the morning, would you give it, or will you stay asleep?

He said: Of course, I will give it because this is the livelihood of my children and I.

I said: Prayer is our livelihood, and for us, it is more significant than millions of dollars. Then followed: How many times does your wife talk to you on the phone a day?

He laughed: She never stops calling.

I inquired: Are you deprecating us for addressing our Lord five times a day?

He said: Why pray, though?

I told him: I wake up for prayer at five in the morning every day, while my non-Muslim friends are doing morning exercises at precisely the same time.

For me, my prayers nourish my body and soul, but exercising is only physical sustenance. Look at how much we take care of our bodies, although our souls are starving from hunger; the result is countless suicide cases for the world's wealthiest people.

Worshipping abolishes the sensation found in the center of the brain, particularly responsible for self-awareness and those around us. As a result, a person will feel a great sense of sublimation, and that is a feeling that you will not understand unless you experienced it.

I went on: Worshipping stimulates the centers of feeling in the brain, and the faith transforms from theoretical information and rituals into subjective, emotional experiences. For example, let's say that a father wants to greet his son after returning from a trip. Would the father be satisfied if he only told his son "Welcome"? He will not feel happy until he hugs and kisses him.

The mind has an innate desire to embody our beliefs and thoughts in a physical form. Therefore, worship rituals were provided to satisfy this craving. Serving and obeying God are manifested in prayer and fasting, and so on.

Dr Andrew Newberg said: 'Worship rituals play a significant role in improving physical, mental and psychological health, along with achieving tranquility and spiritual transcendence. Likewise, turning to the Creator leads to more tranquility and transcendence.

The teacher said: You're right, and we are always depressed, gasping after our worldly pleasures.

During my dialogue with a Muslim who belittled the importance of prayer and supplication, he said: The concept of supplication contradicts the divine laws, and a deity must not be debased as to alter his words and amend his rulings.

I told him: The reality of the laws of nature is endorsed by religion and science. The fact that God exists is not sufficient alone, nor it satisfies our need to communicate with Him. The existence of the laws does not mean that God does not communicate with His creation, nor it says that being connected to Him and segregated from Him are alike.

Oliver Lodge, one of the most acclaimed scientists in Physics, responded to those who claim that supplication contradicts the universal laws by saying: They consider prayer as if they are observing a natural phenomenon outside the boundaries of the universe. It is a cosmic phenomenon to be reckoned within the works of the universe, as it governs all other incidents that occur in our lives without the prayer. Prayer is a psychological education, so why do protesters think that this education is not a reason to achieve some incidents caused by every other rearing method in which a person is being prepared for any other goal?

He said: There is no difference between a person praying for himself, someone else, or his Lord.

I replied: One cannot give what he does not have. How can I ever ask someone for help when he is incapable of helping himself? Besides, appealing to God Almighty is glorifying while doing so with others is degrading. Is it reasonable to equalize the king with the general public when it comes to requests? Both reason and logic refute this concept entirely.

He said: The request is either in conformity with the Divine Will, fulfilled with no claim, or it is contrary to the Divine Will, meaning that there is no meaning to this request.

I countered: The will of God is represented in creating the human's nature, and that it is human nature to seek aid when needed.

But pursuing this from someone other than God is in vain when believing in God Almighty's existence.

He said: The universal laws were an ancient matter that has happened and is done with.

I countered back: The train's whistle blows before its arrival but it is not the reason for arrival, and the light of the missile is seen upon explosion before hearing its sound. There is no relationship between the reason for seeing or hearing.

We did not limit all factors of the universal laws. We achieve what might help us estimate the consequences resulting from them in general, but estimation is only valid through approximation.

Although God has allowed scientists to study the universe which is not limited by laws, God Almighty remains the Doer of whatever He wills.

Creation is a continuous process and not a mechanical one that the Divine Providence has left in negligence without alteration.

Indeed, there is no changing in the laws of God. Although we do not know from these laws except what we are led to with our minds and God's guidance. The laws of God in the humans' destiny might be dependent on psychological breeding through praying. This psychological breeding might be a conditional reason for the Divine laws that the believer may not disable.

Praying for the Unitarians (who worship God alone) is a sign of human progress in understanding the universe's facts, comprehending the Divine Attributes, and communicating with the source of all goodness.

It was not known to the polytheists in that way. They performed their prayers in a bargaining method, as they believed that their gods needed their offerings.

There is no basis for religion without the belief in praying based on request and supplication. Also, believing in its spiritual exercise and its close relevance that links the world of the unseen with our life making the existence of God a reality grander than the validity of the universal laws. In addition, the validity of universal events that concern a person in the pursuing the demands of his livelihood, as well as in the compelling of his conscience.[260]

And allows for them all good things, and prohibits for them wickedness:

I remember being very impressed by the story of a Filipino colleague of mine who converted to Islam. She told me that the reason behind her conversion to Islam was the swine.

I asked her in astonishment: How come?

She said: I knew very well that this animal is very filthy and inflicts the body with many diseases. I've hated this animal for my whole life. I used to think that Muslims worshipped it because they are prohibited from eating it, which caused me to hate them. Until I left the Philippines and lived in an Arabic country, I realized that Muslims forbid pork because it is a filthy animal, and its meat is harmful to health. I then appreciated this religion's greatness, and since then, I am dedicated to reading and searching the content of this hidden gem.

I recall a conversation I'd had with a Brazilian man who was very interested in monotheism. Consuming animal meat prevented him from converting to Islam because he is vegetarian and mistakenly assumed that converting to Islam would force him to eat meat.

---

[260] *What is said about Islam?* Abbas Mahmoud Al-Akkad.

I explained: The fact that the consumption of red or white meat is permissible in Islam does not mean that you are obliged to eat it.

He said: Why is it allowed in the first place?

I said: Meat is an essential source of protein. Humans have incisors, molars, and canines. These teeth are suitable and prepared to cut, chew and grind meat. God created human's teeth for masticating both plants and meat and designed our digestive systems to digest one and the other fully. That is the reason behind the sanctioning of their consumption.

He persisted: Isn't the method of slaughter inhumane?

I corrected: The method of Islamic slaughter, which is severing the animal's neck with a sharp blade, is more merciful than the stunting and strangulation, which the animal suffers from, because once the blood flow to the brain is interrupted, the animal does not feel pain. The animal's convulsions are not from pain, instead due to the blood gushing out of the veins. It facilitates the drainage of all the blood outward, unlike other methods that seal the blood within the animal's tissue, which harms the health of those who devour that meat.

He criticized: Don't these animals have spirits just like us?

I clarified: There is a difference. An animal's soul is the driving force of the body. If it is separated from the body by death, the animals turn into lifeless bodies, and that is a form of life. Plants and trees also have a type of life which is not called a soul, instead, it is a life that passes through its particles with water. If they get separated, they whither and fall.

...And We made from water every living thing. Will they not believe?[261]

---

[261] (Qur'an 21:30).

However, the animal soul is not like a human spirit that has been attributed to God to honor and dignity. Its essence is known only to God and is pertaining only to human beings.

The soul of a person is a divine issue that a man is not required to understand its essence. It is merging the body's force, combined with reasoning power (the mind), perception, knowledge, and faith; and that is what distinguishes it from the spirit of animals.

A person has a visible external nature, which is the body, portraying all the characteristics of matter. It is capable of being weighed and measured. Then there is another nature utterly contrary to the first, characterized by serenity, unlimited by time and place.

He said: This nature, according to my understanding, is supposed to belong to the body?

I replied: The body belongs to it, because when we fast during Ramadan, for example, what motivates us to be patient and refrain from eating? That is due to a strong urge within ourselves that drives us to make this decision.

He said: Why don't we feel it?

I explained: When we use the elevator, for example, we do not feel its movement because we've become part of it, and we can only feel it when it starts moving or when it stops.

He asked: What is the human soul (self)?

I answered: The human soul is the product of the soul's encounter with the body in which a person is defined by his spirit, conscience, his feelings, and his perceptions. The person himself carries the forces of good and evil, therefore a person commits sins or is keen to obey.

He said: What is a human?

I told him: A person is a human personality as a whole, along with flesh, blood and character.

He challenged: What is the difference between the angel, the jinn and Satan?

I answered back: As for the angels, they are one of God's glorious creation; they were created from light. They are compelled for goodness, obedient to the orders of God; they are ever glorifying, ever worshipping, tireless and weariless.

They praise night and day, without ever tiring.[262]

...They never disobey God in anything He commands them, and they carry out whatever they are commanded.[263]

Believing in angels is shared by Muslims, Jews, and Christians. Among them is Gabriel, whom God has assigned to mediate between Him and His messengers. He used to descend with the revelation to them. Michael's assignment is rain and vegetation. Israfil's responsibility is to blow the Horn on the Day of Resurrection, and many others.

I went on: As for the jinn, it is of the realm of the prescience. They live with us on this earth, and they are commanded to obey God, and forbidden to disobey Him, like humankind, but we do not see them. God mentioned stories that show the extent of the power and ability of the jinn, including their ability to influence through whisper or allusion without physical intervention, still, they do not know the invisible nor are they able to harm the firm believer.

---

[262] (Qur'an 21:20).

[263] (Qur'an 66:6).

The devils inspire their followers to argue with you... [264]

The Devil is any dispassionate rebellious, whether human or jinn.

He said: Aren't the sins of Man from Satan?

I said: There are two types of sins; sins that are self-invited and sins committed because of Satan's whispers.

He exclaimed: Which is more dangerous for a person? How can we differentiate between them?

I clarified: The soul is much more dangerous if you do not persevere, just as a baby is weaned from breastfeeding by gradual taming.

The soul that commands evil is the soul that coax a person and pushes him to commit sins. It persists on a specific sin, such as planning and plotting to kill a human being, and there is no rest for it or retreat until it achieves its desired goal.

Likewise, the soul adorns the vile act and shows it right, and it goes overboard in the path of sin and disobedience until its instinct is buried. Then the soul loses the ability to distinguish the good from the bad. For it, the bad deeds look like good deeds, as what happened with the brothers of Prophet Joseph, peace be upon him, when they threw him into the bottom of the well, and they assumed that they were doing well.

And they brought upon his shirt false blood. [Jacob] said, "Rather, your souls have enticed you to something, so patience is most fitting. And God is the one sought for help against that which you describe". [265]

---

[264] (Qur'an 6:121).
[265] (Qur'an 12:18).

Those whose efforts in this world are misguided, while they assume that they are doing well.[266]

What of him whose evil deed was made attractive to him, and so he regards it as good? God leads astray whomever He wills, and He guides whomever He wills. Therefore, do not waste yourself sorrowing over them. God knows exactly what they do.[267]

Speaking of Satan, God Almighty has told us that he is weak. He said: Surely the strategy of the Devil is weak.[268]

So, Satan's plotting is confined to the boundaries of Man's mandatory duties by whispering and displaying falsehood in the appearance of truth, but he has no authority over Man.

So, when you recite the Qur'an, [first] seek refuge in God from Satan, the expelled [from His mercy][269].

He has no authority over those who believe and trust in their Lord. His authority is only over those who follow him, and those who associate others with Him. [270]

The devil's primary concern is to make a person disobey God, no matter how. Therefore, Satan whispers to a person various sins, such as stealing, or committing adultery, lying, adulation, or disbelieving, and other sins. When a person closes the door of disobedience, Satan comes to him from another door, and the obsessive whispering of Satan for a person may be by acting the part of a loving advisor.

---

[266] (Qur'an 18:104).
[267] (Qur'an 35:8).
[268] (Qur'an 4:67).
[269] (Qur'an 16:98).
[270] (Qur'an 16:98:100).

And he swore to them, I am a sincere advisor to you.[271]

Those who are righteous—when an impulse from Satan strikes them, they remind themselves, and immediately see clearly.[272]

Satan knows this and admits it, on the Day of Resurrection he will say to the guilty:

And Satan will say, when the issue is settled, "God has promised you the promise of truth, and I promised you, but I failed you. I had no authority over you, except that I called you, and you answered me. So do not blame me but blame yourselves. I cannot come to your aid, nor can you come to my aid. I reject your associating with me in the past. The wrongdoers will have a torment most painful. [273]

Scholar Ibn al-Qayyim says: "The soul shortens the hearts from reaching the road of the Lord. It is a road only reached after its demise. People are divided into two parts, a group that their selves has triumphed over them only to annihilate them, and another group that has triumphed over their selves, so that they have yielded to their commands."

God glory be to Him, described the human self in the Qur'an as having any one of three characteristics: Tranquil, evil-minded, and reproving.

The Tranquil Soul: Is the one that became serene through the remembrance of God and longed to meet Him, and is addressed upon death.

Return to your Lord, pleased and accepted.[274]

---

[271] (Qur'an 7:21).
[272] (Qur'an 7:201).
[273] (Qur'an 14:22).
[274] (Qur'an 89:28).

The soul then emerges from doubt to certainty, from ignorance to knowledge, from forgetfulness to remembrance, and from showing off to sincerity.

The soul that is evil-minded: Is the one that commands its owner of whatever it desires. This is its nature except if God has guided it and help it, so no one gets rid of the one's evil self except with the Grace of God. The Messenger, peace be upon him, sought refuge from the evil of the soul, saying: We seek refuge in God from the evils of ourselves.

The reproving soul: Is ever self-blaming, yet it turns a lot between remembering and forgetting, advancing and turning away, loving and hating, being content and discontent, being satisfied and angry, and of being good and envious.

Al-Hassan Al-Basri said: "The believer is always reprimanding himself, even on the Day of Resurrection. He always blames himself, whether he was virtuous or not. If he was virtuous, then he blames himself for his dereliction."

He questioner asked: What is the difference between delight and envy?

I answered: Elation is a person disliking another person's superiority over him, and he wishes to be like him or better, so this is jealousy, and it is known as "ghibta".

…This is what competitors should compete for.[275]

I continued: Envy is extremely disliking the blessings bestowed upon the envied. This is the type of jealousy that bears blame. So, when a person detests something, he feels hurt acknowledging what he hates; this becomes a sickness in his heart; he enjoys it when the envied has their blessings taken

---

[275] (Qur'an 83: 26).

away even if this does not result in any benefit to the envious except the single advantage of having the pain that was in his soul removed.

…But the evil plot does not encompass except its own people[276]

He asked: What is the difference between evil occurring from humans and the one that happens from God?

I countered: Evil never comes from God! Evil is not existential matters; existence is pure goodness.

He asked, wanting to know more: How come?

I answered: If a person, for example, beat another person until he loses his ability to move, then he has acquired the attribute of injustice, and injustice is evil. But the presence of strength for someone who grabs a cane and uses it to hit someone else is not wrong. The existence of the will that God has given to him is not wrong as well.

His ability to move his hand is not evil.

The presence of the capacity of beating in the stick is not evil.

All these existential materials are good, and the attribute of evil is not acquired unless it led to harm through its misuse, which is the paralysis in the previous example. Thus, based on that example, the scorpion and snake are not evil if they didn't bite a person that came in front of them. As such, God Almighty is not credited with evil in His actions for those are pure goodness, but rather in their effects that resulted from the misuse of this goodness by humans.

He said: What about people who were born disabled?

I answered: A fifty-year-old disabled person once said: 'I now realize the underlying blessing behind the severe accident that left me crippled.

---

[276] (Qur'an 35 :43).

Before the accident, I intended to turn to atheism. I was too distant from God, and I was hell-bent on immigrating to become an atheist. My injury prevented me from fulfilling my wish, and after thirty years of the accident, I thank God for it, and I see it as one of the greatest blessings that God has bestowed upon me, and that it brought me closer to Him. I am certain that myself was wayward enough to make me not return to God except with such an affliction. God knows the souls of His servants even before they are born.

I said to my inquisitor: Since evil is relative and not absolute, life is a test and not a rewarding place, and the reward is as great as the amount of work. So, handling the difficulties is like someone who travels long distances hoping to reach his goal and his beloved.

He asked, wanting to know: What is the evidence for the resurrection?

I explained: The evidence and phenomena of existence all indicate a constant rebuilding and creation in life all around us. The examples are abundant, such as reviving the earth after its death by rain and other examples.

He brings the living out of the dead, and He brings the dead out of the living, and He revives the land after it had died. Likewise, you will be resurrected.[277]

Did you think that We created you in vain, and that to Us you will not be returned? So Exalted is God, the Ruler, the Real. There is no god except He, the Lord of the Noble Throne.[278]

---

[277] (Qur'an 30:19).
[278] (Qur'an 23:115-116).

Another evidence for the resurrection is the interlocked system of the balanced universe; even the infinitesimally small electron cannot travel from one orb to another in the atom unless it gives or takes an amount of energy equal to its movement. How do you imagine in this system that the killer escapes or that the unjust flees without punishment? I uttered.

Do those who perpetrate the evil deeds assume that We will regard them as equal to those who believe and do righteous deeds, whether in their life or their death? Evil is their judgment! God created the heavens and the earth with justice, so that every soul will be repaid for what it has earned. And they will not be wronged.[279]

I went on: Do you not notice that in this life we lose a lot of our relatives and friends and know that we will die like them one day, but we feel deep in our hearts that we shall live forever? If the human body was a material object within the framework of a worldly life within the material laws, there would be no meaning to this innate sense of freedom that the spirit transcends time and overcomes death.

He asked: How can the Creator resurrect them?

I replied: Just as He created them the first time.

O, people! If you are in doubt about the Resurrection: We created you from dust, then from a drop, then from a clinging clot, then from a lump—developed and undeveloped. To clarify things for you. And We settle in the wombs what We will, for a designated term, and then We bring you out as infants. Then you may reach your maturity. Some of you will pass away, and some of you will reach the vilest age, so that after having known he may not know.

---

[279] (Qur'an 45:21-22).

And you see the earth still, but when We send down water on it, it vibrates and swells, and grows every delightful pair.[280]

Does the human being not consider that We created him from a drop? Yet he becomes a fierce adversary. And he produces arguments against Us, and he forgets his own creation. He says, "Who will revive the bones when they have decayed?" Say, "He who initiated them in the first instance will revive them. And He knows every creation.[281]

So, observe the impact of God's mercy: how He revives the earth after its death. That is the Reviver of the dead, and He is capable of all things.[282]

He challenged: Also, how does He hold them all accountable at the same time?

I rejoined: Just as He provides for them all at the same time.

Those who disbelieve argue with false arguments:

In the dialogue that I've conducted with a large group of French women working in an international organization, I had difficulty dealing with Muslim women of Arab descents who were among these them. The non-Muslim French women were highly interactive and responded effectively, but on the other hand, I was concerned about the Muslim women.

One of them angrily interrupted me while I was answering a non-Muslim woman who asked a question about the headcover's ordinance in the Holy Qur'an saying: The headcover is not an obligation in Islam!

---

[280] (Qur'an 22:5).

[281] (Qur'an 36:77-79).

[282] (Qur'an 30:50).

I challenged: Do you pray the prayers in their due time?

She answered: No, I do not pray.

I said: Then you are right. Praying for you, in this case, is a priority. Pray first, then come to discuss with me the subject of the headcover's ordinance.

I could tell that she felt very embarrassed.

Another one interjected: But when a woman is born, she is bareheaded. Hence the principle is to reveal her head.

I challenged: In that case, she must come out completely naked because she is born without any clothes.

She persisted: The headcover is retardation and backwardness.

I challenged: Is there any backwardness beyond Adam's time? Exposing the head itself is the backwardness. Go back to the photos of your grandmother on her way to school, and see what she was wearing. When the swimming suite appeared for the first time, demonstrations took place all over Europe and Australia that were against it because it violated the human nature and traditions not for religious reasons. Therefore, the manufacturing companies embarked on making extensive advertisements using girls at the age of five, wearing it initially to encourage women to wear it. The first girl who walked out wearing it was too ashamed to continue with the show.

At that time, women and men used to swim in white and black swimwear covering their entire bodies.

She countered back: How did you know that?

I replied: I learned it through my university's education. When I've decided to wear the head cover in high school, I had a strong desire to imitate faithful women throughout history who have taken from the veil a symbol of their righteousness, such as the blessed Virgin Mary, the mother of the Messiah and the wives of the Messenger Muhammad.

At that time, I realized that there was no way for me to find something beautiful and elegant for veiled women in the market, so I decided to study fashion design for this purpose.

I elaborated: what is the difference between the veil of the Catholic nun and the Muslim woman's veil? If you looked at both women from the back, you wouldn't be able to differentiate between them; not until you see them from the front, only then you could tell the difference by noticing if they wear a cross or not. This is the main difference between Muslim and Christian's creed.

Another one cut in: But the nun is religious, she gave herself to God and renounced marriage.

I asked: So, in your opinion, should we choose between marriage and being religious? Isn't this an injustice against ourselves and a great disparagement, forcing our souls to struggle between their physical needs and their spiritual ones? That is a slow destruction of the soul and eternal torment in this life and the Hereafter.

She said: But the headcover is not a normal thing for us.

I smiled and said gently: I'll tell you a symbolic story. There once was a ruler of a village who fell grievously ill, that his nose was amputated because his doctor insisted.

On the following day, the minister came in to check up on the king, but he was so startled by the sight of the nose-less king that he burst out in laughter.

The king was furious and ordered his doctor to cut out the minister's nose.

On the third day, the minister's assistants laughed at the sight of their minister without a nose. So, the minister got offended and told the king what had happened. So, the king ordered his doctor to chop off the noses of all the ministers.

On the fourth day, the ruler went out with his minister and minister's assistants to solve some of the people's problems, and the people laughed at them. Therefore, the king decreed that the doctor should also cut off the noses of all people and noses of any newly-born children.

As a result, all folks of the village became without noses. Later, when a natural person, with a healthy nose from another town came to visit their town, everyone pointed at him and jeered: This one has a nose, he is not a normal human being.

The group laughed out loud at the tale, and someone said: Yes, your story has a lot of truth in it.

Another woman asked: Why does a man not cover his beard just as a woman covers her hair? Why is the dress code worn by a man different than a woman's dress code in Islam? Why do they not cover their bodies in the same way?

I laughed at her question and stated: How peculiar! So why do you wear a two-piece bathing suit, and your husband swims in a one-piece trunk?

The whole group burst out laughing. I continued: A woman covers her hair to ward off sedition; have you heard of a woman raping a man ever in your life?

Women in your countries marsh out in protests demanding for their rights to a safe life without harassment or rape, and we have not heard of a similar demonstration done by men.

One of them had mocked: Why can't a woman be sent as a prophet?

I dared her: Would you want to be sent as a prophet?

She uttered archly: Why not?

I answered: Since your faith is that strong, and you have high endurance, vigor, and determination, then ask God to make you a prophet.

The group laughed again.

Then another lady said: What is the difference between the face cover and headcover?

I clarified: Based on my prior knowledge of their strong reverence to the Virgin Mary, the ones who wear the headcover had emulated the pious women throughout history who took the veil as a symbol of their righteousness such as Virgin Mary, the mother of the Christ, and others. While the women who put on the face cover are following suit with the Messenger's wives, peace and blessings be upon him.

She said: Why does a man marry four women?

I answered: In France, how many women does a man marry?

She uttered: Only one!

I asked her: And how many mistresses does he keep?

The whole group cried out in one voice while laughing: Too many!

I continued: This situation that you are laughing at is the situation that prevailed before Islam. Islam came to set it right; preserving the rights and dignity of women and transforming them from mistresses into wives who have integrity and rights.

She asked irritably: Who would accept to be a second wife? How can a French woman accept to be a second or third wife?

I replied: Whoever accepts to become a mistress with no rights will prefer to become a wife with secured rights for herself and her children.

A mistress lives a degrading life without rights for her and her children, and, oddly, you accept the concept of relationships without marriage and responsibilities, and children without parents or homosexuality, etc.... while you reject a legal marriage between a man and more than one woman.

She persisted: Why does a woman not have the right to marry four men at the same time, just as a man does?

I clarified: A woman can marry a single or a married man as long as he has less than four wives, and that is her right. In contrast, this right does not apply to a man; as he is only allowed to marry someone who is not married, to protect the rights of children in lineage and inheritance.

She said: The children's rights can be preserved by examining their DNA.

I asked her in surprise: If you came into the world and found your mother introducing you to your father through this test, what would your psychological state be?

Regardless, how can a woman play the wife of four men with that temperamental moodiness that she has, not to mention the diseases caused by her relationship with more than one man at the same time?

Another woman said: Why are men the guardians of women in Islam?

I clarified: That is esteem for women and an obligation for men taking care of her affairs and fulfilling her needs. A Muslim woman plays the role of a queen that every woman on earth desires.

She countered: But she is not a queen in reality.

I replied: A smart woman chooses what she should be, either an honored queen or a toiler on the side of the road.

She challenged: Have a look at how men misused that guardianship!

I told her gently: This is not a stigma to the guardianship system, but rather to those who misuse it.

She persisted: Look at the men in some Arab countries, how they oppress their wives at home, then go out to the nightclubs to drink wine and dally with women.

I retorted: How many are they? One thousand two thousand three? Do you know the number of Muslims in any of these countries?

She said sharply: Why did the Qur'an allow them to strike the woman?

I clarified: Who said so? Muhammad, may God bless him and grant him peace, never hit a woman in his life. As for the Qur'anic verse that spoke of the beating, it is meant to be a not severe beating in the case of rebellion, just like when you nudge your son's shoulder when you wake him up from a deep sleep so that he does not miss his test.

I continued: Let's say that you found your daughter standing at the edge of the window to fling herself off. Unintentionally, your hands will reach out to her to grab her and push her backwards so that she does not hurt herself. That is what is intended here by beating a woman; to prevent her from spoiling her life and destroying her children's future. Of course, that is only after several stages, as mentioned in the verse.

As for those from whom you fear disloyalty, admonish them, and abandon them in their beds, then strike them. But if they obey you, seek no way against them. God is Sublime, Great.[283]

---

[283] (Qur'an 4:34).

She said: Why does the woman not hit her husband if he misbehaved?

I explained: If she can take her right on her own, she can do so; but that may cause another harmful effect. But the woman is weak in general; Islam has given her the right to resort to the judiciary.

The basic principle in Islam is that the marital relationship should be based upon affection, serenity, and mercy.

And of His signs is that He created for you mates from among yourselves, so that you may find tranquility in them; and He planted love and compassion between you. In this are signs for people who reflect.[284]

She uttered: My daughter is a homosexual, and I cannot interfere with her decision.

I asked: If she wants to throw herself into fire, would you have interfered or not?

She answered: That is the difference between you and me. You find this behavior dangerous, but I find it natural. Didn't you hear of the relativity theory? Just as there are various theories of human origin and theories of God's concept, likewise morality is relative, and there are no objective moral values.

In France, we find no problem in our daughters having relationships with their schoolmates outside of marriage, for example. I have paid my daughter's costs for staying with her boyfriend in a nearby hotel to spare them meeting up, for instance, in a nearby forest and exposing them to bandits.

---

[284] (Qur'an 30:21).

I told her: having various theories and convictions does not mean that there isn't a one true and correct theory. The numbers of concepts and theories you may collectively have about the means of transportation that I'd use to get here daily, do not negate the fact that I own a black car even if the whole world believes that my car is red. This belief doesn't make it red; there is one truth, which is, I own a black car.

It is illogical to decree the convictions of human beings based on their whims and preferences. For example, there is no doubt that rape is a breach of human rights, a violation of his values and freedom; this indicates that rape is evil, so is homosexuality, which is a violation of the universal laws, and adultery.

The truth can't be denied even if the whole world agreed to invalidate it. A misdeed is as clear as the sun, even if all human beings decided to recognize it as valid.

Also, having various theories of the origin does not negate the presence of one truth, which is: There is only one God "the Creator" the One and Only, who has neither image nor child.

If the entire world wanted to say that the Creator is embodied in the form of an animal or a person, that does not make it so, Exalted be God Almighty.

Hence, your daughter's homosexuality is a wrong and disgraceful act, even if the whole world concurred that it is right. The only and explicit truth is that morality is not relative and does not change with time or place.

One of them interjected: But we must respect the opinions and theories of others.

I declared: We respect the will of choice that God has given to everyone, but we do not respect the disgraceful behavior itself.

Another had questioned: Why did Islam prohibit adoption?

I clarified: Have you heard the story of the Australian girl who accidentally learned, thirty years later, that she was adopted and committed suicide?

If they told her since childhood, they would have spared her and allowed her to search for her family.

Islam urges the sponsorship of orphans, and encourages the sponsor of an orphan to treat him as he treats his children, but upholds the right of the orphan to get to know his real family, to preserve his right in his father's inheritance, and to avoid mixing of lineages.

Another Muslim woman asked next: Why the savagery in the punishment for adultery? Look at the French sophistication.

I countered back: Due to the French sophistication, how many millions do not know where they've come from? Is that sophistication or retardation?

She challenged: Why does a woman inherit half of what a man inherits?

I stated: A Muslim friend had told me one day that she strove so hard to understand this point up until the death of her father-in-law. Her husband inherited twice the amount his sister got, but he had to buy some essentials that he lacked, such as a house for his own family and a car.

His sister, on the other hand, bought jewelry from the amount that she got and saved the rest of the money in the bank, as her husband was obligated to provide housing and other essentials. Only then my friend understood the wisdom behind this rule, and she thanked God.

I explained: Before Islam, a woman was deprived of the inheritance. When Islam came, she was included in the inheritance. Indeed, she even gets more shares than the males or equal to them, or even she gets shares while he does not get anything in many cases, whereas the males only obtain higher proportions according to the degree of kinship and descent.

She insisted: But in many societies, women work and toil to take care of their families. The rule of inheritance here is invalid.

I contradicted: Is the malfunction in your phone, which you caused by not following the operating instructions, evidence of the operating instructions being invalid?

And argued with false arguments to condemn the truth:

The French woman went on with her inquiries: Islam has detracted from the woman's eligibility, by making her testimony half of the man's testimony.

I elucidated: The testimony of a man was never accepted alone even in the most insignificant financial issues. Muslim men did not object to that and considered it a violation of his integrity, except that the woman has the advantage in accepting her testimony alone without a man and in a more crucial subject than the testimony on small matters. That is in the testimony releated to the childbirth and what it entails in inheritance and lineage.

O you who have believed, when you contract (i.e. when you have or contract a debt) a debt one upon another for a stated term, then write it down. And let a writer write it down between you with justice, and let not any writer refuse to write it down, as God has taught him. So let him write and let the one upon whom is the truthful duty of payment (i.e. the debtor) dictate, and let him be pious to Allah (God) his Lord and not depreciate anything therein. So, in case the one upon whom is the truthful duty is foolish, or weak, or unable to dictate himself, then let his patron dictate with justice. And call in to witness two witnesses of your men; yet, in case the two are not two men, then one man and two women from

among the witnesses you are satisfied with, so that (in case) one of the two women errs, then either of the two should remind the other, and let the witnesses not refuse whenever they are called (upon). [285]

The testimony upon which the judiciary system relies on to verify justice based on evidence does not need masculinity or femininity as a criterion to determine its truthfulness or falsehood to decide whether to accept or reject it.

Instead, its criterion fulfills the judge's assurance of the testimony's truth, regardless of the gender of the witness, male or female, and regardless of the number of witnesses.

In any case, we must know that testimony is a responsibility, and when God relieves a woman of it, that is to honor her, not the opposite.

She said: Why does Islam endorse slavery?

I answered: There is not a single verse in the Holy Qur'an that supports slavery! Slavery, which was established before Islam, was a standard system practiced by all populations, without restrictions. Islam's fight against slavery aimed to change the outlook and mindset of the entire society so that slaves become full and active members in society after their liberation without the need to resort to demonstrations, strikes, civil disobedience, or even ethnic revolutions.

Islam's goal was to get rid of this hateful system as quickly as possible and by peaceful measures.

---

[285] (Qur'an 2:282).

She asked: How so?

I explained: Islam did not allow the ruler to enslave his people. Moreover, Islam also granted both the ruler and his people rights and duties within the boundaries of freedom and justice guaranteed to all.

So, slaves were gradually set free through expiations, opening the door for alms, the hasting to do good and through the emancipation of the slaves to draw nearer to God.

The woman who bears a child to her owner was not sold and was automatically granted her freedom upon his death. Contrary to all previous traditions, Islam has decreed that the son of an enslaved woman will be conjoined with his father. Therefore, he is free.

It also decreed that the bondservant purchases himself from his master by paying an amount of money or working for a specified period.

If any of your servants wish to be freed, grant them their wish, if you recognize some good in them.[286]

In the battles that Muslims were forced to fight in defense of themselves, religion, and money, Prophet Muhammad, has instructed his companions to treat prisoners of war with kindness and charity.

The prisoners were also able to buy their freedom by paying a ransom or teaching children how to read and write. Also, Islam's enslavement system did not deprive a child of his mother or a brother from his brother.

Islam has commanded Muslims to show mercy to those fighters who've surrendered.

---

[286] (Qur'an 24:33).

And if anyone of the polytheists asks you for protection, give him protection so that he may hear the Word of God; then escort him to his place of safety. That is because they are a people who do not know.[287]

Islam had also stipulated the possibility of helping slaves to free themselves by funding them from the Muslims' money or from the state treasury. The Prophet, had offered a ransom to free the slaves from the public treasury funds.

She questioned: Aren't the pilgrimage rituals paganistic?

I pointed out: Are we to interpret the respect of the citizens of any country for some monument, in publishing its photos and stamping it on official papers and so on as a worshipping ritual to that monument? There is a massive difference between pagan religions, and the aggrandizing of particular places and sacred landmarks, whether religious, ethnic or national.

She asked: Why do Muslims kiss the Black Stone?

I enlightened her: Would you scold someone for kissing an envelope that has a letter from his father?

She disregarded my question: What about throwing the stones?

I answered her: As for the throwing stones, it shows our opposition to Satan. In this way, we are emulating the actions of our Messenger Ibrahim, peace be upon him, when Satan had intercepted him to prevent him from carrying out his Lord's order and slaughtering his son, so, he cast some stones at him. [288]

---

[287] (Qur'an 9:6).

[288] Imam Al-Hakim in Al-Mustadrak & Imam Ibn Khuzaymah in his book "Sahih" on the authority of Ibn Abbas, may God be pleased with him.

Likewise, walking between the two hills (Al-Safa and Al-Marwah) is following in the footsteps of Hajar (Ibrahim's wife) when she sought to find water for her son Ismail.

All the pilgrimage rituals are for establishing the remembrance of God and denoting obedience and yielding to Him. They are not intended to worship stones, places, nor people. Islam calls for one God who is the Lord of the heavens and earth and what is between them; The Creator and Sovereign of everything.

I have directed my attention towards Him Who created the heavens and the earth—a monotheist—and I am not idolaters.[289]

She exclaimed: For me, these rituals are frightening. Many Muslims died because of excessive crowding.

I informed her: Dozens may die in this annual event due to excessive crowding, yet millions of people die annually because of alcohol consumption. Also, victims die in more significant numbers in soccer field stadiums, carnivals in South America, etc. because of big crowds.

In all cases, death is inevitable. Meeting God is an ascertained reality. Therefore, dying while doing good deeds is better than dying while sinning.

Malcolm X said: "And for the first time after twenty-nine years that I've spent on this earth, I stood before the Creator of everything and felt that I am a complete human being.

I have never witnessed the sincerity of this brotherhood among people of all colors and genders in my life. America needs to understand Islam because it is the only religion that has the solution to the problem of racism."[290]

---

[289] (Qur'an 6:79).

[290] An Islamic herald and an American human rights defender of African origin (African American), he corrected the march of the Islamic movement in America after it deviated strongly from the Islamic faith and called for the correct dogma.

Conclusion:

Evelyn Kobold summarized the greatness of the religion of Islam in these words.

"Islam is a word that means submission to God, and it also means peace. The Muslim is defined as the man who walks in his life according to his Creator's will, and the orders of his Lord, and who lives in peace with God and His servants. Perhaps the most beautiful thing in Islam is the Divine Oneness, devoid of traditions and heretics, and its complete adherence to practical matters of life. Faith in the Qur'an is based on good deeds, and there is no faith in Islam without there being a good deed; ever! This is what one finds in the Qur'an more than once in all its chapters and verses. Islam ordained the pilgrimage on the Muslims who can make the journey, so the sick is excused; the poor, and the slave. It is stipulated in the pilgrimage that the road to be devoid of risks. There should not be disease nor injustice in it. Speaking of the pilgrimage, no one can deny that it's of great importance. It overwhelms the soul from soaring to the realm of supreme spiritualistic ideals and helps it break free from the world's vanities. It allows it turn to God with a sound heart along thousands of people of all kinds with different nationalities, languages, and the diversity of their drinks and tastes. These people come from all over the world enduring on their way all kinds of hardships, the disturbance of pathways, and the far-away distances that cannot be estimated or envisioned. All of that is to only stand in one place before God, May He be exalted, approaching Him with pure hearts, eager cores, and tears a–flowing."[291]

---

[291] Lady Evelyn Zainab Kobold, wrote the book "The Pilgrimage to Macca" (London, 1934), a Scottish orientalist born in Edinburgh in an aristocratic family, converted to Islam and performed the Hajj pilgrimage in 1933.

The Religion in the Sight of God

You are the best nation that has ever emerged for humanity:
I once remember being praised by my German language teacher. She asked: How do you have all this energy to enjoy education, exert effort as well as money and health in studying, working, and take care of your children?
I answered: Prophet Muhammad, may God grant him peace, said: Take advantage of five before five: your youth before your old age, your health before your illness, your riches before your poverty, your free time before your work, and your life before your death.
Then she said: Wondrous! Summit of wisdom, you are a unique type of human being.
After that, I remembered the noble verse: **You are the best nation that has ever emerged for humanity** [292]. I thanked Almighty God very much.

---

[292](Qur'an 3: 110).

There has come to you from God a light and a clear Book:

A group of Ph.D. holders came to attend an international conference, and eventually they visited our center. During a discussion that we had, one of them asked me about Adam's sin. He said sarcastically: Adam did it because of Eve and we endured it for life.

I told him: That's what you believe, but in Islam God forgave Adam, and taught us how to return to Him whenever we sinned during our lifetime. It is not the original sin, but it is the original forgiveness.

Then Adam received from his Lord [some] words, and He accepted his repentance. Indeed, it is He who is the Accepting of repentance, the Merciful.[293]

Thus, women do not bear the burden of Adam's sin, but rather Islam is keen to raise the status of women. Women have played a major role in many of the stories mentioned in the Qur'an, such as Balkis the Queen of Sheba and her story with the Prophet Solomon, which ended with her faith and becoming a Muslim (a worshipper of God alone).

Indeed, I found [there] a woman ruling them, and she has been given of all things, and she has a great throne. [294]

The same group member continued: Can anyone become a Muslim?

I answered: Absolutely.

He asked: How so?

I answered: Every child is born in his right nature, which is being a worshiper of God alone, because without the intervention of parents, schools, or any religious party, he will worship God directly until adulthood.

---

[293] (Qur'an 2:37).
[294] (Qur'an 27: 23).

During his adulthood, he will become entrusted and accountable for his actions. After that, he begins to choose whether to take Jesus as a mediator between him and God, which would make him become a Christian, or to take Buddha as a mediator to become a Buddhist. Other options surrounding him would be taking Krishna for example in order to become a Hindu, or taking Muhammad as a mediator to completely deviate from Islam. Apart from all these options, he still has an option to remain on his nature as a worshiper of God alone (Muslim).

Then, the group applauded.

He asked: Why are non-Muslims not allowed to enter Mecca?

I answered: Even a Muslim who takes Muhammad as a mediator between him and God is not welcome in Mecca. He would be told to stop begging the Messenger or otherwise he should leave the place.

He asked: Do you not find this against tolerance?

I asked: Can you buy vegetables from the bank in your country?

He answered: No.

I asked: Why?

He answered: Because the bank is only for financial transactions while buying vegetables is from the supermarket.

I told him: So, the bank guard is not intolerant when he tells you to go to the supermarket to buy vegetables because this place is for financial transactions. I added: Mecca is a place dedicated to worshiping God alone without an intermediary; it is for worship only and not for tourism.

Whoever wants to worship anyone else apart from God should not come to the house of God.

One of the group members asked: Why does God send human messengers to people like them? Why does he not send them angels instead?

I answered him: What suits human beings, is having another human like them speak in their language and set an example for them. But if God sent a prophet angel to them and did what was difficult for them, they would protest that he is an angel who can do what they cannot.

Say, "If there were angels on earth, walking around in peace, We would have sent down to them from heaven an angel messenger." 295

And if We had made him an angel, We would have made him [appear as] a man, and We would have covered them with that in which they cover themselves.[296]

He said: I believe in God, but I do not believe in the message of Muhammad or in Jesus, and I do not believe that God sends messengers.

I realized from his comment that he is Jewish, then I told him: If you knew the Almighty God properly, you would have known that it is impossible that he creates people, and then leaves them without providing them with the guidance that their souls need. He has provided people with all their bodies' needs of food, drinks, earth, air, sun, and moon, but then He leaves them to fall into confusion, bewilderment, and anxiety? It is not possible. If you do not believe that God sends messengers, then how do you believe in Moses? Who sent him the book that he brought?

---

[295] (Qur'an 17:95).
[296] (Qur'an 6:9).

And they did not appraise God with true appraisal when they said, "God did not reveal to a human being anything." Say, "Who revealed the Scripture that Moses brought as light and guidance to the people? You [Jews] make it into pages, disclosing [some of] it and concealing much. And you were taught that which you knew not – neither you nor your fathers." Say, "God [revealed it]." Then leave them in their [empty] discourse, amusing themselves.[297]

He asked: What is the evidence of Muhammad's prophecy?

I told him: The evidence of his prophecy is found in his biography. He was known as an honest and faithful man before his prophecy; he was an illiterate who did not read or write.

And you did not recite before it any scripture, nor did you inscribe one with your right hand. Otherwise the falsifiers would have had [cause for] doubt.[298]

The Messenger was the first who applied what he called for; he would confirm his words with his deeds. He never asked for worldly rewards for what he used to call for. He was a poor, merciful, and humble person, He sacrificed the most, and he was the most ascetic in what people have.

These are they whom God guided, therefore follow their guidance. Say: I do not ask you for any reward for it; it is nothing but a reminder to the nations.[299]

In addition, he presented evidence that confirms his prophecy, which is shown in the Quranic verses.

---

[297](Qur'an 6: 91).

[298] (Qur'an 29:48).

[299] (Qur'an 6: 90).

The verses are in the Prophet's language; they were rhetoric and eloquent, which makes them rise above the normal words of mankind.

Then do they not reflect upon the Qur'an? If it had been from [any] other than God, they would have found within it much contradiction.[300]

Do they say, 'He has fabricated it?' Say, 'Then bring ten chapters like it, fabricated, and invoke whomever you can, besides God, should you be truthful.[301]

But if they do not respond to you – then know that they only follow their [own] desires. And who is more astray than one who follows his desire without guidance from God? Indeed, God does not guide the wrongdoing people.[302]

The group member asked: What is the difference between the Prophet and the Messenger?

I answered: The Prophet is the one who was inspired by the Creator, but didn't bring a new message or book. The Messenger is the one whom God sent him a book with a method and law that suits his people, for example, the Torah, the Bible, the Qur'an, the scriptures of Abraham, and book of Salms, which was revealed to Prophet David.

He asked: Is the imam in Islam like a priest in Christianity?

I answered: The term Imam means a person who leads people in prayer, or takes care of their affairs and their leadership.

---

[300] (Qur'an 4:82).

[301] (Qur'an 11:13).

[302] (Qur'an 28:50).

It is not a religious rank confined to specific people. There is no hierarchy in Islam; all people are equal. The first to lead the prayer must be the person who memorized Qur'an the most, and knowledgeable of the provisions related to prayer. No matter how much the Imam receives respect from Muslims, he still never listens to confessions, nor does he forgive sins. Hence, his duty is different than the priest's duty.

He asked: What is the difference between Islamic thought and philosophy? I answered: Islamic thought is the set of science and knowledge based on Islamic foundations and controls.

If this knowledge is against the Islam foundations, then it is a non–Islamic thought. But the reality of philosophy is to delve into the science of speech, and the arbitration of mind in beliefs, including divinities, prophecies, metaphysics, and others without believing in revelation, and this contradicts the axioms of belief.

He asked: What is the difference between the prophet and the philosopher? I told him: The knowledge of extreme facts comes from God. The philosopher relies on his reason and logic to elicit realities and introduce philosophical concepts into it, while ignoring the limitations of his thinking as a human being. On the other hand, God reveals the facts to the messenger through revelation. There is no comparison between the messenger and the philosopher. A philosopher should follow the messenger, and the messenger must not follow the philosopher. The messenger is an envoy, and the philosopher is an envoy to him; revelation is the ruler, and the mind is ruled on it.

He asked: What is the new Sharia?

I answered: It is the legislation that contains something new that was not in the previous legislation.

And [I have come] confirming what was before me of the Torah and to make lawful for you some of what was forbidden to you. And I have come to you with a sign from your Lord, so fear God and obey me.[303]

He said: The universe is the only source of knowledge and there is no place for revelation. I told him: They are both together; the universe and the revelation. The creation of God and the revelation of God.

The sources of knowledge for a Muslim are the universe and revelation, and its means are sense and brain. As for the curriculum, it differs according to the type of knowledge and the type of source.

Say, 'Tell me about your partners [you ascribe to God] whom you invoke besides God? Show me what [part] of the earth have they created. Do they have any share in the heavens?' Have we given them a scripture so that they stand on a manifest proof thereof? Rather the wrongdoers do not promise one another [anything] except delusion.[304]

The verse here indicates that worshipping someone else apart from God includes the claim that they are deities, and God must be a creator.

---

[303] (Qur'an 3:50).
[304] (Qur'an 35:40).

The proof that he is the Creator is either witnessed by what He created in the universe, or by witnessing the inspiration from God who proved to be the Creator. So, if this claim does not have evidence from the creation of the universe, nor have evidence from the words of the Creator God, then the claim is necessarily null.

He asked: What is the opinion of Islam in the theory of knowledge and rationality of belief?

I answered: If you mean the theory of knowledge being the exact statement of reality, this is what Islam says.

Some Arabs believed that the smart man had two hearts. If one of the Arabs got angry at his wife, he would tell her you are like my mother. Other Arabs adopted a son from another family, and attributed him to themselves as if he was their biological son, similar to what people do in the West nowadays. So, Almighty God judged all these claims as mere words of the tongue, and it is against the truth.

God did not place two hearts inside any man's body. Nor did He make your wives whom you equate with your mothers, your actual mothers. Nor did He make your adopted sons, your actual sons. These are your words coming out of your mouths. God speaks the truth, and guides to the path. [305]

That is because God is the Truth, and that which they call upon other than Him is falsehood, and because God is the Most High, the Grand. [306]

---

[305] (Qur'an 33:4).
[306] (Qur'an 22:62).

The previous examples show the difference between truth and falsehood, for truth reflects true knowledge that matches reality, and falsehood is an illusion.

The Noble Qur'an affirms the possibility of acquiring knowledge after a person's birth.

God has brought you forth from the bellies of your mothers while you did not know anything. He made for you hearing, eyesight, and hearts so that you may give thanks.[307]

The senses, such as hearing and sight, are all connected to the brain. They are the source of the inputs, and the brain performs the process of dismantling these inputs (the process of reasoning), which produces the idea relating to the feeling that drives a person to a certain behavior. The brain converts the following signals through the senses into things that make sense to a person.

The mind displays the thoughts and ideas in the heart, which activates the heart muscle and then shows an effect. This can be similar to a battery found in the cavity of the brain, and attached to a nerve wire to a lamp located in the heart muscle. The lamp illuminates from this battery in the brain, and therefore we see in the Holy Qur'an the words of Almighty God:

… It is not the eyes that go blind, but it is the hearts, within the chests, that go blind.[308]

In other words, delusion in the human mind extinguishes the light of the heart that is in the chest, which is a reflection of the misguided thoughts in the interior of man.

The sense that is related the most to the brain is hearing.

---

[307] (Qur'an 16:78).
[308] (Qur'an 22:46).

A person hears:

- Sounds of natural things like thunder, wind, and birds.
- Words, which are sounds that denote meanings and the Holy Qur'an often uses hearing by this meaning.

As for the one who does not understand speech and does not benefit from it, the Qur'an resembles it with an animal that can only hear voices.

Do you suppose that most of them listen or apply reason? They are just like cattle; rather they are further astray from the way.[309]

The parable of the faithless is that of someone who shouts after that which does not hear [anything] except a call and cry: deaf, dumb, and blind, they do not apply reason.[310]

As for the speech, some of it is right and some of it is invalid, and there is no way to know this with sense alone, so, the mind must join it and decide first whether the speech is contradictory or consistent, and if it finds it contradictory, it is a judgment that invalidates it.

Although a person comes out of his mother's womb, he does not know anything, but his mind is natively associated with monotheism.

In the saying of the Prophet Muhammad, we read:

Every child that is born, is born upon the Fitrah (natural faith), but his parents make him a Jew, a Christian, or a Zoroastrian.[311]

We now understand that:

- A person is born while having the seed of monotheism planted in his mind, which is the recognition that there is no god worthy of being worshiped except the One God (the Creator).

- A human being is born with a nature that is appropriate only for the facts and rulings that Islam has brought as a belief and behavior.

So set your heart on the religion as a people of pure faith, the origination of God according to which He originated mankind.[312]

Therefore, Man does not feel calm and comfortable unless he is a Muslim, who is a worshiper of God alone.

Those who have faith, and whose hearts find rest in the remembrance of God.' Look! The hearts find rest in God's remembrance! [313]

The group member asked: Is the truth the opposite of beauty, art, and culture in Islam?

I previously read books that discussed this matter, and I confidently answered: The "truth" in Islam was formulated to conform to the delicate aesthetic taste; it addresses human instinct and indicates what achieves his happiness in this world and the Hereafter.

Say, 'Indeed my prayer and my worship, my life and my death are for the sake of God, the Lord of all the worlds. He has no partner, and this [creed] I have been commanded [to follow], and I am the first of those who submit [to God].[314]

The Qur'anic text combines all the aesthetic phenomena with the necessity of thanking their Creator. The texts of the sayings of Prophet Muhammad have shown that the Muslim is required to show God's blessings upon him in apparent and hidden adornment, as showing God's blessings is considered a part of our thanks and love towards God.

---

[312] (Qur'an 30:30).
[313] (Qur'an 13 :28).
[314] (Qur'an 6:162-163).

Messenger of God said:

God is Beautiful, He loves beauty.[315]

Beauty here takes its legitimacy from the teachings of Islam that exhorts a Muslim to take adornments in every detail of his daily life. Taking adornments starts with the purification for prayer, and taking care of appearance beauty, clothing, housing, and transportation through the aesthetics of speech and communication.

The guidance is associated with exaggeration of adornment in marital relations.

Islam surrounds them with numbers of aesthetic recommendations that do not overlook the details of the beautiful word, a caring outlook, and ending with the various etiquette to relieving oneself, cleaning teeth, perfuming and the selection of beautiful clothes. It is a targeted and purposeful aesthetic education that aims to shaping the aesthetic behavior of a Muslim. It is evident in his daily creativity, bowing and prostrating, praying, and invocating, fasting and night prayer (tahajjud), writing and authorship, drawing and engraving, building and architecture.

In fact, the problem of contradicting religion with beauty is a western problem, and not Islamic. The destabilization of religious values in the West, and the bad attitude that intellectuals, writers, and artists have stopped against ecclesiastical perceptions and their history, have helped with trying to exclude them from life, thought and art in general, similar to what happened between the ecclesiastical perceptions, politics, and science.

The world today is in dire need of aesthetic productions that return a person to his humanity, and bring him happiness, which he missed in the midst of

---

[315] (Sahih Muslim).

his physical preoccupations, along with his inability to harmonize the requirements of the soul with the needs of the body.

This lack of humanity occurred after the person's feelings sagged because of consuming all what the media informed him.

This media reached our homes today, restricted human awareness, and made people captive to the small screen in the house.

Brzezinski, the former US National Security Adviser, says in his book "Collapse.": "We have become a society of pornographic permissibility. The individual has violated everything; the words "forbidden" or "prohibited" are no longer in his dictionary.

Thus, civilization will not be righteous and will not continue. The whole ship is sinking and no one has the right to save it, and saving it depends on a return to religion and morals."

The group member commented: Art and beauty are the sources of culture.

I told him: Culture produces art and beauty, not the opposite.

Willis, a cultural ethnographer, says:

"The boundaries between arts and non-arts must be completely redrawn or abolished, so, it is necessary to not just criticize the view that contributes to art producing culture, but we must declare that culture is what actually produces art, not the opposite."

Various philosophies have presented their perceptions of art and beauty since ancient times. These perceptions are contradictive and confusing:

- "Plato" attributes beauty to the eternal example, which is a remnant of memories of the soul, and this is explained by the theory of simulation.

- "Aristotle" vetoed the theory of simulation and the world of example, and he was interested with reality. He believed that beauty had the consistency of composition.
- "Baumgarten" linked beauty with sense and feeling.
- Kant considered art is a target by itself.
- Gauthier said: There is nothing really beautiful unless it is useless and everything that is useful is ugly.
- "Fichte" sees art as self-liberation.
- German philosopher "Schopenhauer" said: Beauty is in spiritually
- pure meditation without mixing it with our will, so it nullifies the will of Man.[316]

Literature in Islam is committed to an obligation of truth and certainty; it is also committed to language and religion. It is an expression of an issue or subject by pure permissible means. It provides halal (permissible) pleasure that God has permitted to His servants, as well as provides security and safety. Literature in Islam also helps a person fulfill his covenant with Almighty God, which is worship, honesty, succession, and architecture for the land by faith and monotheism. Islam has transferred literature to wide scale that has not happened in human history. It has moved the Arabic language from being the language of one people to being the language of the final prophecy, and the language of worship and obedience to God for every Muslim forever throughout the earth and time.

Islamic aesthetic is achieved through conveying the message of monotheism to the world, in order to worship only One God who is impeccable of partners and equals.

---

[316] *Islamic literature on its topics and terminology.* Adnan Bin Ali Rida Bin Muhammad Al Nahawi.

Who has a better call than him who summons to God and acts righteously and says, 'Indeed I am one of the Muslims ? [317]

Beauty is manifested in the human instinct, which was originated by God. It is also manifested in the soul of the believer and the way he was created, then it's manifested in his work, along with his words and statement: beautiful patience, beautiful forgiveness, beautiful release, beautiful abandonment, etc. So, beauty extends in the perception of the believer until he lives with true beauty in all things, and that's according to his faith, his connection with the universe, the awareness of his beauty, and his connection with the Creator of the universe.[318]

We certainly created man in the best of forms, then We relegated him to the lowest of the low, except those who have faith and do righteous deeds. There will be an everlasting reward for them.[319]

He created the cattle, in which there is warmth for you and [other] uses and some of them you eat. There is in them a beauty for you when you bring them home for rest and when you drive them forth to pasture.[320]

And you see the mountains, thinking them rigid, while they will pass as the passing of clouds. [It is] the work of God, who perfected all things. Indeed, He is Acquainted with that which you do.[321]

The group member said: How did the language arise? Is it similar to what scientists say, emerging from the sounds of apes?

---

[317] (Qur'an 41: 33).

[318] *Islamic literature on its topics and terminology*. Adnan Bin Ali Rida Bin Muhammad Al Nahawi.

[319] (Qur'an 95: 4-6).

[320] (Qur'an 16:5-6).

[321] (Qur'an 27:88).

His question made me laugh; I recently read about this topic, so I confidently told him: It has been proven that the language nature is inherently (genetically) programmed in the structure of our brains, and that all the languages of the world share the same rules that govern them.[322]

Among His signs is the creation of the heavens and the earth, and the difference of your languages and colors. There are indeed signs in that for those who know.[323]

The Noble Qur'an mentioned that Almighty God taught Adam all the names.

And He taught Adam the Names, all of them; then presented them to the angels and said, 'Tell me the names of these, if you are truthful".[324]

God taught Adam the names means that Adam learned that everything has a name, whether it is a physical thing like water and sky, or something immaterial like pain and light, or an abstract meaning like freedom and happiness. This is called coding, and the ability to code is one of the finest human mental talents which is practiced by himself and no one else. It is considered one of the fundamental differences between humans and other beings.

He created man, [and] taught him articulate speech.[325]

The statement is the formulation of ideas rationally and according to the rules. The human being uses the symbols which he gave to things. In addition, he uses the rules of the language programmed in his mind.

---

[322] Naom Chomsky, was the greatest linguist of the twentieth century.

[323] (Qur'an 30:22).

[324] (Qur'an 2: 31).

[325] (Qur'an 55:3-4).

By the Lord of the heaven (sky) and the earth, it is indeed the truth, just as [it is a fact that] you speak.[326]

Pronunciation is the next stage in the spoken language, and it is performed by the speech organs (larynx, pharynx, and mouth), and the brain centers which are responsible for the work of this device.

This system will not have a benefit and value if it does not have a receiver of this spoken information, so Almighty God created hearing for us.

Say, 'It is He who created you, and made for you hearing, eyesight, and hearts. Little do you thank'.[327]

The human language system is complemented by the rationalization of what a person hears and understands.

…Thus, do we elaborate the signs for a people who apply reason.[328]

Modern medicine has reached types of imbalances that can affect the pronunciation system. For example, there can be a person who does not understand what he hears, or another person might be unable to hear. In addition, there can be someone else who is unable to pronounce, someone who cannot formulate his thoughts, or someone who looks at something and does not find its name in his mind.[329]

The group member asked: What do you think of Einstein's time relativity concept when he said: "We do not have to talk about time without space, nor about place without time, and as long as everything moves, it must carry its time, and when the object moves faster, its time will shrink in comparison to other times which associated with other movements slower than it"?

---

[326] (Qur'an 51: 23).

[327] (Qur'an 67: 23).

[328] (Qur'an 30: 28).

[329] *Illusion of Atheism*. Dr. Amr Sharif.

I answered: The Holy Qur'an referred to the relativity of time, and mentioned that there is a day of a thousand years in length, and a day of fifty thousand years in length.

He directs the command from the heaven to the earth; then it ascends toward Him in a day whose span is a thousand years by your reckoning. [330]

The angels and the Spirit ascend to Him in a day whose span is fifty thousand years. [331]

The time, as Einstein says, does not have a single, self-standing fact as characteristic of matter. Also, the universe is like a book in which incidents are accurately recorded, so every movement, action or saying is recorded in this universe. In addition, everything that a person utters from the day of his birth until his death is preserved, and this is what is mentioned with an amazing accuracy in the Holy Qur'an.

He says no word but that there is a ready observer beside him. [332]

We also have other signs that indicate the Holy Qur'an addressing the concept of time relativity.

They remained in the Cave for three hundred years, and added nine more [to that number]. [333]

Say, 'God knows best how long they remained. To Him belongs the Unseen of the heavens and the earth. How well does He see! How

---

[330] (Qur'an 32: 5).

[331] (Qur'an 70 :4).

[332] (Qur'an 50: 18).

[333] (Qur'an 18: 25).

well does He hear! They have no guardian besides Him, and none shares with Him in His judgment.[334]

Almighty God mentioned here that they stayed 300 years and increased nine.

The Qur'an preceded all the sciences of astronomy when it estimated the period that the cave people stayed in the cave. They stayed three hundred years, which equals to 309 years.

Every 300 solar years equal to 300 x 365,25 = 109575 days, and 300 lunar years equal to 300 x 354,37 = 106311 days.

The difference between the two calendars is 109575 –106311 = 3264 days = 9 years. So, 309 lunar years correspond to 300 Gregorian years, with a difference of 9 years.

In addition, 300 years (109575) equals to 88 109575 in Mercury (Mercury year 88 Earth days) 1245 years.

Also, these 300 years on Earth equals to 109575 243 = 451 years on planet Venus, and equals to 109575 687 = 59.5 years on planet Mars.

Thus, time remains relative, but the true value does not exist except for Almighty God, who surrounded time and space.

Say, 'God knows best how long they remained. To Him belongs the Unseen of the heavens and the earth.[335]

The Holy Qur'an also mentions the relativity of worldly life.

He will say, 'How many years did you remain on earth?' They will say, 'We remained for a day, or part of a day; yet ask those who keep

---

[334] (Qur'an 18: 26).
[335] (Qur'an 18: 26).

the count.' He will say, 'You only remained a little; if only you had known.[336]

And on the day when the Hour sets in the guilty will swear that they had remained only for an hour. That is how they were used to lying [in the world]. [337]

It will be, on the Day they see it, as though they had not remained [in the world] except for an afternoon or a morning thereof. [338]

Then the group member said: Many scholars say that every era must document history from its point of view, because each generation's appreciation of what is important and meaningful to them differs from the other generation. Every generation tries to see the past through its interests and ideas prevailing in it, which means history is relative.

I replied: This is true, but this does not negate the fact that events have one truth, whether we like it or not. The documentation of human beings was subjected to distortion and inaccuracy of events, and it was based on whims, unlike the documentation of the God, which has very accurate past, present, and future.

Byzantium has been vanquished in a nearby territory (lowest), but following their defeat they will be victors in a few years. All command belongs to God, before and after, and on that day the faithful will rejoice at God's help. He helps whomever He wishes, and He is the All-mighty, the All-merciful.[339]

These verses mention the defeat of the Byzantines against the Persians at the Battle of Antioch. God the Almighty promised the Muslims that the defeat

---

[336] (Qur'an 23: 112-114).

[337] (Qur'an 30:55).

[338] (Qur'an 79: 46).

[339] (Qur'an 30: 2-5).

would turn into a victory for the Byzantines in a few years. The Byzantines' victory was important for the Muslims because they were Christians, and Christians were followers of a heavenly religion, while the Persians were a follower of the Zoroastrian religion which is a pagan religion. The battle took place in the area surrounding the Dead Sea (located in the groove of the Jordan Valley).

The most interesting fact for non-Muslims, which was recently discovered through satellites and modern technology, is that the area surrounding the Dead Sea is the lowest on the earth, and this is a Qur'anic miracle. This fact was not known or expected for the non-Muslims in the seventh century, as satellites and modern technology were not available at that time. The only possible explanation is that the Prophet Muhammad received a divine revelation from God – the Creator of the universe.

After about 7 years of revealing these verses God's promise in the Qur'an was fulfilled by victory for the Romans miraculously. The Qur'an preceded the theory of history relativity, too, in the codification of events in the Preserved Tablet.

We have attached every person's omen to his neck, and We shall bring it out for him on the Day of Resurrection as a wide–open book that he will encounter. 'Read your book! Today your soul suffices as your own reckoner'. [340]

The group member asked: How do you see the concept of enlightenment?

I answered him: The Islamic concept of enlightenment is based on a firm foundation of faith and science, which combines enlightenment of mind

---

[340] (Qur'an 17: 13-14).

with the enlightenment of the heart, with faith in God first, and with the knowledge that is inseparable from faith.

The concept of European enlightenment has been transferred to Islamic societies like other western concepts. Enlightenment in the Islamic concept does not depend on the abstract mind that is not guided by the light of faith.

In addition, Man does not benefit his faith if he does not use his mind, the gift that God gave him, in thinking, meditating, forethinking, and doing things in a way that fulfills the public interest, benefits people, and stays forever.

In the dark medieval, Muslims restored the light of civilization and advancement that had been extinguished in all countries of the West and East until Constantinople.

The Enlightenment movement in Europe was a natural reaction to the despotism exercised by the ecclesiastical authorities against reason and human will. This situation was not known nor it existed in the Islamic civilization.

God is the Guardian of the faithful: He brings them out of darkness into light. As for the faithless, their patrons are the Rebels, who drive them out of light into darkness. They shall be the inmates of the Fire, and they shall remain in it [forever].[341]

Reflecting on these Qur'anic verses, we find that God's Will takes out a person from darkness. This is known as the "Divine Guidance" for a person. It does not take place except with God's permission because a person who God brings out from the darkness of ignorance, polytheism,

---

[341] (Qur'an 2: 257).

and superstition to the light of faith, science, and true knowledge is a person who has a bright mind, insight, and conscience. The Almighty God referred to the Noble Qur'an as light as well.

… Certainly, there has come to you a light from God, and a manifest Book.[342]

The Noble Qur'an and the non–distorted (Torah and Gospel) were sent by Almighty God to His messengers for guiding people to get out of the darkness to the light, and thus, God associated the guidance with light.

We sent down the Torah containing guidance and light…[343]

…We gave him the Evangel containing guidance and light, confirming what was before it of the Torah, and as guidance and advice for the God wary.[344]

There is no guidance without God's light, and there is no light that can illuminate a person's heart and his life without God's permission.

God is the Light of the heavens and the earth…[345]

Here, we note that in Qur'an the light comes single in all situations, while darkness comes in plural, and this is very accurate in describing these conditions.[346]

As for those who strive in Us, We shall surely guide them in Our ways:

I remember that I received a call from a colleague of mine on the weekend, and he told me that a South American boxer, during his participation in an international boxing competition, wanted to know about Islam. He was

---

[342] (Qur'an 5: 15).

[343] (Qur'an 5: 44).

[344] (Qur'an 5:46).

[345] (Qur'an 24: 35).

[346] https://www.albayan.ae/five-senses/2001-11-16-1.1129413

only free on a Friday, and he didn't speak English; they wanted someone who speaks Spanish to be able to talk to him.

I asked my husband, and he said that we can meet him together in a public place.

Eventually, I met him with my husband and daughter on Friday in a nearby cafe. He was accompanied by a delegation from the club who hosted him, and he announced his conversion to Islam at the end of the meeting.

Among his questions, he asked me: Are there saints in Islam?

I answered: No.

He exclaimed: So, you do not have righteous people? You do not sanctify the companions of the Prophet Muhammad?!!

I answered: We follow the righteous and the companions of the Messenger. We love them and try to be good like them, and we worship God alone as they did, but we do not sanctify them nor make them a mediator between us and God.

He said: For example, I carry a necklace with the Star of David because my name is David, so if I become a Muslim, should I take it off?

I told him: First of all, the Prophet David, peace be upon him, was one of the honored prophets in the Qur'an like other prophets. In the Holy Qur'an, God has cleared all the bad traits which were attributed to them from distortions in books of the Old and New Testament. The Qur'an mentioned how creatures praised God with Prophet David for the beauty of his voice.

We bestowed upon David favor from Us: "O mountains, and birds: echo with him." And We softened iron for him.[347]

Muslims have no problem with the prophets; they have a problem with those who distorted God's religion, and turned this star into a political symbol.

He said: What is the difference between Shiites and Sunnis?

I told him: Prophet Muhammad was not a Sunni nor a Shiite, but he was a true Muslim. Also, Christ was not a Catholic nor any other, but he was Muslim. Both worshipped God without a mediator. Christ did not worship himself nor worship his mother, nor did Prophet Muhammad beg himself, his daughter, or her husband.

In addition, when someone in Medina rumored that the sun was eclipsed by the death of Abraham who was the son of the Prophet, the Prophet spoke to them fourteen centuries ago. He said a valuable phrase, which was a message for everyone who adopts countless myths about the eclipse of the sun these days. He said:

The sun and the moon do not eclipse because of someone's death. So whenever you see these eclipses pray and invoke God (Allah) till the eclipse is over.[348]

The emergence of many different groups due to political problems or any other problem is possible, but it has nothing to do with religion. However, this term "Sunnah" means that you follow the Messenger's approach entirely, and the term "Shiites" means a group of people who have defected from the approach which was taken by the Muslim consensus.

Indeed, those who have divided their religion and become sects – you, [O Muhammad], are not [associated] with them in anything.

---

[348] (Sahih Al Bukhari)

Their affair is only [left] to God; then He will inform them about what they used to do.[349]

But who is better than God in judgment for a people who have certainty?

The young man asked persistently: What is the meaning of jihad?

I told him: "Jihad" means striving to stop oneself from sin. The mother's Jihad in her pregnancy is to bear the pain of pregnancy. The student's diligence in his studies, the struggle of the defender of his money, his family and his religion are examples of jihad. Even persevering in acts of worship such as fasting and praying on time is considered a type of jihad.

Islam appreciates life, so it is not permissible to fight both peaceful people and civilians. Additionally, property, children, and women must be protected even during wars. It is also not permissible to mutilate the bodies of the dead people, as it is not an ethic of Islam.

Allah does not forbid you from those who do not fight you because of religion and do not expel you from your homes – from being righteous toward them and acting justly toward them. Indeed, Allah loves those who act justly. God only forbids you from those who fight you because of religion and expel you from your homes and aid in your expulsion – [forbids] that you make allies of them. And whoever makes allies of them, then it is those who are the wrongdoers.[350]

Because of that, We decreed upon the Children of Israel that whoever kills a soul unless for a soul or for corruption [done] in the land – it is as if he had slain mankind entirely. And whoever saves

---

[349] (Qur'an 6: 159).
[350] (Qur'an 60:8-9).

one – it is as if he had saved mankind entirely. And our messengers had certainly come to them with clear proofs. Then indeed many of them, [even] after that, throughout the land, were transgressors.[351]

A non-Muslim is one of four:

The secured people:

They are the ones who were given safety by Muslims.

The rule includes those who entered our country with a tourist visa, and those who resided on our land.

And if any one of the polytheists seeks your protection, then grant him protection so that he may hear the words of God. Then deliver him to his place of safety. That is because they are a people who do not know.[352]

People of the treaty "Ahd":

They are the ones who are promised by Muslims to leave the fighting

The rule includes most of the countries of the world in our time.

Except those idolaters with whom you have a treaty, who have not failed you in the least, nor helped anyone against you. Fulfil your obligations to them during the term (of the treaty). God loves those who take heed for themselves.[353]

People of the "Dhimma":

"Dhimma" is a historical term referring to non-Muslims living in an Islamic state with legal protection by paying Al "Jizia", which is a type of a (Poll Tax), imposed on non-Muslim citizens of an Islamic state, for

---

[351] (Qur'an 5: 32).
[352] (Qur'an 9: 6).
[353] (Qur'an 9:4).

which their lives, progeny, possessions, are protected by the State. They are entitled to practice their religion without any interference by anyone not from their faith. In addition, they are guaranteed to settle their intra community disputes according to their own traditions and laws, not according to the Islamic law (Sharia). They are exempted from military service while being entitled to full protection from alien enemies. It is similar to the tax paid by millions during our time in exchange for the state's care of their affairs.

Fight those who do not have faith in God nor [believe] in the Last Day, nor forbid what God and His Apostle have forbidden, nor practice the true religion, from among those who were given the Book, until they pay the tribute out of hand, degraded.[354]

The fighters:

They are the ones who declared the fight against Muslims, as these have no covenant, no obligation, and no safety. They are the ones in whom Almighty God said:

And fight with them until there is no more persecution and religion should be only for God; but if they desist, then surely God sees what they do. [355]

This category of fighters is the one that we must fight only. God did not command killing, but fighting, and there is a big difference between them. Fighting here means confrontation along with war for self-defense, and this is what all statutory laws stipulate.

---

[354] (Qur'an 9:29).
[355] (Qur'an 8: 39).

Fight in the way of God those who fight you, but do not transgress. Indeed, God does not like transgressors.[356]

He asked: Isn't the term infidel contempt for the other side?

I answered: Am I not considered infidel for a Christian because I do not believe in the Trinity doctrine? The term disbeliever means the person who denies the truth. The truth for me as a Muslim is Monotheism, and for Christians its Trinity.

He asked: Why does Islam reward those people who carry out suicide operations by obtaining virgins after death?

I answered: It is illogical for the giver of life (God) to order Man to end his life, and to take lives of others without guilt, while at the same time He says "Do not kill yourselves". There are also other verses that forbade killing other souls unless there is a justification, such as retribution, or counteracting aggression without violating the rights of others. Suicide operations were found to serve the interests of groups that are not related to religion or its purposes. They are away from the grace and morals of this great religion. The bliss of heavens should not be based on that narrow view of obtaining virgins only, for Paradise has what no eye has seen, nor an ear heard, and no heart has perceived.

Young people today suffer from economic conditions, and the inability to earn money that should help them with marriage. This kind of suffering makes them become easy prey for the promoters of these heinous acts, especially those who are addicted and those who suffer from psychological disorders. If the promoters believed in this idea, first they would start by themselves, before they sent the youth to this task.

---

[356] (Qur'an 2: 190).

Conclusion:

We conclude that only Islam provides renaissance and real science within the framework of a rational understanding of the function of religion in life. Islam provided harmony between reason and religion, reason and the information transformed through narrated chains (Qur'an and sayings of Prophet Muhammed), along with harmony between the mind and heart. Therefore, there is no enlightenment, renaissance, progress, beauty, or true science except by embracing the religion of Islam.

There is also conscious balance between the requirements of Sharia (Islamic Law) and the requirements of life without violating the rule of the true religion, or giving away one of the established principles of religion.

The sense alone could not help those who depended on it to reach the whole truth, but rather it led to deviation and corruption of their opinions, because the sense is a part of a complete truth that is only completed by other factors.

Also, those who ignored the mind but they sought inner knowledge through intuition or conscience alone failed to reach the whole truth. Hence, the Islamic theory of knowledge provided a connection between the mind and the heart, and a connection between this world and the unseen world.

The Qur'an introduces the Creator to people with words that they do not find in the philosophy books or books of other religions. It also guides them to the way in which they should worship this Creator, and to the morals that people should take in treating each other. In addition, it also guides them to transcend their spirit, and forbids them to degrade their status.

The Qur'an provided them with an integrated life approach, from beliefs, worship, and morals, to the social system as an individual, family and society, and to relations with non-Muslims, in a balanced manner that meets the mental, physical, and spiritual needs

....**Thus, He completes His blessings upon you, so that you may submit.**[357]

---

[357] (Qur'an 16: 81).

Whoever Seeks a Religion Other Than Islam?

The Instinct God instilled in Humanity:

I was having a conversation with a British family consisting of a father, mother, and a ten-year-old child. While I was answering the mother's question about the Muslim faith, the beautiful and smart boy asked me: So according to what I understand from your words, if I was taking an exam at school and there was a difficult question, if I supplicated directly to God without Christ, I am a Muslim? I answered him: Yes. I then remembered the noble verse: **So, devote yourself to the religion of monotheism – the natural instinct God has instilled in mankind...** [358]and I rejoiced with joy as I was able to tell from his understanding that the message I wanted to deliver arrived successfully.

---

[358] (Qur'an 30:30).

And the mercy of your Lord is better than whatever they accumulate:

I was having a dialogue with a famous Latin soccer player, his mother, and his doctor. The concept of monotheism entirely convinced them. One of the questions they had was about Muslims' failure to express themselves and report the correct religion.

The player said: Cartoons that offend the Messenger Muhammad are a series of cartoons that also happen to offend Christ and the Creator himself. The people who draw these cartoons are atheists who devote their time and effort to mocking all critical symbols in religions. Why do Muslims not protest in anger when they offend the Creator, for example, or even Christ, and only demonstrate for the Prophet Muhammad's sake? These actions resulted in a great misunderstanding, as we are sure that Muhammad is a god of Muslims.

I told him: This is true, but Muslims are imperfect. They are people who sin and strike.

I told them: I, myself, am very shocked at the fact that there are a vast number of Muslims in Europe, for example, and Europeans still don't know about Islam except for the pillars of Islam, such as prayer, Zakat (giving alms), and fasting. They don't know about the pillars of faith, including the belief in Jesus's prophecy and the true Bible.

I remember the story of a large group from the State of Panama. A big bus brought them to us, and they came very late after a busy day. It was clear that the tour guide who accompanied them brought them late because she didn't want to allow them to listen to a brief presentation about Islam.

She told me that time is limited, and then she jokingly said: You look tired. There is not much time left for the call to Maghreb (sunset) prayer; the tourists will have to leave the mosque hall immediately.

I told her: No, I am not tired. I can end the visit before the call to Maghreb (sunset) prayer starts.

She reluctantly accepted. I began talking to them and was surprised when everyone sat on the ground. They then brought me questions that include the difference between Islam, Judaism and Christianity, the prophecy of Prophet Muhammad, etc.

I told them: The religion of Islam is the religion of monotheism practiced by many in your country by nature. It means worshipping God alone without a mediator, and the belief that Christ is one of the messengers of God.

They said: Who is Allah?

I told them: Christians, Jews and Muslims in the Middle East use the word {Allah} to refer to God, which means the One True God, the God of Moses and Jesus. The word {Allah} was mentioned 89 times in the old version of the Old Testament.

Someone said: I read the Qur'an. Why does the Creator refer to Himself in plural form if He is One and not a Trinity?

I told him: The reference of God to Himself as WE or US in many verses of the Qur'an denotes Grandeur and Power in Arabic. In the English language, this is known as the royal WE, where a plural pronoun refers to a single person holding a high office, such as a monarch.

For avoiding doubt, the Qur'an has consistently reminded us of the SINGULAR pronoun about God, when called upon by His servants.

The tour guide then became angrier when the tourists kept refusing every time she asked them to leave because of the limited time. When it was eventually time for prayer, they still refused to leave because of the many questions they had. They consistently kept saying: We found the truth, and our years of life were lost without knowing it.

I also remember the story of a Mexican basketball team who were a group of young people under twenty years old that were carefully selected for their height. Their crew accompanied them as well.

I told them: A Muslim is whoever believes in One God and worships Him alone without a **mediator**, and believes that Muhammad is a messenger, along with Jesus.

They shouted in one voice and said: This is what we believe in; more than half of the team declared shahada: "I bear witness there is no god but One God (Allah), **and Muhammad is the final Messenger of God**". The rest rushed to ask for a Spanish translation of the Qur'an, including booklets for reading. Some of them wept too; I said to myself: What did I say that made them glow with joy? I spoke for only a few minutes. **Glory be to Allah who created the pure hearts for the correct religion.**

I met with a ninety-year-old British woman, a widow of a distinguished person in society. She came with her British friend and her Indian driver. The woman cried as soon as I started talking, and said: I believe that there is no god but God and that Jesus is the Messenger of God.

Then she said: I love my husband very much, and he died ten years ago. If I converted to Islam now, what would be the fate of my husband? Will I meet him in heaven?

I told her: What was your husband's belief in Christ? Did he also believe that he is a prophet? Or did he believe that he is a god?

She said: Will you believe me if I tell you that I do not know? Our marriage lasted sixty years, and I do not remember discussing this issue. Then the lady's cry increased until I felt sorry for her.

I told her: God is more merciful with his creation than the mother with her son. He has mercy on those who have in their hearts an **atom's weight** of faith. Perhaps your husband is among them, and that is according to God's will.

The lady left the mosque because her friend urged that she didn't like the dialogue and wanted to go. The lady never asked me to convert to Islam.

The lady returned about three months later with her grandson, his girlfriend, and the lady's driver who came last time. She asked the reception staff about me, and I was thrilled to see her.

Her driver told me: Ever since she left that meeting, she never stopped talking about it. She wants to announce her Islam, because she is convinced that it is the true religion, and frankly, I am also very convinced of that.

After the **woman declared the testimony, I** told him: **Do** you want to witness the same?

He said: Unfortunately, I am deeply convinced of this religion, but I cannot change the faith of my fathers and grandparents.

Should We treat the true believers and the wrongdoers alike?

An atheist once asked me: Why does God punish His servants if they do not believe in Him?

I told him: We must differentiate between faith and submission to the Lord of the Worlds.

The right required for the Lord of the Worlds, which no one can leave, recognizes His oneness and His worship alone. He has no partner; the Creator alone has the Kingship along with the command, whether we are satisfied or not; this is the origin of faith. We do not have another option, and accordingly, Man is accountable and punished.

Anything opposite to submission is a crime.

Shall We then treat the (submitting) Muslims like the criminals (polytheists and disbelievers, etc.)? [359]

Injustice is worshipping a partner along with the Lord of the Worlds.

...So do not attribute to God equals while you know [that there is nothing similar to Him. [360]

They who believe and do not mix their belief with injustice – those will have security, and they are [rightly] guided. [361]

He said: What would I lose if I disbelieved in the Creator?

---

[359] (Qur'an 68:35).
[360] (Qur'an 2:22).
[361] (Qur'an 6:82).

I told him: The condition of any disbeliever in the worldly life:

The saddest among people, even if he's pretending to be happy.

And whoever turns away from My remembrance – indeed, he will have a depressed [i.e., difficult] life, and We will gather [i.e., raise] him on the Day of Resurrection blind.[362]

When calamity happens to a disbeliever, he is not rewarded.

And We will approach [i.e., regard] what they have done of deeds and make them as dust dispersed.[363]

When no one can help the disbeliever, he does not know who else to ask.

…And those they call upon besides Him do not respond to them with a thing, except as one who stretches his hands toward water [from afar, calling it] to reach his mouth, but it will not reach it [thus]. And the supplication of the disbelievers is not but in error [i.e., futility].[364]

The disbeliever's best helpers are the weak creatures.

…And for (the ones) who have disbelieved, their constant patrons are the Taghut (i.e., false gods, idols, devils, and seducers) who bring them out of the light into the darknesses; those are the companions of the Fire; they are therein eternally (abiding).[365]

---

[362] (Qur'an 20:124).
[363] (Qur'an 25:23).
[364] (Qur'an 13:14).
[365] (Qur'an 2:257).

If something makes the disbeliever happy, he still knew that he would die; hence it won't last.

…And they exult with (the present) life; (Literally: the lowly "life", i.e., the life of this world) and in no way is the present life, besides the Hereafter, (anything) except a (passing) enjoyment (Literally: belongings).[366]

If the disbeliever suffers from injustice, he does not think that all the Ever–Living Sustainer of all creatures will support him.

Whosoever thinks God will not help him in the present world and the world to come; let him stretch up a rope to heaven, then let him sever it, and behold whether his guile does away with what enrages him. [367]

After all that, how does he not commit suicide?

The condition of a disbeliever in the afterlife:

He asks for safety, but he does not find any.

But those who disbelieved – their deeds are like a mirage in a lowland which a thirsty one thinks is water until, when he comes to it, he finds it is nothing but finds God before Him, and He will pay him in full his due; and God is swift in account. [368]

---

[366] (Qur'an 13:26).
[367] (Qur'an 22:15).
[368] (Qur'an 24:39).

The disbeliever would ask for help from those who worshipped other than God, so they abandon him.

And it will be said, "Invoke your 'partners'" and they will invoke them; but they will not respond to them, and they will see the punishment. If only they had followed guidance![369]

The disbeliever would seek bliss, but he does not find.

And the companions of the Fire will call to the companions of Paradise, "Pour upon us some water or from whatever God has provided you." They will say, "Indeed, God has forbidden them both to the disbeliever.[370]

The disbeliever asks to win bliss, but he ends up losing.

On the [same] Day the hypocrite men and hypocrite women will say to those who believed, "Wait for us that we may acquire some of your light." It will be said, "Go back behind you and seek light." And a wall will be placed between them with a door, its interior containing mercy, but on the outside of it is torment.[371]

He even requests **permission** to get rid of the torment, yet he cannot.

And they will call, "O Malik, let your Lord put an end to us!" He will say, "Indeed, you will remain."[372]

---

[369] (Qur'an 28:64).
[370] (Qur'an 7:50).
[371] (Qur'an 57:13).
[372] (Qur'an 43:77).

Even the devil abandons him.

And Satan will say when the matter has been concluded, "Indeed, God had promised you the promise of truth. And I promised you, but I betrayed you. But I had no authority over you except that I invited you, and you obeyed me. So do not blame me; but blame yourselves. I cannot help you, nor can you help me. I reject the way you associated me with God before.' A bitter torment awaits such wrongdoers.[373]

The disbeliever will forever be immortalized in the fire.

As for those who were [destined to be] wretched, they will be in the Fire. For them therein is [violent] exhaling and inhaling. [They will be] abiding therein as long as the heavens and the earth endure, except what your Lord should will. Indeed, your Lord is an effecter of what He intends.[374]

If stones spoke, along with trees birds, they would have said: There is no god but God (Allah), the Mighty King.

If We had sent down this Qur'an upon a mountain, you would have seen it humbled and coming apart from fear of God. And these examples We present to the people that perhaps they will give thought.[375]

---

[373] (Qur'an 14:22).
[374] (Qur'an 11:106-107).
[375] (Qur'an 59:21).

The sentence "There is no god but God", is the Fort of God, the Key to Heaven, and Safety from torment. It is the best remembrance, and there is no barrier between it and God, and it is required for the **Messenger's** intercession.

The Messenger of God said:

The happiest with my intercession on the Day of Resurrection is he who says: There is no god but God (Allah) pure from his heart or soul.[376]

The Messenger of God said:

The best remembrance is to say: There is no god but God (Allah), and the best supplication is to say: Praise be to God.[377]

The atheist asked: What do I gain if I convert to Islam?

I answered: The condition of the believer in this world and the Hereafter:

There is no fear for him or sadness.

Indeed, those who have said, "Our Lord is God," and then remained on a right course – there will be no fear concerning them, nor will they grieve. [378]

God promised the believer safety.

They who believe and do not mix their belief with injustice – those will have security, and they are [rightly] guided. [379]

---

[376] (Sahih Al Bukhari).
[377] (Narrated by Al Tirmizi).
[378] (Qur'an 46:13).
[379] (Qur'an 6:82).

God promised the believer the reward for calamity.

Rejoicing in what God has bestowed upon them of His bounty, and they receive good tidings about those [to be martyred] after them who have not yet joined them – that there will be no fear concerning them, nor will they grieve. [380]

And We will surely test you with something of fear and hunger and a loss of wealth and lives and fruits, but give good tidings to the patient. [381]

Who, when disaster strikes them, say, "Indeed we belong to God, and indeed to Him we will return". Upon these are blessings and mercy from their Lord. These are the guided ones. [382]

The believer finds shelter in adversity.

And when My servants ask you, [O Muhammad], concerning Me – indeed I am near. I respond to the invocation of the supplicant when he calls upon Me. So, let them respond to Me [by obedience] and believe in Me that they may be [rightly] guided. [383]

God is the believer's guardian.

God is the Protecting Guardian of those who believe. He bringeth them out of darkness into light. As for those who disbelieve, their patrons are false deities. They bring them out of light into darkness. Such are rightful owners of the Fire. They will abide therein. [384]

---

[380] (Qur'an 3:170).
[381] (Qur'an 2:155).
[382] (Qur'an 2:156-157).
[383] (Qur'an 2:186).
[384] (Qur'an 2:257).

The believer will be rewarded for his patience in this world and the Hereafter.

And those who emigrated for [the cause of] God after they had been wronged – We will surely settle them in this world in a good place; but the reward of the Hereafter is greater, if only they could know. [385]

Say, O My servants who have believed, fear your Lord. For those who do good in this world is good, and the earth of God is spacious. Indeed, the patient will be given their reward with– out account [i.e., limit]. [386]

God promised the believer victory in this world and the Hereafter. Indeed, We will support Our messengers and those who believe during the life of this world and on the Day when the witnesses will stand. [387]

God promised the believer eternal bliss.

And as for those who were [destined to be] prosperous, they will be in Paradise, abiding therein as long as the heavens and the earth endure, except what your Lord should will – a bestowal uninterrupted". [388]

---

[385] (Qur'an 16:41).
[386] (Qur'an 39:10).
[387] (Qur'an 40:51).
[388] (Qur'an 11:108).

The atheist said: How do I practice monotheism in my life?

I told him: If you want to practice monotheism, then follow what the Messenger of God said:

O young man, I shall teach you some words [of advice]: Be mindful of God and God will protect you. Be mindful of God and you will find Him in front of you. If you ask, then ask God (Allah) [alone]; and if you seek help, then seek help from God [alone]. Know that if the nation were to gather to benefit you with anything, they would not benefit you except with what God had already prescribed for you. If they were to gather to harm you with anything, they would not harm you except with what God had already prescribed against you. The pens have been lifted and the pages have dried. [389]

I continued: Whenever you feel afraid, say:

...Sufficient for us is God, and [He is] the best Disposer of affairs.[390] So, they returned with favor from God and bounty, no harm having touched them. And they pursued the pleasure of God, and God is the possessor of great bounty.[391]

If you are deceived, then say:

... I entrust my affair to God. Indeed, God is Seeing of [His] servants.[392]

So, God protected him from the evils they plotted. [393]

---

[389] (Narrated by Al Tirmizi).

[390] (Qur'an 3:173).

[391] (Qur'an 3:174).

[392] (Qur'an 40:44).

[393] (Qur'an 40:45).

 If you want to ask for the present life and its enjoyment, then say:

…**What God willed [has occurred]; there is no power except in God**. [394]

…**It may be that my Lord will give me [something] better**…[395]

If you feel sad, then say:

There is no deity except You; exalted are You. Indeed, I have been of the wrong doers.[396]

So, **We responded to him and saved him from the distress**. **And thus, do We save the believers**.[397]

Faith is an unseen issue that requires faith in God, His Angels, His Books and His messengers, the Last Day, and acceptance to God's destiny.

The Bedouins say, **"We have believed." Say**, **"You have not [yet] believed; but say [instead]**, **'We have submitted,' for faith has not yet entered your hearts**. **And if you obey God and His Messenger**, **He will not deprive you from your deeds of anything**. **Indeed, God is Forgiving and Merciful**.[398]

The verse above indicates that faith is of a higher rank and degree, contentment, acceptance, and conviction. Religion has different levels and degrees that increase and decrease. A person's ability and the capacity of his heart to accommodate metaphysical matters vary from person to person.

---

[394] (Qur'an 18:39).

[395] (Qur'an 18:40).

[396] (Qur'an 21:87).

[397] (Qur'an 21:88).

[398] (Qur'an 49:14).

Human beings are distinguished according to their understanding of the characteristics of Beauty and Majesty, along with their knowledge of their Lord.

A person will not be punished for his lack of realization of his narrow horizon. But God will hold Man accountable for the minimum acceptable level for him to avoid an eternity in Hellfire. He must accept monotheism, which means believing that God (Allah) is the Creator, and He is the only One worthy of worship. By this submission, God forgives all other sins of whom He wills. There is no other option for a person, either faith and victory, or disbelief and loss.

Indeed, God does not forgive association with Him, but He forgives what is less than that for. whom He wills.[399]

Faith is a concept related to the unseen. It stops when the unseen is revealed or the signs of the Hour appear.

... On the Day some of the signs of your Lord come up, its belief will not profit a self that did not believe earlier or earned some charity, (i.e., benefits) in its belief. Say, "Wait! Surely, we (too) are waiting.[400]

If a person wants to benefit from his faith by doing good deeds and wants to increase them, this must be done before the day of Judgment, and the Unseen are exposed.

---

[399] (Qur'an 4:116).
[400] (Qur'an 6:158).

As for a person who does not have good deeds, he should not leave the world except when he submits to God, by accepting the concept of monotheism, which means worshipping God alone, and that's if he hopes to escape the eternity in the Hellfire. Other than disbelieving or associating with a mediator apart God, some people who sinned may temporarily fall in the Hellfire. It is under the will of God, if He decides to forgive them or to send them to the Hellfire temporarily.

O you who have believed, fear God as He should be feared and do not die except as Muslims [in submission to Him]. [401]

Faith in Islam should be practiced by both verbally (faith) and physically (actions). It shouldn't be only verbally, similar to the teachings of Christianity today, nor should be only actions, identical to the concept of atheism.

Actions of someone who believes in the unseen in this life and his patience, are not equal to whoever believed in the Hereafter, when the unseen is revealed. Also, whoever works for God's sake in the stage of distress and weakness of Islam is different from the actions of whoever works for the sake of God when Islam is widespread and robust.

...Not equal among you are those who spent before the conquest [of Makkah] and fought [and those who did so after it]. Those are greater in degree than they who spent afterwards and fought. But to all God has promised the best [reward]. And God, with what you do, is Acquainted. [402]

---

[401] (Qur'an 3:102).
[402] (Qur'an 57:10).

The Lord of the Worlds does not punish without reason. Man is either held accountable and punished for **messing with** people's rights, or His rights.

- The minimum we must do to escape from eternal life in the Hellfire is to give the Lord of the Worlds his right, which is by worshipping Him alone, and acknowledge that He has no partner nor son. We must also say: "I bear witness that there is no god but Allah alone who has no partner nor son, and I bear witness that Muhammad is His servant and Messenger, and I testify that God's messengers are true and I testify that Paradise is true and Hellfire is true."

- We are not allowed to stop the path of God or support any action intended to stand in the face of **advocacy** or the spread of God's religion.

- We are not allowed to **mess with people's rights** or commit injustice.

- We must stop doing evil things to creatures; if necessary, Man should distance himself from people.

- A person may not have many good deeds, but he has not harmed anyone, nor is preoccupied with any harmful activity to himself or people, and he has witnessed to God's oneness. Hence, he is to be saved from the torment of Hell.

What would God do with [i.e., gain from] with your punishment if you are grateful and believe? And ever is God Appreciative and Knowing.[403]

Humans are classified into ranks and degrees, starting from their deeds in the real world until the rise of the Hour, the exposure of the unseen world, and the beginning of judgement in the Hereafter.

Some people will be tested in the Hereafter, as mentioned in the Prophet's saying.

The Lord of the Worlds punishes people separately each according to his evil deeds and actions. He either punishes people in the world or delays it to the afterlife. The punishments depend on the severity of the act whether it has repentance or not, and the extent of its impact and its harm on plants, offspring, and other creatures, and that's because God does not like corruption.

The people at the time of other prophets, such as the people of Noah, Hood, Saleh, Lot, etc. didn't believe in messengers, so God punished them during their lifetime because of their reprehensible actions and their tyranny. It's not only that they never stopped their evil acts, but they also exceeded the limit. The people of Prophet "Saleh" killed the camel; people of the Pharaoh wronged the people of Prophet "Moses" and tortured them. Also, the people of Prophet "Lot" insisted on the obscene; the people of Prophet "Shoaib" insisted on corruption, and they committed injustice against people's rights in the measure and the scale.

---

[403] (Qur'an 4:147).

Also, the people of Prophet "Hood" were tyrants; the people of Prophet "Noah" insisted on polytheism, which is worshipping partners apart from the Lord of the Worlds.

So each We seized for his sin; and among them were those upon whom We sent a storm of stones, and among them were those who were seized by the blast [from the sky], and among them were those whom We caused the earth to swallow, and among them were those whom We drowned. And God would not have wronged them, but it was they who were wronging themselves. [404]

Whoever does righteousness – it is for his [own] soul; and whoever does evil [does so] against it. And your Lord is not ever unjust to [His] servants. [405]

The atheist said: You are defending Islam because you were born in a Muslim family. If you were born in a Christian family, you would now preach to Christianity. No one can change the religion of his fathers and grandfathers.

I told him: You have made a person dependent on others, and decided that he will not leave his family's religion! You robbed his right to intellectual independence and to distinguish between the right and wrong. You also monopolized his request for information! Not allowing him to access this information is a grave mistake because a person has the right to seek knowledge and research the horizons of this universe.

---

[404] (Qur'an 29:40).
[405] (Qur'an 41:46).

God Almighty has deposited in us these minds to use them, and not to disable them. Every person follows his father's religion without using his mind, and without thinking and analyzing this religion, he is undoubtedly unjust to himself and despises himself. He hates this great grace that God Almighty has placed in him, namely, the mind.

I continued: Some people grew up in a polytheistic or Christian family that believed in the Trinity, yet eventually rejected this belief and said: There is no god but One God.

I went on: I will tell you a symbolic story to explain this point. A wife cooked a fish for her husband, but she cut off the head and tail before she cooked it, and when her husband asked her: Why did you cut off the head and tail? She said: My mom cooks it this way. The husband asked the mother: Why do you cut the tail and head when you cook fish? The mother answered: My mom cooks it this way. Then the husband asked Grandma: Why do you cut off the head and tail? She replied: The cooking pot in the house was small, and I had to cut the head and tail to insert the fish into the pot.

The reality is that many of the previous events that took place a long time ago stick to that age and time, and have their reasons associated with them. It's catastrophic to imitate actions without rethinking despite changing conditions and changing times.

...God will not change the condition of a people until they change what is in themselves... [406]

---

[406] (Qur'an 13:11).

The atheist asked: What is the fate of those whom the message of Islam didn't reach them?

I answered: God Almighty will not oppress these people, but He will test them on the Day of Resurrection.

He said: How about the people who did not get the opportunity to explore Islam well?

I told him: These people have no excuse because they should not fail to search and think as we mentioned. If God Almighty's judgment is torture, then it is not unjust after all these arguments that he made against them, from reason, instinct, messages and signs in the universe and themselves. The least they were supposed to do is getting to know Allah and worship only Him. If they had done that, they would escape eternity in Hellfire, and they would achieve happiness in this world and the Hereafter. Do you think this is difficult?

The right of God Almighty over His servants whom He created is to worship Him alone; the right of servants is not to torture those who do not worship anything with Him. The matter is simple. They are words that a person says, believes in them, acts accordingly, and is enough to survive the fire. Is this not justice? This is God Almighty's rule, and He is the Judge, the Just, the Gentle, and the Expert. This is the religion of God Almighty.

The real problem is not committing sins, because it is the nature of Man to make mistakes, but the best of sinners is the one who repents.

But the problem is the persistence in committing sins and insisting on them while the person is continuously advised. He still wouldn't listen to advice, nor work accordingly. He would be reminded, but did not benefit from the reminder. He would be preached, and did not hear, consider, repent nor seek forgiveness, but rather insists and walks away arrogantly.

And when our verses are recited to him, he turns away arrogantly as if he had not heard them, as if there was in his ears deafness. So, give him tidings of a painful punishment.[407]

The atheist asked: Why don't we disobey God?

I told him: If you want to disobey God, do not eat from His provision, get out of His land, and look for a safe place where God does not see you. If the Angel of death comes to you to seize your soul, tell him to delay me until I repent a sincere repentance and do good deeds. If the angels of torture come on the Day of Resurrection to take you to the Hellfire, do not go with them; resist them and refrain from going with them, and take yourself to heaven[408]. Can you do that?

I continued: When you have a pet at home, the most you want from it is obedience, and this is because you only bought it and did not create it. So, what about your Creator? Is He not worthy of your obedience, worship, and submission? We are submitting in our worldly journey to a lot of things. Our heart is beating, our digestive system is working, and our senses are fully aware. We only must submit to God during the rest of our affairs in which we have been given a choice to arrive in safety.

He asked: What is safety?

I answered: The end of the journey and the arrival to safety are summed up in these verses.

---

[407] (Qur'an 31:7).
[408] The story of Abrahin bin Adham.

And the earth will shine with the light of its Lord, and the record [of deeds] will be placed, and the prophets and the witnesses will be brought, and it will be judged between them in truth, and they will not be wronged. (69) And every soul will be fully compensated [for] what it did; and He is most knowing of what they do. (70) And those who disbelieved will be driven to Hell in groups until, when they reach it, its gates are opened and its keepers will say, "Did there not come to you messengers from yourselves, reciting to you the verses of your Lord and warning you of the meeting of this Day of yours?" They will say, "Yes, but the word of punishment has come into effect upon the disbelievers. (71) [To them] it will be said, "Enter the gates of Hell to abide eternally therein, and wretched is the residence of the arrogant." (72) But those who feared their Lord will be driven to Paradise in groups until, when they reach it while its gates have been opened and its keepers say, "Peace be upon you; you have become pure; so enter it to abide eternally therein," [they will enter]. (73) And they will say, "Praise to Allah, who has fulfilled for us His promise and made us inherit the earth [so] we may settle in Paradise wherever we will. And excellent is the reward of [righteous] workers." Or [lest] it say, "If only Allah had guided me, I would have been among the righteous." [409]

---

[409] (Qur'an 39:69-57).

The Message of Islam

Nothing in Islam's teachings lead people to atheism; there are no mysteries or ambiguities in Islam that confuse the mind. Islam is simple and solid. The teachings of Islam are summarized as follows:

- Islam teaches that the universe has one God. He is the Creator of the universe and what it contains. Nothing is like Him. The Muslim must worship his Creator alone by communicating with Him directly upon repentance from sin or seeking help, not through a priest, saint, or mediator. God is the Most Merciful to His creatures, more than a mother to her children, so He forgives them whenever they sincerely repent to Him. It is the Creator's right to be worshipped alone, and Man's right to have a direct relationship with his Lord.

- Islam teaches that the Creator does not come to earth in human, animal, stone, or idol form. He has neither a partner nor child. God the Almighty sent many prophets like Jesus, Moses, and Muhammad to spread monotheism. Jesus was created without a father, and Adam was created without a father or mother. So, God creates but does not give birth. He instructed us to worship Him and go to Him alone as the prophets worshiped Him. The Muslim must worship God like what Jesus did, but must not worship Jesus himself. He also must worship God like what Muhammad did, but must not worship Muhammad himself.

- Islam teaches that the belief in the Creator is based on the fact that things do not appear without a cause or by chance, not to mention this vast inhabited material universe and its creatures who possess an intangible consciousness, and obey the laws of non-material mathematics. In addition, we need an independent, immaterial, eternal source to explain a finite, material universe.

- Islam teaches that God is Perfect; He does not need to die for us. He gives life and death. He does not incarnate in anyway. So, He did not die in the person of Jesus Christ nor was He resurrected. He saved His Prophet Jesus and protected him from the crucifixion as He helps and protects His chosen believers.

- Islam teaches that the lesson God gave to all humanity when He accepted Adam's repentance for eating the forbidden fruit is the first instance of God's forgiveness to humanity. There is no issue of the original sin; every soul bears the burden of its corruption. The lesson shows the merciful nature of God. People are born free of sins; they are held accountable for their sins after reaching puberty or maturity.

- Islam teaches that humans cannot be blamed for sins they did not commit, nor they can gain salvation for not attempting to be good. One's life is a test, and each soul is responsible for its actions. God gave Man life and gave him the will to test him. Man is only responsible for his actions. The human being has the freedom to choose only within the limits of his knowledge and capabilities. Judgment follows responsibility. Thus, God will not judge us for our physical appearance, our social status, or tribal affiliations. Freedom with strife is more honorable to Man than slavery with happiness; judgment and reward is meaningless without choice.

- Islam involves believing in all the messengers of God sent to different people in different eras without differentiating between them;

denying one of God's prophets violates Islam. The belief establishes a powerful common bond with people of other faiths. [410]

- Islam involves believing in all earlier revelations of God (Abraham's scriptures, the book of David, the Torah, The Gospel). Islam teaches that the original message in all sacred texts is Pure Monotheism (Unifying God in worship). Unlike the Divine scriptures that preceded, the Qur'an is not kept in the hands of any particular group or Muslims clergymen which could have led to its misinterpretation or alteration. The Qur'an's text is still in its original language (Arabic) without any change, distortion, or alteration, and it is still preserved as it is until our time. It will remain so, as God promised to keep it. It is available to all Muslims. It's known by heart to many Muslims. Current Qur'an translations in multiple languages are nothing but a translation of the Quran's meanings. The Prophet Muhammad's teachings were transmitted through confirmed chains of authenticated narrators.

- Islam teaches that all what exists in the universe is under God's possession and domination. He has comprehensive knowledge, prevalent power, and absolute control. Everything is subjected to His Absolute Knowledge and Will. The Sun, planets and galaxies operate in precision without failure ever since they were created. This same precision applies to humans' creation. Perfect harmony and order between body and soul show that God never puts human beings' souls into animal bodies.

---

[410] While many of the prophets and messengers that God has sent to different nations are mentioned by name in the Qur'an (i.e. Jesus, Moses, Abraham, Noah, David, Solomon, Ismail, Isaac, Joseph, etc.), others are not mentioned. Therefore, the possibility that other famous religious teachers such as the Hindu Lords Rama, Krishna, and Gautama Buddha were prophets of God cannot be outrightly negated.

He never lets them wander between plants and insects (reincarnation), in a case which the person will never know what his past was in his previous life. God made the human civilized innately, gave him mind and knowledge, and assigned him vicegerent for earth and commander over other creatures. God will never humiliate human beings.

- Islam teaches that the true religion of God is always in harmony with human nature. It is one religion, easy, understandable, and straightforward. It is suitable for every time and place. The plurality of religions results from taking mediators between the Creator and humans in worship. The key to humanity towards harmony is when people worship the Creator directly without an intermediary, along with believing in Muhammad the final Messenger and following his teachings, then hearts will unite on one religion.

- Islam teaches doing good deeds and avoiding bad ones, such as the parents' right by being kind to them, the children's right by providing them a decent life, preserving the orphan's money, observing correct measure, weigh with justice, and not cheat the balance, justice in words and deeds, the fulfilment of covenants, the prohibition of committing immorality or even approaching it, and the prohibition of killing the human soul unjustly. All these values are innate moral principles. Therefore, people are naturally and instinctively aware of these values.

- Islam teaches that treating each other with good manners to benefit humanity and reconstruct the earth does not substitute believing in the Creator and adherence to universal morals under religion's umbrella. The reconstruction of the earth and good manners are not the purpose of religion, but they are means. The purpose of religion is to tell the human about his Lord, then about his source, path, and destiny. The excellent end and future are only achieved by obtaining God's satisfaction. The way to that is through the reconstruction of the earth and good manners.

- Islam teaches that there is no priesthood in God's religion, and faith is for all. People are equal, like the teeth of a comb before God, so there is no difference between an Arab or a non-Arab except with piety and good deeds.

- Islam teaches that one of God's greatest attributes is 'The All-Wise'; He does not create anything in vain, exalted be He! He creates things for reasons that reflect His Great Wisdom. He created us to have mercy on us, and to give us happiness. All beautiful human qualities are derived from His qualities. Our existence in this world is for a noble goal: knowing God Almighty, and turning to Him by repentance and seeking His direct help.

- Islam teaches that benevolence is the rule, while evil is the exception. Organized things will always collapse and dissolve unless something collects them from the outside, or to be good on a grand scale as it is, without the Creator organizing these random phenomena that appear in the beautiful things like beauty, wisdom, joy, and love.

- Islam teaches that the Creator established the laws of nature and the laws that govern them. It protects itself by itself when environmental corruption or imbalance appears, and it maintains this balance to reform the earth and continue living better. Therefore, what benefits people and life is what stays and remains on the earth. When calamities occur on earth, such as diseases, volcanoes, earthquakes, and floods, God's names and attributes are revealed, such as the Strong, the Healer, and the Protector for example, when He heals the sick or preserves the survivor, or His name, the Just, in the oppressor's punishment and the sinner. His name, Wise, is evident as well in the trials and tests of the non-sinner, for which he is rewarded for his patience and tortured if he complained instead. So, the person knows the Lord's Majesty from calamities, similar to how he knows the Attributes of Beauty from gifts. If a person only knows Divine Beauty, it is as if he did not know God, the Exalted.

- Islam teaches that the worldly life that a person lives is only a moment compared to the eternal life. From then he forgets all that he suffered in this world with one dip in the bliss of paradise, as this worldly life is the beginning of an eternal journey that Man will resume after death by resurrection and Judgment, and then the reward.

- Islam teaches that the human in his freedom may act contrary to what satisfies God, but he cannot do anything in contradiction to His Will. God granted us freedom to transgress against His wishes (we disobey Him) but He gave no one the freedom to transcend His Will. This freedom is further affirmed by our experience that it is impossible under any pressure to compel the heart to accept anything it does not want to. We can force anyone through threats and force them to stay with us but no pressure whatsoever can make them love us. God has safeguarded our hearts from all forms of compulsion and duress. Therefore, God judges according to what is in the heart and rewards according to the intention, which is visible to no-one but Him.

- Islam teaches that the greatness of Islam is in its simplicity and universality. Islam's name is not connected to any person or place or a particular group but reflects humans' relationship with their Creator (submission to God).

- The teachings of Islam include:

   Performing the ritualistic prayers to keep the connection with the Creator.

   Fasting the month of Ramadan to developing better self-control and appreciate God's blessings.

   Giving a certain specific percentage of certain types of a person's saved wealth annually, reaching the poor people to keep economic balance in society, purify the wealth, and revive the economy.

   Performing the pilgrimage to Mecca[411] once in a lifetime symbolizes all believers' unity regardless of their classes, backgrounds, cultures, or languages.

- Islam teaches that some people believe it is enough to be kind and charitable to other human beings. It makes no sense for an employee to keep his relationship with his colleagues perfect while ignoring his relationship with the manager. Our relationship with the Creator should be the best in our life.

- Islam teaches that many people go through a search and doubt period before finding a path to the Creator; they are like a lost child searching for his mother. Once they start the relationship with God, they finally find peace.

---

[411] A city in Saudi Arabia where Muslims believe that it has the first House of God (Ka'aba) was appointed for humanity to worship God a lone without intermediary.

I bear witness that there is no god worthy of worship except one God; the Creator (Allah), that He has no partner nor son, and I bear witness that Muhammad is His servant and His final messenger.

I bear witness that the messengers of God are true, I bear witness that heavens (Paradise) and Hellfire are true.

Books of the author:

- The True Message of Jesus Christ in the Qur'an and Bible. 2017.

  Published in English and translated into 15 languages.

- The Original Concept of God. 2018.

  Published in English and translated into 7 languages.

- Why Islam? 2019.

  Published in English and translated into 13 languages.

- Eye on the Truth. 2020.

  Published in English and translated into 4 languages.

- Why Religion? 2020.

  Published in German and translated to Spanish.

الحمد لله

www.ingramcontent.com/pod-product-compliance
Lightning Source LLC
LaVergne TN
LVHW020112070726
842525LV00018B/2944